AFRICA TO AMERICA

FROM THE MIDDLE PASSAGE THROUGH THE 1930s

AFRICAN AMERICAN HISTORY AND CULTURE

AFRICA TO AMERICA

FROM THE MIDDLE PASSAGE THROUGH THE 1930S

EDITED BY JEFF WALLENFELDT, MANAGER, GEOGRAPHY AND HISTORY

IN ASSOCIATION WITH

ROSEN
EDUCATIONAL SERVICES

Published in 2011 by Britannica Educational Publishing
(a trademark of Encyclopædia Britannica, Inc.)
in association with Rosen Educational Services, LLC
29 East 21st Street, New York, NY 10010.

Distributed exclusively by Rosen Educational Services.
For a listing of additional Britannica Educational Publishing titles, call toll free (800) 237-9932.

First Edition

Britannica Educational Publishing
Michael I. Levy: Executive Editor
J.E. Luebering: Senior Manager
Marilyn L. Barton: Senior Coordinator, Production Control
Steven Bosco: Director, Editorial Technologies
Lisa S. Braucher: Senior Producer and Data Editor
Yvette Charboneau: Senior Copy Editor
Kathy Nakamura: Manager, Media Acquisition
Jeff Wallenfeldt: Manager, Geography and History

Rosen Educational Services
Hope Lourie Killcoyne: Senior Editor and Project Manager
Nelson Sá: Art Director
Cindy Reiman: Photography Manager
Matthew Cauli: Designer, Cover Design
Introduction by Therese Shea

Library of Congress Cataloging-in-Publication Data

Africa to America: From the Middle Passage Through the 1930s / edited by Jeff
Wallenfeldt, Manager, Geography and History. — 1st ed.
    p. cm. — (African American history and culture)
Includes bibliographical references and index.
ISBN 978-1-61530-126-3 (library binding)
1. African Americans—History. 2. African Americans—Biography. 3. African Americans—
Intellectual life. I. Wallenfeldt, Jeffrey H.
E185.A2513 2010
973'.0496073—dc22

                                                                    2009054299

Manufactured in the United States of America

On the cover: From the agonies of Middle Passage, depicted in this engraving, to the
ascendancy of leaders such as sociologist and civil rights activist W.E.B. Du Bois, pictured
here in 1918, the centuries-long odyssey from Africa to America was marked by great
sorrow, hard-won advances, and eventual achievement. *Herbert Orth/Time & Life Pictures/
Getty Images (Du Bois); Hulton Archive/Getty Images (slave ship illustration)*

On pages 19, 37, 68, 87, 112, 131, 183, 188, 203: A sharecropper and his first child in Person
County, N.C., Jan. 1, 1939. *Buyenlarge/Hulton Archive/Getty Images*

CONTENTS

Introduction 12

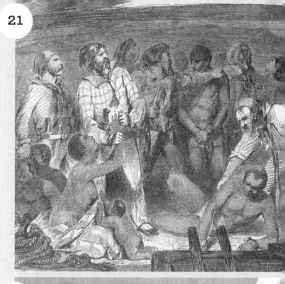

21

27

30

CHAPTER 3: AFRICAN ROOTS: ART 68

CHAPTER 4: RACE AND RACISM 87

CHAPTER 5: SLAVERY, ABOLITIONISM, AND RECONSTRUCTION 112

92

116

117

CHAPTER 6: LAW AND SOCIETY 131

120

129

146

CHAPTER 7: RELIGION 183

CHAPTER 8: EDUCATION 188

149

153

193

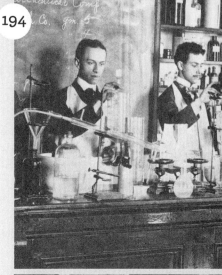

CHAPTER 9: LITERATURE AND THE ARTS 203

230

242

INTRODUCTION

At the beginning of the 21st century, the United States counted more than 36 million African Americans among its citizens. At different times in American history a variety of terms have been used to refer to the people now most often identified as African American or black, including "Afro-American," "Negro," and "Colored," as well as an execrable list of derisive epithets that are indicative of the ignorance and intolerance African Americans encountered in their long struggle for freedom and full participation in American political, economic, social, and cultural life. The African American journey through history has been often tragic, laden with frustration, and fraught with peril, but also sustained by heroism, determination, and triumph.

The roots of most African Americans extend back far beyond the plantations of colonial America and the republic in the first half of 19th century to the rich cultures of Western Africa. Sophisticated, thriving empires dating from at least the Ghana in about 500 CE developed from wealth centred on gold and salt mines. The famed city of Timbuktu originated around 1100 as a trading centre and developed into a bastion of Islamic society. Later, the great cultures of the Mali, Songhai, and Hausa city-states arose largely in accordance with their military strength. To the south, on the Guinea Coast, major empires such as the Asante and the Oyo bolstered their power through trade with Europeans.

The social hierarchies of some African kingdoms included slaves, and the willingness of some African peoples to deport their enemies as slaves facilitated the slave trade that developed between the New World and Africa. In the 18th and 19th centuries, the area along the Gulf of Guinea became the focus of European and African slave trade, earning the label the Slave Coast. Slaves were handed over primarily to British and Dutch traders, frequently in exchange for firearms.

While African identity defies a single characterization, it is safe to say that all African cultures have a reverence for the arts. Sub-Saharan African crafts have included sculpture, painting, pottery, rock art, textiles, masks, body decoration, jewellery, and colourful appliqué. Today, as in the past, much African art is based on tradition. Just as prized as the visual arts, the literary tradition of the African peoples—specifically oral literature—includes riddles, proverbs, praise songs, and epic poems. The legacy of the African tradition in oral literature and especially of the ancient trickster tales can be seen in the African American stories that revolve around the character of Brer Rabbit.

Notwithstanding the complexity and sophistication of many African civilizations, many Europeans, and later Americans, came to view African peoples

This Jan. 1901 Harper's Monthly *magazine illustration depicts the arrival of African captives in Jamestown, 1619.* Library of Congress Prints and Photographs Division

and cultures as inferior. This view encouraged these Europeans and Americans to embrace the concept of "race," which, in turn, led some to attempt to correlate phenotypic features with intellect and temperament. In the process, a single physical characteristic, dark skin—the simple result of evolution in equatorial climates—became the determining factor in enslavement. (By the early 21st century, many scholars had dismissed the genetic validity of characterization by "race" and had come to see "race" as a social construct.) By the middle of the 18th century, slavery had established a firm foothold in colonial America. Though slaves represented tremendous potential profits, the slave traders' inhumane treatment of them encompassed brutal shipboard deprivations that resulted in the deaths of almost one-sixth of all Africans forced to make the voyage to the New World.

Slavery was a boon to the economic prosperity of the American colonies—not just the Southern plantations on which it was most widely practiced but also for Northern businesses. For the sake of unifying the colonies, the objections of those who opposed slavery were subverted, and the "peculiar institution" was enabled by the U.S. Constitution, though tension would remain between slave and free states until the Civil War. Many early American leaders embodied this symbiotic conflict. Thomas Jefferson, for example, owned many slaves but stated that slavery violated the very principles of the American Revolution. During his

presidency, legislation established 1808 as the end date for the importation of slaves into the United States. Yet the "breeding" of slaves became more important, further degrading the unity of black families and prompting anguished filicide as a means of preventing the enslavement of offspring. With each generation, the slave codes—laws prohibiting the education of slaves and giving absolute control to owners—further entwined slavery and the Southern culture. Slave revolts, such as Nat Turner's Virginia uprising in 1831, were bloody though ineffectual in producing mass change.

Slave narratives, such as that written by Olaudah Equiano, provide evocative first-hand accounts of the evils of slavery. Perhaps the most famous of these slave narratives is the 1845 *Narrative of the Life of Frederick Douglass, an American Slave, Written by Himself*. Douglass, who had fled slavery, seemed to epitomize the potential that could be realized with the manumission and education of slaves. Similarly eloquent and shedding light on the heartbreaking predicament of the female slave and mother, Sojourner Truth told her story in an 1861 autobiography titled *Incidents in the Life of a Slave Girl*. All of these works not only were important tools of the abolition movement but together became one of the most influential traditions in American literature.

Several religious organizations, including the Quakers and Free Methodists, were active abolitionists vehemently opposed to slavery. Some of their members acted as "conductors" on the Underground Railroad, the surreptitious trail to the North, Canada, and freedom; others supported efforts to resettle slaves in Africa, which led to the founding of the country Liberia. The militant opposition of one white abolitionist, John Brown, culminated in a raid in 1859 on the federal arsenal at Harpers Ferry, Va. (now in West Virginia), that was intended to spark a massive slave revolt. However, the development of dedicated African American churches actually stemmed from discrimination within wider religious organizations. The African Methodist Episcopal Church, for example, formed in 1816 in response to restrictions on where African American parishioners in a Philadelphia church were allowed to sit.

The American Civil War was a product of years of many uneasy compromises, among them one that resulted in the U.S. Constitution counting slaves as three-fifths of a person for purposes of determining representation in Congress (though slaves, of course, were denied the franchise). Others included the Missouri Compromise in 1820, the Compromise of 1850, and the Kansas-Nebraska Act of 1854, the last grounded in the principle of popular sovereignty, by which new states were to determine by a vote whether slavery would be permitted in them. Congressional legislation regarding the institution of slavery itself was stifled by "gag rules." The division of the country on the slavery issue led to political schisms in the U.S. presidential election of 1860, which resulted in the ascension to the country's highest office of Abraham Lincoln, a Republican running on an anti-slavery platform. The secession of a number of Southern states was followed by the formation of the Confederate States of America.

Lincoln's first priority was the preservation of the Union. His initial inclination to gradually free the slaves gave way to the Emancipation Proclamation, which freed all slaves in rebelling states in 1863. The Union Army's ranks swelled with more than 186,000 African Americans by the end of the war. Yet even in uniform, black soldiers experienced discrimination. Moreover, Confederate outrage at the militarization of African Americans was demonstrated in the Fort Pillow Massacre, wherein Southern forces massacred not only black troops stationed at the fort in Tennessee but also women and children. In all more than 300 African Americans were slain in the incident.

The reunification of the United States following the Union victory in 1865 brought significant if largely temporary respite to the plight of African Americans in the South. But at the same time it fanned the flames of reaction. White Southerners replaced slave codes with restrictive black codes; without the benefit of land redistribution, and still lacking real economic opportunity, former slaves were forced into exploitative sharecropping relationships that looked a lot like slavery. Whites turned violently on blacks in race riots that made abundantly clear that it was necessary for the federal government to step in.

The second stage of Reconstruction (the first, Presidential Reconstruction, had been relatively conciliatory), overseen by the Radical Republicans in Congress, resulted in the military occupation of most of the former Confederacy. The Freedmen's Bureau was founded in 1865 for the purpose of finding jobs and providing aid and shelter for African Americans. It also helped establish over 1,000 schools. The Fisk School in Tennessee and the Hampton Institute in Virginia (both now universities) were two of the most successful. It was during this period that the Fourteenth Amendment, guaranteeing African Americans the right to citizenship, and the Fifteenth Amendment, guaranteeing them the right to vote, were enacted.

What followed was a brief but heady period of widespread African American involvement in local and state government in the South. However, many former Confederates resumed their political positions once they were, by 1872, again permitted to vote and hold office. Legislation in Southern states called Jim Crow laws segregated whites from "people of colour" in places such as in schools, on transportation, in theatres, and in cemeteries. The U.S. Supreme Court upheld this concept in the 1896 *Plessy* v. *Ferguson* decision. "Separate but equal" became the mantra of institutionalized racism. At the same time restrictions were introduced that prevented African Americans from exercising their right to vote. The Ku Klux Klan, which had arisen during Reconstruction, intimidated—and

lynched—blacks as well as terrorized those who opposed white supremacy. Journalist and teacher Ida Bell Wells-Barnett, the daughter of a slave, led an anti-lynching movement in the 1890s. She also founded perhaps the first black women's suffrage group. Not until Mary McLeod Bethune and the advent of the National Council of Negro Women in the 1930s did black women and children have such a strong advocate.

The work of black writers continued to mirror the challenges faced by African Americans. In the late 19th century, Paul Laurence Dunbar became the first African American professional writer. His works, which employed both dialect and standard diction of the time, reflect the demands of a black artist writing for a predominantly white audience. Charles W. Chestnutt's novels and stories addressed white supremacy bluntly, thereby limiting the overall commercial success and appeal of his work.

Around the turn of the 20th century, Booker T. Washington took over Douglass's mantle as the country's most influential African American leader. He minimized the advantages to be gained from the pursuit of political equality and instead encouraged African Americans to work toward economic equality through trades and crafts, an approach that appeased many anxious whites, whom Washington called upon not to impede this progress, a strategy that became known as the Atlanta Compromise. Washington's Tuskegee Institute was a centre of industrial training, and his autobiography, *Up from Slavery* (1901), was seen as a prescriptive guide. On the other hand, another hugely influential African American leader, W.E.B. Du Bois, criticized Washington's abandonment of the fight for civil rights as being "accommodationist," and questioned the rationale of training African Americans in only certain disciplines. Du Bois and like-minded leaders formed the Niagara Movement in 1905 and the NAACP (National Association for the Advancement of Colored People) in 1909.

In the aftermath of the Civil War, most African Americans still lived in the South, where they worked as sharecroppers and menial labourers. Beginning in 1916, labour shortages caused by World War I lured millions of African Americans to urban areas in the North and West in what would be called the Great Migration. However, there was no escaping racial tension. Race riots occurred all over the United States during and following the war. The court system sometimes failed in prosecuting violence against African Americans, and the legal arm of the NAACP became instrumental in working toward legislative and constitutional reform.

Marcus Garvey, born in Jamaica and head of the Universal Negro Improvement Association, arrived in the United States in 1916. Garvey called for a "New Negro" to rise in society, one who embraced "racial" pride, although his belief in the separation of races helped diminish his influence. Concurrently, Harlem, a section of New York City, was becoming a hub of black intellectualism. From this relatively small Manhattan neighbourhood came the Harlem Renaissance of the 1920s, an explosion of African American literature, arts, and music. Those who participated in the movement believed that the black experience was a rich store of material for uniquely African American art. The popularity of jazz and blues music soared, and poets and novelists such as Claude McKay, Langston Hughes, and Nella Larsen enjoyed critical acclaim.

The success of this subset of African Americans belied the state of black America overall. By the 1930s, the Great Depression had hit the United States and African Americans worst of all. A new creative movement called urban realism, exemplified by the work of Richard Wright, mirrored and critiqued the plight of the great majority of African Americans. As World War II approached, the cry for change that echoed throughout African American literature —and among African Americans generally— became more urgent, more organized, and more politically charged.

CHAPTER 1

Overview: From African Roots to World War II

This overview of the first phase of African American history starts with a high-angle survey of a centuries-long period spanning the arrival of the first Africans in North America up to the onset of World War II. Its primary purpose is to introduce the people, events, organizations, and concepts that will be the focus of more detailed treatment in ensuing chapters, but it is also intended as a summary that provides sufficient background to allow readers to jump into the rest of the book at any point.

THE EARLY HISTORY OF BLACKS IN THE AMERICAS

Africans assisted the Spanish and the Portuguese during their early exploration of the Americas. In the 16th century some black explorers settled in the Mississippi valley and in the areas that became South Carolina and New Mexico. The most celebrated black explorer of the Americas was Estéban, who traveled through the Southwest in the 1530s.

The uninterrupted history of blacks in the United States began in 1619, when 20 Africans were landed in the English colony of Virginia. These individuals were not slaves but indentured servants—persons bound to an employer for a limited number of years—as were many of the settlers of European descent (whites). By the 1660s large numbers of Africans were being brought to the English colonies. In 1790 blacks numbered almost 760,000 and made up nearly one-fifth of the population of the United States.

Attempts to hold black servants beyond the normal term of indenture culminated in the legal establishment of black chattel slavery in Virginia in 1661 and in all the English colonies by 1750. Easily distinguished by their skin colour from the rest of the populace—the result of evolutionary pressures favouring the presence in the skin of a dark pigment called melanin in populations in equatorial climates—black people became highly visible targets for enslavement. Moreover, the development of the belief that they were an "inferior" race with a "heathen" culture made it easier for whites to rationalize black slavery. Enslaved blacks were put to work clearing and cultivating the farmlands of the New World.

Of an estimated 10 million Africans brought to the Americas by the slave trade, about 430,000 came to the territory of what is now the United States. The overwhelming majority were taken from the area of western Africa stretching from present-day Senegal to Angola, where political and social organization as well as art, music, and dance were highly advanced. On or near the African coast had emerged the major kingdoms of Oyo, Ashanti, Benin, Dahomey, and Kongo. In the Sudanese interior had arisen the empires of Ghana, Mali, and Songhai; the Hausa states; and the states of Kanem-Bornu. Such African cities as Djenné and Timbuktu, both now in Mali, were at one time major commercial and educational centres.

With the increasing profitability of slavery and the slave trade, some Africans themselves sold captives to the European traders. The captured Africans were generally marched in chains to the coast and crowded into the holds of slave ships for the dreaded Middle Passage across the Atlantic Ocean, usually to the West Indies. Shock, disease, and suicide were responsible for the deaths of at least one-sixth during the crossing. In the West Indies the survivors were "seasoned"—taught the rudiments of English and drilled in the routines and discipline of plantation life.

SLAVERY IN THE UNITED STATES

Black slaves played a major, though unwilling and generally unrewarded, role in laying the economic foundations of the United States—especially in the South. Blacks also played a leading role in the development of Southern speech, folklore, music, dancing, and food, blending the cultural traits of their African homelands with those of Europe. During the 17th and 18th centuries, African and African American (those born in the New World) slaves worked mainly on the tobacco, rice, and indigo plantations of the Southern seaboard. Eventually slavery became rooted in the South's huge cotton and sugar plantations. Although Northern businessmen made great fortunes from the slave trade and from investments in

Southern plantations, slavery was never widespread in the North.

Crispus Attucks, a former slave killed in the Boston Massacre of 1770, was the first martyr to the cause of American independence from Great Britain. During the American Revolution, some 5,000 black soldiers and sailors fought on the American side. After the Revolution, some slaves—particularly former soldiers—were freed, and the Northern states abolished slavery. But with the ratification of the Constitution of the United States, in 1788, slavery became more firmly entrenched than ever in the South. The Constitution counted a slave as three-fifths of a person for purposes of taxation and representation in Congress (thus increasing the number of representatives from slave states), prohibited Congress from abolishing the African slave trade before 1808, and provided for the return of fugitive slaves to their owners.

In 1807 Pres. Thomas Jefferson signed legislation that officially ended the African slave trade beginning in January 1808. However, this act did not presage the end of slavery. Rather, it spurred the growth of the domestic slave trade in the United States, especially as a source of labour for the new cotton lands in the Southern interior. Increasingly, the supply of slaves came to be supplemented by the practice of "slave breeding," in which women slaves were persuaded to conceive as early as age 13 and to give birth as often as possible.

Laws known as the slave codes regulated the slave system to promote absolute control by the master and complete submission by the slave. Under these laws the slave was chattel—a piece of property and a source of labour that could be bought and sold like an animal. The slave was allowed no stable family life and little privacy. Slaves were prohibited by law from learning to read or write. The meek slave received tokens of favour from the master, and the rebellious slave provoked brutal punishment. A social hierarchy among the plantation

Scene aboard a slave ship, engraving by H. Howe, 1855. Library of Congress, Washington, D.C.

slaves also helped keep them divided. At the top were the house slaves; next in rank were the skilled artisans; at the bottom were the vast majority of field hands, who bore the brunt of the harsh plantation life.

With this tight control there were few successful slave revolts. Slave plots were invariably betrayed. The revolt led by Cato in Stono, S.C., in 1739 took the lives of 30 whites. A slave revolt in New York City in 1741 caused heavy property damage. Some slave revolts, such as those of Gabriel Prosser (Richmond, Va., in 1800) and Denmark Vesey (Charleston, S.C., in 1822), were elaborately planned. The slave revolt that was perhaps most frightening to slave owners was the one led by Nat Turner (Southampton, Va., in 1831). Before Turner and his co-conspirators were captured, they had killed about 60 whites.

Individual resistance by slaves took such forms as mothers killing their newborn children to save them from slavery, the poisoning of slave owners, the destruction of machinery and crops, arson, malingering, and running away. Thousands of runaway slaves were led to freedom in the North and in Canada by black and white abolitionists who organized a network of secret routes and hiding places that came to be known as the Underground Railroad. One of the greatest heroes of the Underground Railroad was Harriet Tubman, a former slave who on numerous trips to the South helped hundreds of slaves escape to freedom.

FREE AFRICAN AMERICANS AND ABOLITIONISM

During the period of slavery, free blacks made up about one-tenth of the entire African American population. In 1860 there were almost 500,000 free African Americans—half in the South and half in the North. The free black population originated with former indentured servants and their descendants. It was augmented by free black immigrants from the West Indies and blacks who had been freed by individual slave owners.

But free blacks were only technically free. In the South, where they posed a threat to the institution of slavery, they suffered both in law and by custom many of the restrictions imposed on slaves. In the North, free blacks were discriminated against in such rights as voting, property ownership, and freedom of movement, though they had some access to education and could organize. Free blacks also faced the danger of being kidnapped and enslaved.

The earliest African American leaders emerged among the free blacks of the North, particularly those of Philadelphia, Boston, and New York City. Free African Americans in the North established their own institutions—churches, schools, and mutual aid societies. One of the first of these organizations was the African Methodist Episcopal (AME) church, formed in 1816 and led by Bishop Richard Allen of Philadelphia. Among other noted free African Americans was the astronomer and mathematician Benjamin Banneker.

BENJAMIN BANNEKER: REFLECTIONS OF A FREE BLACK MAN

Benjamin Banneker was one of the most accomplished black men in the early life of the country. Through self-education he became adept in the fields of mathematics, engineering, and astronomy. These abilities brought him to the attention of Thomas Jefferson, who suggested he be named as one of the engineers to lay out the new national capitol at Washington. In 1791 Banneker began publishing almanacs, the best-known of his activities. He sent a copy of his first almanac to Jefferson, along with the following letter. Source: Copy of a Letter From Benjamin Banneker to the Secretary of State With His Answer, Philadelphia, 1792.

I am fully sensible of the greatness of that freedom, which I take with you on the present occasion; a liberty which seemed to me scarcely allowable, when I reflected on that distinguished and dignified station in which you stand, and the almost general prejudice and prepossession, which is so prevalent in the world against those of my complexion.

I suppose it is a truth too well attested to you to need a proof here, that we are a race of beings who have long labored under the abuse and censure of the world; that we have long been looked upon with an eye of contempt; and that we have long been considered rather as brutish than human, and scarcely capable of mental endowments.

Sir, I hope I may safely admit, in consequence of that report which hath reached me, that you are a man far less inflexible in sentiments of this nature, than many others; that you are measurably friendly, and well disposed toward us; and that you are willing and ready to lend your aid and assistance to our relief, from those many distresses and numerous calamities to which we are reduced.

Now sir, if this is founded in truth, I apprehend you will embrace every opportunity to eradicate that train of absurd and false ideas and opinions, which so generally prevails with respect to us; and that your sentiments are concurrent with mine, which are, that one universal Father hath given being to us all; and that He hath not only made us all of one flesh, but that He hath also, without partiality, afforded us all the same sensations and endowed us all with the same faculties; and that however variable we may be in society or religion, however diversified in situation or color, we are all of the same family, and stand in the same relation to Him.

Sir, if these are sentiments of which you are fully persuaded, I hope you cannot but acknowledge that it is the indispensable duty of those who maintain for themselves the rights of human nature, and who possess the obligations of Christianity, to extend their power and influence to the relief of every part of the human race, from whatever burden or oppression they may unjustly labor under; and this, I apprehend, a full conviction of the truth and obligation of these principles should lead all to.

Sir, I have long been convinced that if your love for yourselves and for those inestimable laws which preserved to you the rights of human nature was founded on sincerity, you could not but be solicitous that every individual, of whatever rank or distinction, might with you equally enjoy the blessings thereof; neither could you rest satisfied short of the most active effusion of your exertions, in order to their promotion from any state of degradation to which the unjustifiable cruelty and barbarism of men may have reduced them.

Sir, I freely and cheerfully acknowledge that I am of the African race, and in the color which is natural to them of the deepest dye; and it is under a sense of the most profound gratitude to the Supreme Ruler of the universe, that I now confess to you that I am not under that state of tyrannical thralldom and inhuman captivity to which too many of my brethren are doomed, but that I have abundantly tasted of the fruition of those blessings, which proceed from that free and unequaled liberty with which you are favored; and which, I hope, you will willingly allow you have mercifully received from the immediate hand of that Being from whom proceedeth every good and perfect gift.

Sir, suffer me to recall to your mind that time, in which the arms and tyranny of the British crown were exerted with every powerful effort, in order to reduce you to a state of servitude: look back, I entreat you, on the variety of dangers to which you were exposed; reflect on that time in which every human aid appeared unavailable, and in which even hope and fortitude wore the aspect of inability to the conflict, and you cannot but be led to a serious and grateful sense of your miraculous and providential preservation; you cannot but acknowledge that the present freedom and tranquility which you enjoy you have mercifully received, and that it is the peculiar blessing of Heaven.

This, sir, was a time when you clearly saw into the injustice of a state of slavery, and in which you had just apprehensions of the horrors of its condition. It was now that your abhorrence thereof was so excited that you publicly held forth this true and invaluable doctrine, which is worthy to be recorded and remembered in all succeeding ages: "We hold these truths to be self-evident, that all men are created equal; that they are endowed by their Creator with certain unalienable rights, and that among these are, life, liberty, and the pursuit of happiness."

Here was a time, in which your tender feelings for yourselves had engaged you thus to declare, you were then impressed with proper ideas of the great violation of liberty, and the free possession of those blessings to which you were entitled by nature; but, sir, how pitiable is it to reflect that although you were so fully convinced of the benevolence of the Father of mankind, and of His equal and impartial distribution of these rights and privileges, which He hath conferred upon them, that you should at the same time counteract His mercies, in detaining by fraud and violence so numerous a part of my brethren under groaning captivity and cruel oppression, that you should at the same time be found guilty of that most criminal act, which you professedly detested in others, with respect to yourselves.

I suppose that your knowledge of the situation of my brethren is too extensive to need a recital here; neither shall I presume to prescribe methods by which they may be relieved otherwise than by recommending to you and all others to wean yourselves from those narrow prejudices which you have imbibed with respect to them, and as Job proposed to his friends, "put your soul in their souls' stead"; thus shall your hearts be enlarged with kindness and *benevolence towards them; and thus shall you need neither the direction of myself or others, in what manner to proceed herein.*

And now, sir, although my sympathy and affection for my brethren hath caused my enlargement thus far, I ardently hope that your candor and generosity will plead with you in my behalf, when I make known to you that it was not originally my design; but having taken up my pen in order to direct to you, as a present, a copy of an Almanac, which I have calculated for the succeeding year, I was unexpectedly and unavoidably led thereto.

This calculation is the production of my arduous study, in this my advanced stage of life; for having long and unbounded desires to become acquainted with the secrets of nature, I have had to gratify my curiosity herein through my own assiduous application to astronomical study, in which I need not recount to you the many difficulties and disadvantages which I have had to encounter.

And although I had almost declined to make my calculation for the ensuing year, in consequence of that time which I had allotted therefore being taken up at the federal territory, by the request of Mr. Andrew Ellicott, yet finding myself under several engagements to printers of this state, to whom I had communicated my design, on my return to my place of residence I industriously applied myself thereto, which I hope I have accomplished with correctness and accuracy; a copy of which I have taken the liberty to direct to you, and which I humbly request you will favorably receive; and although you may have the opportunity of perusing it after its publication, yet I choose to send it to you in manuscript previous thereto, that thereby you might not only have an earlier inspection, but that you might also view it in my own handwriting.

Free blacks were among the first abolitionists. They included John B. Russwurm and Samuel E. Cornish, who in 1827 founded *Freedom's Journal*, the first African American–run newspaper in the United States. Black support also permitted the founding and survival of the *Liberator*, a journal begun in 1831 by the white abolitionist William Lloyd Garrison. Probably the most celebrated of all African American journals was the *North Star*, founded in 1847 by the former slave Frederick Douglass, who argued that the antislavery movement must be led by black people.

Beginning in 1830, African American leaders began meeting regularly in national and state conventions. But they differed on the best strategies to use in the struggle against slavery and discrimination. Some, such as David Walker and Henry Highland Garnet, called on the slaves to revolt and overthrow their masters. Others, such as Russwurm and Paul Cuffe, proposed that a major modern black country be established in Africa. Supported by the American Colonization Society, whose membership was overwhelmingly white, African Americans founded Liberia in West Africa in 1822. Their ideas foreshadowed the development of Pan-African nationalism under the leadership of AME Bishop Henry M. Turner a half century later. However, most black leaders then and later regarded themselves as Americans and felt that the problems of their people could be solved only by a continuing struggle at home.

THE CIVIL WAR ERA

The extension of slavery to new territories had been a subject of national political controversy since the Northwest Ordinance of 1787 prohibited slavery in the area now known as the Midwest. The Missouri Compromise of 1820 began a policy of admitting an equal number of slave and free states into the Union. But the Compromise of 1850 and the Kansas-Nebraska Act of 1854 (both grounded in the doctrine of popular sovereignty), along with the Supreme Court's Dred Scott decision of 1857, opened all the territories to slavery.

By the end of the 1850s, the North feared complete control of the country by slaveholding interests, and whites in the South believed that the North was determined to destroy its way of life. White Southerners had been embittered by Northern defiance of the 1850 federal Fugitive Slave Act and had been alarmed in 1859 by the raid at Harpers Ferry, Va. (now in West Virginia), led by the white abolitionist John Brown. After Abraham Lincoln was elected president in 1860 on the antislavery platform of the new Republican party, the Southern states seceded from the Union and formed the Confederate States of America.

The Civil War, which ultimately liberated the country's slaves, began in 1861. But preservation of the Union, not the abolition of slavery, was the first objective of President Lincoln. He initially believed in gradual emancipation, with the federal government compensating the slaveholders for the loss of their "property." But in September 1862 he issued the Emancipation Proclamation, declaring that all slaves residing in states in rebellion against the United States as of Jan. 1, 1863, were to be free. Thus the Civil War became, in effect, a war to end slavery.

African American leaders such as author William Wells Brown, physician and author Martin R. Delany, and Frederick Douglass vigorously recruited blacks into the Union armed forces. Douglass declared in the *North Star*, "Who would be free themselves must strike the blow." By the end of the Civil War more than 186,000 African American men were in the Union army. They performed heroically despite discrimination in pay, rations, equipment, and assignments as well as the unrelenting hostility of the Confederate troops. Slaves served as a labour force for the Confederacy, but thousands of them dropped their tools and escaped to the Union lines.

RECONSTRUCTION AND AFTER

As a result of the Union victory in the Civil War and the ratification of the Thirteenth Amendment to the Constitution (1865), nearly four million slaves were freed. The Fourteenth Amendment (1868) granted African Americans citizenship, and the Fifteenth Amendment (1870) guaranteed their right to vote. Yet the Reconstruction period (1865–77) was one of disappointment and frustration for African Americans, for these new provisions of the Constitution were often ignored, particularly in the South.

After the Civil War, the freedmen were thrown largely on their own meagre resources. Landless and uprooted, they moved about in search of work. They generally lacked adequate food, clothing, and shelter. The Southern states enacted black codes, laws resembling the slave codes that restricted the movement of the former slaves in an effort to force them to work as plantation labourers—often for their former masters—at absurdly low wages.

The federal Freedmen's Bureau, established by Congress in 1865, assisted the former slaves by giving them food and finding jobs and homes for them. The bureau established hospitals and schools, including such institutions of higher learning as Fisk University and Hampton Institute. Northern philanthropic agencies, such as the American Missionary Association, also aided the freedmen.

During Reconstruction, African Americans wielded political power in the South for the first time. Their leaders were largely clergymen, lawyers, and teachers who had been educated in the North and abroad. Among the ablest were Robert B. Elliott of South Carolina and John R. Lynch of Mississippi. Both were speakers of their state House of Representatives and were members of the U.S. Congress. Pinckney B. S. Pinchback was elected lieutenant governor of Louisiana and served briefly as the

Blanche Kelso Bruce, Frederick Douglass, and Hiram Rhoades Revels are featured in this late-19th-century print of heroes of African American life. Library of Congress Prints and Photographs Division

AMERICAN COLONIZATION SOCIETY

The American Colonization Society (full name: American Society for Colonizing the Free People of Color of the United States American) was founded in 1816 by Robert Finley, a Presbyterian minister, and some of the country's most influential men, including Francis Scott Key, Henry Clay, and Bushrod Washington (nephew of George Washington and the society's first president). Support for it came from local and state branches and from churches, and the federal government provided some initial funding. The membership was overwhelmingly white—with some clergymen and abolitionists but also a large number of slave owners—and all generally agreed with the prevailing view of the time that free blacks could not be integrated into white America.

The society's program focused on purchasing and freeing slaves, paying their passage (and that of free blacks) to the west coast of Africa, and assisting them after their arrival there. In 1821, after a failed colonizing attempt the previous year and protracted negotiations with local chiefs, the society acquired the Cape Mesurado area, subsequently the site of Monrovia, Liberia. Some saw colonization as a humanitarian effort and a means of ending slavery, but many antislavery advocates came to oppose the society, believing that its true intent was to drain off the best of the free black population and preserve the institution of slavery. Reviled by extremists on both sides of the slavery debate and suffering from a shortage of money, the society declined after 1840. In 1847 Liberia, until then virtually an overseas branch of the society, declared its independence. Between 1821 and 1867 some 10,000 black Americans, along with several thousand Africans from interdicted slave ships, were resettled by the group, but its involvement with transport to Liberia ended after the American Civil War. The society focused on education and missionary activities until the early 20th century. It was dissolved in 1964.

state's acting governor. Jonathan Gibbs served as Florida's secretary of state and superintendent of education. Between 1869 and 1901, 20 African American representatives and two African American senators—Hiram R. Revels and Blanche K. Bruce of Mississippi—sat in the U.S. Congress.

But black political power was short-lived. Northern politicians grew increasingly conciliatory to the white South, so that by 1872 virtually all leaders of the Confederacy had been pardoned and were again able to vote and hold office. By means of economic pressure and the terrorist activities of violent anti-black groups, such as the Ku Klux Klan, most African Americans were kept away from the polls. By 1877, when Pres. Rutherford B. Hayes withdrew the last federal troops from the South, Southern whites were again in full control. African Americans were disfranchised by the provisions of new state constitutions such as those adopted by Mississippi in 1890 and by South Carolina and Louisiana in 1895.

Only a few Southern black elected officials lingered on. No African American was to serve in the U.S. Congress for three decades after the departure of George H. White of North Carolina in 1901.

The rebirth of white supremacy in the South was accompanied by the growth of enforced "racial" separation. Starting with Tennessee in 1870, all the Southern states reenacted laws prohibiting marriage between blacks and whites. They also passed Jim Crow laws, segregating blacks and whites in almost all public places. By 1885 most Southern states had officially segregated their public schools. Moreover, in 1896, in upholding a Louisiana law that required the segregation of passengers on railroad cars, the U.S. Supreme Court in the case of *Plessy* v. *Ferguson* established the doctrine of "separate but equal."

In the post-Reconstruction years, African Americans received only a small share of the increasing number of industrial jobs in Southern cities. And relatively few rural African Americans in the South owned their own farms, most remaining poor sharecroppers heavily in debt to white landlords. The largely urban Northern African American population fared little better. The jobs they sought were given to European immigrants. In search of improvement, many African Americans migrated westward.

During and after the Reconstruction period, African Americans in cities organized historical, literary, and musical societies. The literary achievements of African Americans included the historical writings of T. Thomas Fortune and George Washington Williams. *The Life and Times of Frederick Douglass* (1881) became a classic of autobiography. Blacks also began to make a major impact on American mass culture through the popularity of such groups as the Fisk Jubilee Singers.

THE AGE OF BOOKER T. WASHINGTON

From 1895 until his death in 1915, Booker T. Washington, a former slave who had built Tuskegee Institute in Alabama into a major centre of industrial training for African American youths, was the country's dominant black leader. In a speech made in Atlanta in 1895, Washington called on both African Americans and whites to "cast down your bucket where you are." He urged whites to employ the masses of black labourers. He called on African Americans to cease agitating for political and social rights and to concentrate instead on working to improve their economic conditions. Washington felt that excessive stress had been placed on liberal arts education for African Americans. He believed that their need to earn a living called instead for training in crafts and trades. In an effort to spur the growth of African American business enterprise, Washington also organized the National Negro Business League in 1900. But black businessmen were handicapped by insufficient capital and by the competition of white-owned big businesses.

Booker T. Washington, c. 1912. Hulton Archive/Getty Images

NEW YORK DRAFT RIOT OF 1863

Being in the North offered no guarantee of freedom from racism and brutality. The draft riot of 1863 was a major four-day eruption of violence in New York City resulting from deep worker discontent with the inequities of conscription during the U.S. Civil War. Although labouring people in general supported the Northern war effort, they had no voice in Republican policy and occasionally deserted from the army or refused reenlistment. Because of their low wages—often less than $500 a year—they were particularly antagonized by the federal provision allowing more affluent draftees to buy their way out of the Federal Army for $300. Minor riots occurred in several cities, and when the drawing of names began in New York on July 11, 1863, mobs (mostly of foreign-born, especially Irish, workers) surged onto the streets assaulting residents, defying police, attacking draft headquarters, and burning buildings. One of the targets was the Colored Orphan Asylum on Fifth Avenue; though the crowd set fire to the building, the 200-plus young residents were led to safety by asylum workers, and remained unharmed by the mob.

The New York draft riot was also closely associated with racial competition for jobs. Northern labour feared that emancipation of slaves would cause an influx of African American workers from the South, and employers did in fact use black workers as strikebreakers during this period. Thus the white rioters eventually vented their wrath on the homes and businesses of innocent African Americans, and Civil War freedmen's associations were forced to send aid to their brethren in New York. (This racial ill feeling in the ranks of urban labour persisted into the second half of the 20th century.) The four-day draft riot was finally quelled by police cooperating with the 7th N.Y. Regiment, which had been hastily recalled from Gettysburg, and the drawing of names proceeded on August 19 without incident. Property damage of the riot eventually totalled $1,500,000.

Washington was highly successful in winning influential white support and became the most powerful African American in the country's history at the time. But his program of vocational training did not meet the changing needs of industry, and the harsh reality of discrimination prevented most of his Tuskegee Institute graduates from using their skills. The period of Washington's leadership proved to be one of repeated setbacks for African Americans: more blacks lost the right to vote, segregation became more deeply entrenched, and antiblack violence increased. Between 1900 and 1914 there were more than 1,000 known lynchings. Antiblack riots raged in both the South and the North, the most sensational taking place in Brownsville, Tex. (1906); Atlanta (1906); and Springfield, Ill. (1908).

Meanwhile, African American leaders who opposed Washington's approach began to emerge. The historian and

SARAH BREEDLOVE WALKER

One African American businessperson who did find great success was Sarah Breedlove Walker, generally acknowledged to be the first black female millionaire in the United States. She was already a widow when, at age 20, she moved to St. Louis, where she worked as a washerwoman for some years while experimenting at home with various hair dressings. In 1905 she developed a formula for creating a smooth, shiny coiffure for African American women. She quickly achieved local success with what later became known as the "Walker Method" or "Walker System." Moving to Denver, Colo., in 1906, she married Charles J. Walker, and thenceforward she was known as Madame C.J. Walker.

Walker organized agents to sell her hair treatment door-to-door and in 1910 transferred her business—by then the Madame C.J. Walker Manufacturing Co.—to Indianapolis, Ind. Her company at its peak employed some 3,000 people, many of them "Walker agents"—saleswomen dressed in long black skirts and white blouses who became familiar figures in the black communities of the United States and the Caribbean. Walker was president and sole proprietor of her company, and she soon became one of the best-known figures in America. Through the example of entertainer Josephine Baker, the Walker System coiffure became popular in Europe as well.

Walker augmented her fortune with shrewd real estate investments. Generous with her money, she included in her extensive philanthropies educational scholarships, the National Association for the Advancement of Colored People, homes for the aged, and the National Conference on Lynching. She bequeathed her estate to various charitable and educational institutions and to her daughter, A'Lelia Walker, who was later known for supporting an intellectual salon—known as the Dark Tower—that helped to stimulate the cultural Harlem Renaissance of the 1920s.

sociologist W.E.B. Du Bois criticized Washington's accommodationist philosophy in *The Souls of Black Folk* (1903). Others who questioned Washington's methods included William Monroe Trotter, the militant editor of the Boston *Guardian*, and Ida B. Wells-Barnett, a journalist and a crusader against lynching. They insisted that African Americans should demand their full civil rights and that a liberal education was necessary for the development of black leadership. At a meeting in Niagara Falls, Ont., in 1905, Du Bois and other black leaders who shared his views founded the Niagara Movement. Members of the Niagara group joined with concerned liberal and radical whites to organize the National Association for the Advancement of Colored People (NAACP; initially known as the National Negro Committee) in 1909. The NAACP journal *Crisis*, edited by Du Bois, became an effective advocate for African American civil rights. The NAACP won its first major legal case in 1915, when the

U.S. Supreme Court outlawed the "grandfather clause," a constitutional device used in the South to disfranchise African Americans.

Black contributions to scholarship and literature continued to mount. Historical scholarship was encouraged by the American Negro Academy, whose leading figures were Du Bois and the theologians Alexander Crummell and Francis Grimké. Charles W. Chesnutt was widely acclaimed for his short stories. Paul Laurence Dunbar became famous as a lyric poet. Washington's autobiography *Up from Slavery* (1901) won international acclaim.

In New York City during World War I the NAACP led a march protesting brutality against African Americans. One of the many banners read: "Mr. President, why not make America safe for democracy?" Encyclopædia Britannica, Inc.

THE IMPACT OF WORLD WAR I AND AFRICAN AMERICAN MIGRATION TO THE NORTH

When slavery was abolished in 1865, African Americans were an overwhelmingly rural people. In the years that followed, there was a slow but steady migration of African Americans to the cities, mainly in the South. Migration to the North was relatively small, with nearly eight million African Americans—about 90 percent of the total black population of the United States—still living in the South in 1900. But between 1910 and 1920, crop damage caused by floods and by insects—mainly the boll weevil—deepened an already severe economic depression in Southern agriculture. Destitute African Americans swarmed to the North in 1915 and 1916 as thousands of new jobs opened up in industries supplying goods to Europe, then embroiled in World War I. Between 1910 and 1920 an estimated 500,000 African Americans left the South.

African Americans who fled from the South soon found that they had not escaped segregation and discrimination. They were confined mainly to over-crowded and dilapidated housing, and were largely restricted to poorly paid, menial jobs. Again there were antiblack riots, such as that in East St. Louis, Ill., in 1917. But in the Northern cities the economic and educational opportunities for African Americans were immeasurably greater than they had been in the rural South. In addition, they were helped by various organizations, such as the National Urban League, founded in 1910.

Some African Americans opposed involvement in World War I. The black Socialists A. Philip Randolph and Chandler Owen argued that the fight for democracy at home should precede the fight for it abroad. But when the United States entered World War I in April 1917, most African Americans supported the step. During the war about 1,400 black officers were commissioned. Some 200,000 African Americans served abroad, though most were restricted to labour battalions and service regiments.

THE GARVEY MOVEMENT AND THE HARLEM RENAISSANCE

Many African Americans became disillusioned following World War I. The jobs that they had acquired during the war all but evaporated in the postwar recession, which hit African Americans first and hardest. The Ku Klux Klan, which had been revived during the war, unleashed a new wave of terror against blacks. Mounting competition for jobs and housing often erupted into bloody "race riots" such as those that spread over the nation in the "red summer" of 1919.

In the face of such difficulties, a "new Negro" developed during the 1920s—the proud, creative product of the American city. The growth of racial pride among African Americans was greatly stimulated by the black nationalist ideas of Marcus Garvey. Born in Jamaica, he had founded the Universal Negro Improvement Association there in 1914. He came to the United States in 1917 and established a branch of the association in the Harlem district of New York City. By 1919 the association had become the largest mass movement of African Americans in the country's history, with a membership of several hundred thousand.

The Garvey movement was characterized by colourful pageantry and appeals for the rediscovery of African heritage. Its goal was to establish an independent Africa through the return of a revolutionary vanguard of African Americans. Garvey's great attraction among poor African Americans was not matched, however, among the black middle class, which resented his flamboyance and his scorn of their leadership. Indeed, one of Garvey's sharpest critics was Du Bois, who shared Garvey's basic goals and organized a series of small but largely ineffectual Pan-African conferences during the 1920s. The Garvey movement declined after Garvey was jailed for mail fraud in 1925 and deported to Jamaica in 1927.

The flowering of African American creative talent in literature, music, and the arts in the 1920s was centred in New York City and became known as the Harlem Renaissance. Like the Garvey movement, it was based on a rise in "race consciousness" among African Americans. The principal contributors to the Harlem Renaissance included not only well-established literary figures such as Du Bois and the poet James Weldon Johnson but also new young writers such as Claude McKay, whose militant poem "If We Must Die" is perhaps the most-quoted African American literary work of this period. Other outstanding writers of the Harlem Renaissance were the novelist Jean Toomer and the poets Countee Cullen and Langston Hughes. During the 1920s painters Henry Ossawa Tanner and Aaron Douglas and performers Paul Robeson, Florence Mills, Ethel Waters, and Roland Hayes were also becoming prominent. The black cultural movement of the 1920s was greatly stimulated by African American journals, which published short pieces by promising writers. These journals included the NAACP's *Crisis* and the National Urban League's *Opportunity*. The movement was popularized by African American philosopher Alain Locke in *The New Negro*, published in 1925, and by African American historian Carter G. Woodson, founder of the Association for the Study of Negro (now African American) Life and History and editor of the *Journal of Negro History*.

AFRICAN AMERICAN LIFE DURING THE GREAT DEPRESSION AND THE NEW DEAL

The Great Depression of the 1930s worsened the already bleak economic situation of African Americans. They were the first to be laid off from their jobs, and they suffered from an unemployment rate two to three times that of whites. In early public assistance programs African Americans often received substantially less aid than whites, and some charitable organizations even excluded blacks from their soup kitchens.

This intensified economic plight sparked major political developments among African Americans. Beginning in 1929, the St. Louis Urban League launched a national "jobs for Negroes" movement by boycotting chain stores that had mostly black customers but hired only white employees. Efforts to unify African American organizations and youth groups later led to the founding of the National Negro Congress in 1936 and the Southern Negro Youth Congress in 1937.

Virtually ignored by the Republican administrations of the 1920s, black voters drifted to the Democratic Party, especially in the Northern cities. In the presidential election of 1928 African Americans voted in large numbers for the Democrats for the first time. In 1930 Republican Pres. Herbert Hoover nominated John J. Parker, a man of pronounced antiblack views, to the U.S. Supreme Court. The NAACP successfully opposed the nomination. In the 1932 presidential race African Americans overwhelmingly supported the successful Democratic candidate, Franklin D. Roosevelt.

The Roosevelt administration's accessibility to African American leaders and the New Deal reforms strengthened black support for the Democratic Party. A number of African American leaders, members of a so-called "black cabinet," were advisers to Roosevelt. Among them were the educator Mary McLeod Bethune, who served as the National Youth Administration's director of Negro affairs; William H. Hastie, who in 1937 became the first black federal judge; Eugene K. Jones, executive secretary of the National Urban League; Robert Vann, editor of the *Pittsburgh Courier*; and the economist Robert C. Weaver.

African Americans benefited greatly from New Deal programs, though discrimination by local administrators was common. Low-cost public housing was made available to black families. The National Youth Administration and the Civilian Conservation Corps enabled African American youths to continue their education. The Works Progress Administration gave jobs to many African Americans, and its Federal Writers Project supported the work of many black authors, among them Zora Neale Hurston, Arna Bontemps, Waters Turpin, and Melvin B. Tolson.

The Congress of Industrial Organizations (CIO), established in the mid-1930s, organized large numbers of black workers into labour unions for the first time. By 1940 there were more than 200,000 African Americans in the CIO, many of them officers of union locals.

CHAPTER 2

AFRICAN ROOTS: CULTURES AND KINGDOMS

T oday African Americans can trace their roots to virtually all reaches of the African continent, many as recent immigrants. The origins of most African Americans, however, stem from western and west-central Africa, whence came the great majority of the people who were captured, often by other Africans, and conveyed to slavery in the Americas. A large number of those Africans who became slaves in North America began their servitude in the New World in the Caribbean region; others were brought directly to North America. Of the latter group, most came from an area that stretched from the Senegal River in the north to modern-day Angola in the south, from along the western African coastline to several hundred miles inland. More specifically they came from modern-day Senegal and the Gambia, a region often referred to as Senegambia; from the Bight of Biafra, comprising most of modern-day Cameroon and Nigeria; from along the Bight of Benin, including southeastern Ghana, Togo, Benin, and southwestern Nigeria; from the Congo-Angola region (modern-day Republic of the Congo, Democratic Republic of the Congo, and Angola); and from the Windward (Liberia and Ivory Coast) and Gold (Ghana) coasts. Among those peoples enslaved were the Kongo, Mbundu, Yoruba, Fon, Nupe, Igbo, Wolof, Fulani, and Serer.

The rich history and culture of western Africa includes many of these peoples. The section that follows considers the traditional cultures of the two principal regions of

western Africa—the western portion of the Sudan, a geographic area that stretches across the entire width of Africa, and the Guinea coast, the coastal region of western Africa.

TRADITIONAL CULTURE OF THE WESTERN SUDAN

The major ethnic groups of the western Sudan are the Wolof of Senegal, the Serer to the south, and the Mande-speaking peoples to the east, comprising such subgroups as the Malinke, the Khasonke, the Bambara (Bamana), the Wasulunka, the Dyula, the Marka, and the Soninke (Serahuli). The Songhai are located largely in the region south of Timbuktu along the Niger, the Mossi are in the Volta basin, and a variety of smaller groups, such as the Dogon, Lobi, and Bobo, live within the great bend of the Niger. Other small groups, such as the Diola (Jola), Landuma, and Baga, are to the southwest. The Hausa are concentrated largely in northern Nigeria, though they are scattered in all the major trade centres of western Africa. The Fulani (Fulbe, or Peul) are distributed widely from the west Atlantic coast to Chad and Cameroon, though particularly concentrated in Senegal, Guinea, and northern Nigeria.

The continuous movements of people over the centuries have led to a complicated pattern of languages, but most authorities consider these languages to be branches of one great Niger-Congo family. These branches are the Mande, Kordofanian, Gur, Kwa, Ijoid, Adamawa-Ubangi, Benue-Congo, Kru, and Atlantic. The last includes such varied languages as Wolof, Serer, Fulani, and Diola. The Kordofanian languages are spoken in the area of the Nuba Hills. Other major language families that have been distinguished are the Nilo-Saharan languages, which include Songhai, and the Afro-Asiatic languages, which comprise Ancient Egyptian, Berber, Cushitic, Oromo, and Hausa, among others. French is the language of communication among the elite of most nations of the western Sudan—namely, Senegal, Mali, Niger, Chad, and Guinea—but English is used in the Gambia, Ghana, and Nigeria.

SOCIAL ORGANIZATION

In the period from about 500 to 1470 CE the Sudanic zone was characterized by the rise and fall of a series of states and empires. The first to achieve eminence was Ghana (not to be confused with the modern state of that name), situated between the Sénégal and Niger rivers. It derived great wealth from trade in gold from the south and salt from the mines of the Sahara to the north. Ruins excavated at Koumbi Saleh are believed to be its capital, a town that could have contained 20,000 inhabitants. Ghana's power declined during the 11th century after nearly 20 years of attacks from the Almoravids, a Berber military and religious order from the Sahara, devoted to converting nonbelievers to Islam. The Mande-speaking people of Mali, on the Niger, developed the next great state, expanding rapidly in the mid-13th century, absorbing Ghana, and then gaining power over the trading cities of Timbuktu and Gao at the end of the major trans-Saharan trade routes. In the early 14th century the emperor of Mali, Mansa Mūsā, visited Egypt and Mecca. A large number of Arab scholars—teachers, lawyers, architects, doctors—established themselves in Mali at this time. After the death of Mansa Mūsā the empire began to break up. The city-state of Gao, under the Songhai, broke away toward the end of the 14th century and by the early 16th century had taken over control of the central region of the western Sudan. The power of Gao was extended over Timbuktu and Djenné, which were then at their height as centres of trade, learning, and religion. The power of the Songhai, however, was broken in 1591 by an invading army from Morocco, whose firearms provided a great advantage over the swords and spears of the Songhai.

Farther east, the Chad region received various waves of immigrants—hunters, fishermen, and farmers who introduced weaving, bronze work, and pottery. They came under the influence of two states: that of Kanem, north and east of Lake Chad, which was powerful between the 11th century (when Islam began to make itself felt) and the 15th; and that of Bornu, to the west of Lake Chad, the dominant state in the 16th and 17th centuries. Bornu's army had a strong cavalry force, wore chain mail, quilted armour, and iron helmets, and retained its medieval splendour down to the 19th century, with something of its former pageantry still to be seen at Islamic festivals.

Society in all of these states was highly stratified, with a powerful ruling class controlling the wealth. A central ruler appointed regional governors or obtained the allegiance of outlying vassal chiefs, who were obliged to pay annual tribute and supply labour as needed. Well-organized armies both suppressed rebellion within the state and defended the boundaries against external enemies. War captives became slaves and performed much of the physical labour, carrying loads and working on farms. Islamic religious teachers often formed part of the ruler's court, and gradually the people were converted to Islam. The ruler himself often filled a sacred role, as it was believed that the vital forces of the kingdom—rain, good harvests, and fertility—depended on him. The rulers were patrons of various arts and crafts, and the courts included musicians, praise singers, storytellers, goldsmiths, leatherworkers, and so on. Men of slave origin could rise to high rank as court officials and enjoy power over the freeborn.

BELIEF SYSTEMS

Indigenous systems of belief that were unaffected by Islam—which, as has already been made clear, had a strong presence in the region—involved the concept of the essential unity of the visible and invisible worlds, humanity being accorded the dominant position in the system. Forces in plants, animals, and minerals were believed to be made known to humans through ancestors and could be used for either good or evil, humans having the moral responsibility for making the choice. Living persons were seen as a continuation of the life stream of the first beings. Ancestors were thought to watch over the living and act as intermediaries between them and the creator of the universe, who, though remote from humans, had supreme power. The ancestors indicated their wishes through dreams sent to the elders, while the living communicated with the ancestors through prayer and sacrifice, the blood of sacrificed animals setting in motion certain latent spiritual forces. The spirit world was also evoked by persons wearing carved masks during special ceremonies; associated dances and drumming were intended to cleanse, reinvigorate, and protect the community. The masks themselves were the abode of spirits, and carvers felt inspired by supernatural powers.

These religious beliefs reinforced—and continue today in the region to reinforce—the traditional values of society, for it was (and is) believed that lack of harmony in the community and breaches of traditional law and custom resulted in disasters such as drought, disease, and crop failure. In this system of belief, society is threatened by forces outside the community—evil spirits that cause mental disorders and physical abnormalities—and by people inside the community in whom evil grows—witches, who can cause harm to both human beings and crops through a witch substance inside them, and sorcerers, who perform deliberate acts of evil magic. Charms were worn and protective devices set up to guard against such dangers, while diviners sought to detect both witches and sorcerers. Individuals with problems consulted diviners, whose role it was to trace the causes of troubles, using such techniques as casting cowrie shells or reading patterns in sand to see into the spiritual world, and then to indicate the proper measures to be taken. Diviners provided treatment at the physical level by prescribing herbs and medicines, at the psychological level by listening to confessions and providing reassurance, and at the social level by trying to disperse tensions between individuals.

TRADITIONAL CULTURE OF THE GUINEA COAST

Guinea is a term used originally for the coastlands and adjacent forests of western Africa between the Republic of Guinea on the west and Equatorial Guinea on the east, including the whole, or the southern parts, of Guinea-Bissau, Sierra Leone, Liberia, Côte d'Ivoire, Ghana, Togo, Benin, Nigeria, and Cameroon. There have been conflicting accounts of the derivation of the name Guinea, but it would seem to be a version of the Berber word *aguinaw*, or *gnawa*, meaning "black man," or "Negro."

THE ENVIRONMENT AND THE PEOPLE

In western Africa, in the general absence of major mountainous areas, natural regions were determined primarily by climate and vegetation, and the Guinea Coast societies were associated with the equatorial forest zone. This forest has now long been cleared for agriculture in some areas, but in the east heavy forest formerly extended from the borders of the Cameroon highlands to the area west of the Niger River. In the west, forest stretched from Sierra Leone to western Ghana. Between these two belts of forest was a drier region where tree cover was thin. Societies in this area, while culturally similar to true forest societies, have historically been different in significant ways.

The forest greatly influenced the cultural development of the Guinea Coast by affecting the movements of peoples and the development of agriculture and commerce. People occupied the forest areas relatively late because farming there had to await the development of suitable tools and crops. Iron axes are needed to clear equatorial forests and only with the introduction of the shade-tolerant crops—the plantain and the cocoyam (taro and eddo), brought from Asia in the 9th century CE—could forest farming become an economic alternative to hunting and gathering. Moreover, forest farming did not include animal husbandry, for the forest harboured species of tsetse fly that are particularly dangerous to cattle and horses. This had advantages for the forest people, however, because the tsetse fly and the dense vegetation protected them from marauding cavalry. Gradually the forest gave its inhabitants commercial advantages: kola nuts and, later, palm oil were so highly desired by distant peoples that traders by sea, and overland from the north, were drawn to the Guinea Coast.

The cultural significance of the original forest environment is shown even today in the linguistic map of western Africa. In detail there are many different languages in the forest area, some spoken by millions, some by a few thousand people. What is striking, however, is that the boundaries between the major language families roughly coincide with the old boundaries of the forest. Only in the extreme east does this clear division disappear. The linguistic division between the forest societies and the hinterland is good evidence for the long historical distinctiveness of the Guinea Coast cultures.

HISTORICAL BACKGROUND OF TRADE AND POLITICS

Before the end of the 15th century, most of the region's external contacts were made through the savanna kingdoms to the north, whose merchants wanted slaves, gold, and kola nuts (a stimulant lawful for Muslims). From the end of the 15th century, however, the interests of the Guinea Coast peoples were partly reoriented toward trade with European merchants, who sought successively gold, slaves, and palm oil. European trade was significant partly because, unlike the northern trade, it was controlled within the Guinea area entirely by local people. Europeans were prevented from penetrating inland by climate, disease, and the express action of African authorities. The merchants at the coast provided inducements to sell; how their wants were supplied was a matter for local traders. These overseas merchants were also significant because of the nature of the goods they brought to sell. They were mainly consumer goods, but they also included such capital goods as iron, guns, and gunpowder, and these gradually introduced a crucial new factor into local warfare. Political authorities were forced into trade because it became militarily vital to acquire the new weapons. Even imported consumer goods had a political significance, for it was normally the political authorities, able to tax European merchants and the local traders, who could acquire most goods. They thus had the best resources with which to exert general influence; consequently new power was put into their hands with important political consequences.

The development of Guinea Coast societies was radically influenced by the nature of their exports, especially the slaves. Slave trading did not everywhere lead to raiding, but where it did it led to changes in military and political organization. In Dahomey a strong government sent its army to raid slaves in every dry season; in Yoruba areas one factor in the violent relations between the city-states in the 18th and 19th centuries was probably their involvement in the trade, and new political forms were bred in response to this situation. Wherever war captives were traded as slaves, those central authorities who controlled captives developed an economic advantage over their rivals.

In the 19th century palm oil gradually became the most important Guinea Coast export because of its increased use as an industrial lubricant and because European humanitarians were successful in applying political pressure on their governments, especially the British, to end overseas transport of slaves. Nevertheless, slave dealing and raiding remained important internally throughout the century. Even when slave exports declined, the growing palm-oil traffic in itself stimulated these activities, for the transport of the bulky oil required slaves to paddle the canoe transports or to head-load the oil to the ports. Moreover, a trader using many men to transport oil needed others, often slaves, to produce food for them; thus, slaves were important economically and politically to the Mende of Sierra Leone in the west and the Fante (Fanti), Dahomean, Yoruba, Niger delta, and Efik peoples in the south.

The growth of the palm-oil trade brought other economic and political changes. African traders exporting palm oil needed more capital than slave traders did, because slaves transported themselves and worked while awaiting shipment, whereas oil was expensive to transport and constituted idle capital while at the ports. An unanticipated result of the change to the oil trade was, therefore, that the exporters, needing capital, became increasingly reliant on European firms that advanced them goods on credit and therefore took increasing interest in local political affairs. This was one factor leading to colonialism. Paradoxically, in the rural areas many men who could never have been slave traders could easily gather and sell palm produce. Apart from the exceptional case of Dahomey, where most palm oil came from large government-fostered plantations, oil was drawn mainly from the fruit of trees growing naturally in the bush. In the eastern forest areas especially, participation in this production and trade was very general.

By the end of the 19th century a network of local markets had been developed over much of the hinterland of the Guinea Coast. The great centralized kingdoms were naturally associated with great trade routes, but there is evidence that traders were protected by the common interest of many people—and almost all political authorites—that the routes should be kept open. It is remarkable that for the most part, even in the absence of strong governments and in areas where adjacent peoples might be regarded as fair game for attacks, the accredited trader passed unharmed; appropriate punishment was dealt out by local authorities to any person who robbed or injured them.

KINGDOMS AND CHIEFDOMS OF GUINEA

Although trade could flow across political boundaries, the political development of western African societies was much influenced by the growth of trade and through the warfare and the struggle for trade routes that accompanied it. Where trade was limited, most political units seem to have remained weak and small in scale. This was true in the earlier part of the 19th century in much of the area of Sierra Leone and Liberia and is a major reason that it was possible to settle freed slaves there without their being dominated by indigenous powers. Later, however, hinterland Mende tribes, located in rich oil-palm areas, fought for the control of trade routes and developed into more centralized groups under warrior chiefs. At the other end of the western forest, and at the other extreme regarding trade, the Asante Confederation of kin-based states developed much earlier and quite differently. The area had early commercial importance in the northern trade as a source of gold and of the best kola nuts. From the 17th century the Asante exploited their gold resources, which were easily made a government monopoly, in order to gain local control over the import of firearms. Extending their influence over their immediate neighbours by diplomacy and over those more distant by warfare, they eventually subjugated peoples as far southeast as Accra, on the coast, and as far north as the savanna. It has been shown that in the 19th century the authorities—with remarkable insight into their own social structure, which was based on matrilineal clans—created a semiprofessional civil service in which offices were passed from father to son; this ensured that new officials were trained but that the offices escaped the clutches of the major kin groups.

In the eastern forest, northwest of the Niger delta, was the kingdom of Benin, whose rulers claimed to have come originally from the Yoruba area. It was of medieval origin and was so well established in the late 15th century that the king of Benin sent an emissary to the king of Portugal, who in turn sent missionaries to Benin. Its internal political development from that time involved complex power struggles between the party of the ruler, the oba, and the nobles. In theory there existed a complex balance between different interest groups, but that balance shifted in different generations. Interestingly, it seems that the central authorities were so well aware of the dangers of allowing power to pass to locally based kin groups that much ingenuity was exerted in creating structures that ensured that commoners' kin groups did not develop and that politically ambitious individuals had to seek advancement by moving to the capital of Benin and could not create power bases in their home areas. In this the social structure of

Benin was almost the reverse of the adjacent Yoruba areas.

To the east of the city of Benin lies the Niger delta, one of the greatest mangrove swamps in the world. In the 18th and 19th centuries, in that area and farther east at the mouth of the Cross River, there developed small, independent trading settlements. At first most were villages exchanging fish for agricultural produce; later, wherever deepwater anchorages existed—suitable for European ships and close to rivers giving good access to the interior—these settlements became large trading centres interested in exerting commercial control over the palm-oil-rich and slave-rich hinterlands.

Throughout much of the Guinea Coast the king or chief was the keystone of the political system because, although his actual powers varied enormously, his ritual relation to his predecessors and, usually, the gods provided the ideological framework for that system. In some cases he was the only appropriate intercessor with his deceased ancestors who were believed to exercise a controlling influence over group affairs. In other cases he was transformed, by his installation rites, into a person so sacred that all his actions had to be circumscribed lest, by breaking taboos, he brought disaster on his people.

In Oyo, one of the best-described Yoruba kingdoms, the king, at the culmination of his installation rituals, ate the heart of his predecessor and was transformed into a personification of his ancestors. Thereafter, on his only public appearances, at rituals held three times a year, he appeared veiled, his face hidden by a beaded fringe. Those who formally represented him in judicial, religious, military, and administrative capacities were slave eunuchs, chosen because, having neither kin nor affines, they were presumed to have no interests to serve but their master's. Although secluded, it appears that the king was involved in important political maneuverings, playing one group of hereditary chiefs off against a second and trying to avoid the great danger that would ensue if both groups were to unite against him.

Such political structures can be described as if they were frictionless systems of checks and balances persisting unaltered for generations, but modern research suggests that these structures were changed in detail whenever the balance of political power shifted. Points of particular struggle were the rules for choosing the successor to king or chief. In polygynous societies even a rule of inheritance by the eldest son does not necessarily indicate the true heir as there is room for dispute over the status of the mother. Any rule that widened the choice—e.g., to any member of a lineage—gave increased powers to the selectors. Furthermore, military success could bring great problems, for if new territories were conquered there might be great competition between king and barons over claims to control the offices essential for the administration of these areas.

These structures, based on similar beliefs in the ritual powers of chiefs, were found in many chiefdoms of the Guinea Coast, even very small ones. Nevertheless, there were some political units that might be called essentially secular. Mende chiefs, for example, were explicitly leaders whose rule was based on military prowess. In Niger delta and Efik towns senior priests had ritual headship but lacked any political importance, for power was held by rich traders. Leadership in many Igbo villages often lay de facto with wealthy men who were members of influential societies; there were few formal political offices, and decisions were reached through public discussions at village meetings.

KIN GROUPS AND OTHER ASSOCIATIONS

Kinship ties have been almost invariably of great significance in all traditional African societies, and the Guinea Coast was no exception. For the individual, ties through both the father and the mother were significant, but for inheritance and for political and legal purposes kin groups were commonly organized by singling out a particular line of descent. The bases of these kin groups might have been patrilineal or matrilineal, or both these lines of descent might be recognized simultaneously in different contexts. Most Yoruba kin groups were patrilineal, the Asante groups were matrilineal. Kin structures such as clans were usually of great significance in the administration of groups even in large and complex kingdoms although, as in the case of the Benin kingdom, there were exceptions. Even in matrilineal societies almost all important offices were held by men but, because women in such groups determined the group affiliation of their children and were of great formal significance in establishing a man's rights (as he claimed political office through his mother), women commonly attained a freedom of action and a degree of public significance that was difficult for them to acquire in patrilineal kin groups.

The rights of women in marriage varied considerably from group to group, but in many Guinea Coast societies, even patrilineal ones, it would generally be a mistake to regard women as having been particularly downtrodden in the past. Even when this superficially appears to have been the case, careful research reveals that, as very active economic partners of their farmer husbands, wives might exercise much influence over the allocation of crops and even of patrilineally inherited land. Among the Yoruba the husbands and their sons did almost all the farm work, and the women were responsible for marketing.

Age was an important basis for group formation in western African societies, though by no means did it have the same political significance that was attached to it in some East African societies, where age stratified the male population into groups with markedly different levels of rights and authority. In the Guinea Coast, age-groups tended to be more important in societies with weakly developed formal political structures; Igbo groups, for example, attached considerable importance to status given by membership in age-sets (compulsory groupings of individuals of roughly similar age who advance through life together). In the Benin kingdom groups structured by age were, similarly to most other aspects of life, subjected to manipulation from the centre. If a man remained in his village his age-status was determined solely by his birth; if he went to Benin City and served in one of the so-called palace societies he might return home after a period and be entitled to promotion to an age-set beyond his years. This was a distinct inducement to go to work at the capital, and, since ultimately elders held sway in the village, the effect was probably that the most vigorous and, therefore, leading elders were relatively young men who had been influenced by the Benin City "establishment." Quite apart from the political significance of age-sets, however, they might provide very significant personal ties for individuals who existed independently of any kin group organization to which they were attached. The links between age-mates where they united individuals in different kin groups, did, however, have a political aspect, for they were of great value when kin-group elders met to deal with intergroup arguments; often the elders were age-mates and had the closest personal ties with one another.

One of the most characteristic of Guinea Coast institutions, especially in areas in which central government was weakly developed, was the so-called secret society. Such societies had a significance similar to that of age-sets because they cut across kin-group lines and united people in different settlements or of different political groups. Moreover, the fact that membership was often graded and the higher grades were open to those who could pay the fees meant that in societies where new wealth from trade became important it was often through these societies that wealthy men (few were open to women) achieved political influence to which they might not otherwise have had access. In two major areas—in Sierra Leone and Liberia, and in the area east of the Niger delta—these associations achieved such power that they were crucial to the precolonial systems of law and order. Among the peoples in the former area, there was a women's society, Sande, but Poro, for men, was the major organization responsible for punishing such serious offenses as incest and homicide. There were local Poro councils composed of members of the highest grade, and a chief's authority often rested on his Poro rank. Poro spread among the Gola, Kpelle, and Mano of Liberia and the Mende of Sierra Leone.

The most interesting example of the politically powerful secret society, however, was probably that of Ekpe in 19th-century Calabar, the Efik capital at the mouth of the Cross River. There the Ekpe society was the main instrument of the governing oligarchy of wealthy traders. There was no strong central government to ensure that traders honoured their commitments either to one another or to European traders, but the threat of Ekpe action usually ensured compliance. The power of Ekpe is credited with having made Calabar society one of the most stratified on the Guinea Coast. Its membership was reserved almost exclusively for freemen, and its power was used to subordinate the large slave population. In the neighbouring delta area many able slaves who escaped exportation were eventually incorporated into local groups and became almost indistinguishable from the local population. In Calabar, perhaps because there was more agricultural land available, unexported slaves were kept as serfs. A few became prosperous and had slaves of their own (no one who had any pretensions did his own manual work). Ekpe members, however, banded together to maintain the free–slave distinction. Not surprisingly perhaps, Calabar was a place of bitter friction and saw slave uprisings in the middle of the century.

In general, secret societies were institutions for translating slight advantages of wealth into political influence, and wherever they occurred they indicated the existence of a measure of social stratification greater than that which commonly distinguished the successful elder from his junior kinsmen. The idea that small-scale tribal societies were essentially egalitarian has become much less tenable with recent research. It is recognized that, even in apparently unstratified societies, successful men usually depended for their position on their ability to control the labour of junior male kin and wives. Often they used their positions to increase their control over both at once, for by marrying polygynously while keeping young men wifeless they ensured an excellent labour supply for themselves.

Stratification was most obvious among wealthy and centralized states. However, because wealthy men were always polygynous and usually had many offspring, the wealth of one generation was commonly dispersed in the next, so that class formation was limited—the hereditary basis of high status was lacking.

In the 19th century new forms of stratification emerged in Sierra Leone and Liberia when freed slaves educated in North America were settled in these areas to become the "Creoles," shopkeepers and white-collar workers—an elite vis-à-vis the natives. Some Sierra Leonians moved to other British West African possessions on the coast, where they joined with tiny indigenous elites drawn from wealthy, educated coastal families to form with them a new bureaucratic class.

BELIEF SYSTEMS

There are, at least in outline, similarities between the various belief systems on the Guinea Coast. Most systems contained these features: belief in a withdrawn high god; belief in lesser gods that were useful because they were easily manipulated; concern with the dead, usually but not necessarily ancestors, who were thought to exercise influence over the groups to which they belonged in life; and belief in witches and sorcerers, whose existence explained undeserved misfortune. Finally, there was common acknowledgment of the power of diviners who could determine the cause of a particular misfortune. Beliefs as to what constituted the basis of diviners' powers varied widely, but there was such a pragmatic attitude that what mattered was the apparent success of the divination, not its conceptual foundation. Diviners traveled widely between societies. They often advertised the power of distant cults, and sometimes priests were brought long distances to establish new local shrines. In this way famous cults spread widely, and this fact may help to account for the existence of broadly similar beliefs between societies that had apparently rather little contact with one another. In general, however, these religious beliefs were broadly compatible with the type of society in which they were found, so that there tended to be complex pantheons of gods in hierarchical and stratified kingdoms such as Dahomey, but small-scale, stateless societies lacked that kind of complexity among their deities.

These beliefs accounted not only for misfortune but also for individual success. There was a widespread belief that individuals, in an existence before birth, had to choose whether their earthly lives should be fortunate or unlucky, and consistent lack of success might be ascribed to wrong choices—so-called pre-natal fate. In some societies particularly fortunate individuals were presumed to have established a relationship with a luck-bestowing supernatural being—for example, the water spirit of the Niger delta. In other societies undue prosperity was suspect and might be ascribed to membership in a sorcerers' society, which was believed to give wealth to its initiates in return for a sinister fee: the life of a relative. In such societies the implication was that the individual could get ahead only at the expense of his kin.

KINGDOMS, EMPIRES, AND CENTRES

Long before the Pilgrims landed at Plymouth or the Jamestown colony was established, long even before Christopher Columbus reached the New World, Africa was the home of a panoply of complex, highly developed kingdoms and empires that included thriving centres of commerce, militarism, and learning. Aspects of some of them have already been considered above in a regional context. What follows is a more detailed look at a collection of the most significant of these societies (and some their most prominent cities), most of which were located in portions of western and west-central Africa from which the majority of the ancestors of African Americans hailed. Many of these early states were grounded in the tradition of Islamic belief and culture.

GHANA

The first of the great medieval trading empires of western Africa, Ghana flourished in the 7th–13th centuries. It was situated between the Sahara and the headwaters of the Sénégal and Niger rivers, in an area that now comprises southeastern Mauritania and part of Mali. Ghana was populated by Soninke clans of Mande-speaking people who acted as intermediaries between the Arab and Amazigh (Berber) salt traders to the north and the producers of gold and ivory to the south. (Again, the empire should not be confused with the modern Republic of Ghana.)

An unconfirmed tradition dates the origins of the kingdom to the 4th century CE. Nothing is known of the political history of Ghana under its early kings. The first written references to the empire are those of Arabic geographers and historians from the 8th century, and it seems certain that, by 800, Ghana had become rich and powerful. Called Wagadu by its rulers, it derived its more familiar name from the king's title of *ghāna*. The king was able to enforce obedience from lesser groups and to exact tribute from them. Much of the empire was ruled through tributary princes who were probably the traditional chiefs of these subject clans. The Ghanaian king also imposed an import-export tax on traders and a production tax on gold, which was the country's most valuable commodity.

According to the 11th-century Spanish-Arab chronicler Abū ʿUbayd al-Bakrī, the king welcomed to his capital many of the northern African traders of the Sahara, who, after the Arab conquest in the 8th century, had been converted to Islam. In the course of Ghana's history the capital was moved from one place to another: that of the 11th century has been tentatively identified by archaeologists as Kumbi (or Koumbi Saleh), 200 miles (322 km) north of modern Bamako, Mali.

The principal raison d'etre of the empire was the desire to control the trade in alluvial gold, which had led the nomadic Amazigh peoples of the desert to develop the western trans-Saharan caravan road. Gold was secured, often by mute barter, at the southern limits of the empire. From there it was conveyed to the empire's capital, where a Muslim commercial town developed alongside the native city. There the gold was exchanged for commodities, the most important of which was salt, which had been transported southward by northern African caravans.

As Ghana grew richer it extended its political control, strengthening its position as an entrepôt by absorbing lesser states. It also incorporated some of the gold-producing lands to its south and such south-Saharan cities to the north as Audaghost, a famous market that has since disappeared.

Ghana began to decline in the 11th century with the emergence of the Muslim Almoravids, a militant confederation of the Ṣanhājah and other Amazigh groups of the Sahara who combined in a holy war to convert their neighbours. Abū Bakr, the leader of this movement's southern wing, took Audaghost in 1054 and, after many battles, seized Kumbi in 1076. The Almoravids' domination of Ghana lasted only a few years, but their activities upset the trade on which the empire depended, and the introduction of their flocks into an arid agricultural terrain initiated a disastrous process of desertification. The subject peoples of the empire began to break away, and in 1203, one of these, the Susu, occupied the capital. In 1240 the city was destroyed by the Mande emperor Sundiata, and what was left of the empire of Ghana was incorporated into his new empire of Mali.

Kanem-Bornu

Another of the great African trading empires, Kanem-Bornu was ruled by the Sef (Sayf) dynasty that controlled the area around Lake Chad from the 9th to the 19th century. Its territory at various times included what is now southern Chad, northern Cameroon, northeastern Nigeria, eastern Niger, and southern Libya.

Kanem-Bornu was probably founded around the mid-9th century, and its first capital was at Njimi, northeast of Lake Chad. Toward the end of the 11th century, the Sef *mai* (king) Umme (later known as Ibn ʿAbd al-Jalīl) became a Muslim, and from that time Kanem-Bornu was an Islamic state. Because of its location, it served as a point of contact in trade between North Africa, the Nile Valley, and the sub-Sahara region.

In the late 14th century the Bulala people forced the Sef to abandon Kanem, and the capital was moved to Birni Ngazargamu in Bornu, west of Lake Chad. It remained there even after Kanem was retaken in the early 16th century.

Under its able rulers of the 16th century (Muḥammad Dunama, 'Abd Allāh, and especially Idrīs Alawma, who reigned c. 1571–1603), Kanem-Bornu (thereafter sometimes called simply Bornu) was extended and consolidated.

At the beginning of the 19th century, the Fulani of Nigeria disputed Bornu's suzerainty over the Hausa states to the west of Lake Chad and drove *mai* Aḥmad from his capital in c. 1808. They were expelled by the intervention of Muḥammad al-Kanamī, a scholar, warrior, and diplomat of Kanem, to whom Aḥmad had been forced to appeal for aid. Obliged also to assist Aḥmad's successor, Dunama, against the raiding Fulani, al-Kanamī assumed implicit control of Bornu but was never able to reestablish its power. The Sef dynasty died out in 1846.

KATSINA

According to tradition, the historic kingdom and emirate Katsina, one of the Hausa Bakwai ("Seven True Hausa States"), was founded in the 10th or 11th century in northern Nigeria. Islam was introduced in the 1450s, and Muhammad Korau (reigned late 15th century) was Katsina's first Muslim king. During his reign camel caravans crossed the Sahara from Ghudāmis (Ghadames), Tripoli, and Tunis southward to Katsina and brought such prosperity to the state that it became caught in the rivalry between the great West African empires of Songhai (Gao) and Kanem-Bornu. In 1513 Katsina was conquered by the Songhai.

The original walls around Katsina town, the kingdom's capital, were built in the mid-16th century. In 1554 Katsina defeated the forces of Songhai and, in 1570, those of Kano, its principal rival in the trans-Saharan trade. After Moroccan armies had vanquished Songhai in 1591, Katsina was (until the end of the 18th century) a tributary state of Bornu. Katsina entered its greatest period of prosperity in the early 18th century. Besides being the leading Hausa commercial state, it replaced Timbuktu (Tombouctou) as the chief west African centre of Islamic studies. Later in the century, wars with Gobir, a Hausa state to the northwest, marked the beginning of Katsina's decline.

Fulani herdsmen settled in Katsina by the 15th century, and in 1804 the Fulani jihad (holy war) leader, Usman dan Fodio, led a revolt (beginning in Gobir) against the Hausa overlords. The Fulani leader Umaru Dallaji captured Katsina town in 1806 and was named the first Katsina emir with Katsina as his seat. The emirate was governed by the representative of the sultan of Sokoto (a town 160 miles [258 km] west) as well as the local emir.

Many of the Hausa nobility and people fled to Dankama (25 miles [40 km] northeast) and to Tassawa (Tessaoua) and Maradi in Niger, where they proclaimed a Hausa Katsina chiefdom. Their raids throughout the 19th century weakened the Fulani emir and Katsina town (which was surpassed by Kano).

In 1903 Katsina's emir pledged allegiance to the British rulers of Northern Nigeria. When the British and French set the present Niger-Nigeria boundary in 1904, Katsina emirate was reduced in size and made a part of Kano province. Much of its former territory is now in Katsina state.

MALI

The West African empire of Mali developed from the state of Kangaba, on the Upper Niger River east of the Fouta Djallon, and is said to have been founded before 1000 CE. It flourished from the 13th to the 16th century. The Malinke inhabitants of Kangaba acted as middlemen in the gold trade during the later period of ancient Ghana. Their dislike of the Susu chief Sumanguru's harsh but ineffective rule provoked the Malinke to revolt, and in 1230 Sundiata, the brother of Kangaba's fugitive ruler, won a decisive victory against the Susu chief. (The name Mali absorbed the name Kangaba at about this time.)

In extending Mali's rule beyond Kangaba's narrow confines, Sundiata set a precedent for successive emperors.

Imperial armies secured the gold-bearing lands of Bondu and Bambuk to the south, subdued the Diara in the northwest, and pushed along the Niger as far north as Lac Débo. Under Mansa Mūsā (1307–32?) Mali rose to the apogee of its power. He controlled the lands of the Middle Niger, absorbed into his empire the trading cities of Timbuktu and Gao, and imposed his rule on such south Saharan cities as Walata and on the Taghaza region of salt deposits to the north. He extended the eastern boundaries of his empire as far as the Hausa people, and to the west he invaded Takrur and the lands of the Fulani and Tukulor peoples. In Morocco, Egypt, and elsewhere he sent ambassadors and imperial agents and on his return from a pilgrimage to Mecca (1324) established Egyptian scholars in both Timbuktu and Gao.

By the 14th century the Dyula, or Wangara, as the Muslim traders of Mali came to be called, were active throughout West Africa. The tide that had carried Mali to success, however, impelled it ineluctably to decline. The empire outgrew its political and military strength: Gao rebelled (c. 1400); the Tuareg seized Walata and Timbuktu (1431); the peoples of Takrur and their neighbours (notably the Wolof) threw off their subjection; and the Mossi (in what is now Burkina Faso) began to harass their Mali overlord. By about 1550 Mali had ceased to be important as a political entity.

WOLOF EMPIRE

The Wolof (Ouolof) empire dominated what is now inland Senegal during the early period of European contact with West Africa, flourishing from the 14th to the 16th century. Founded soon after 1200, the Wolof state was ruled by a king, or *burba,* whose duties were both political and religious. During the 14th century, it began to develop satellite states, of which the most important was Cayor. During the 15th century Wolof was a powerful empire, on the border of which lay the tributary state of Sine-Solum, ruled by the Serer, a kindred people to the Wolof.

With the advent of the Portuguese in about 1440, the Wolof were drawn first into a profitable trading partnership and then into a political alliance—though they remained sufficiently independent to repel Portugal's more blatant attempts at infiltration.

In 1556 the nobles of Cayor threw off Wolof domination and established an independent state of their own on the Senegal coast. This action cut off Wolof's access to the sea and to the European trade; its importance subsequently declined.

TIMBUKTU

Located on the southern edge of the Sahara, just north of the Niger River, in the present-day country of Mali, Timbuktu (French: Tombouctou) was one of the most renowned cities of the medieval world. Its historical importance rests on its preeminence as a trading post on the trans-Saharan caravan route and as a centre of Islamic culture from 1400 to 1600.

Timbuktu was founded about 1100 CE as a seasonal camp by Tuareg nomads. There are several stories concerning the derivation of the city's name. According to one tradition, Timbuktu was named for an old woman left to oversee the camp

Minaret of the 15th century Sankore mosque, Timbuktu, Mali. Bloomberg/Getty Images

while the Tuareg roamed the Sahara. Her name (variously given as Tomboutou, Timbuktu, or Buctoo) meant "mother with a large navel," possibly describing an umbilical hernia or other such physical malady. Timbuktu's location at the meeting point of desert and water made it an ideal trading centre. In the late 13th or early 14th century it was incorporated into the Mali empire.

By the 14th century it was a flourishing centre for the trans-Saharan gold-salt trade, and it grew as a centre of Islamic culture. Three of West Africa's oldest mosques—Djinguereber (Djingareyber), Sankore, and Sidi Yahia—were built there during the 14th and early 15th centuries. After an extravagant pilgrimage to Mecca in 1324, the Mali emperor Mansa Mūsā built the Great Mosque (Djinguereber) and a royal residence, the Madugu (the former has since been rebuilt many times, and of the latter no trace remains). The Granada architect Abū Isḥāq as-Sāḥili was then commissioned to design the Sankore mosque, around which Sankore University was established. The mosque still stands today, probably because of as-Sāḥili's directive to incorporate a wooden framework into the mud walls of the building, thus facilitating annual repairs after the rainy season. The Tuareg regained control of the city in 1433, but they ruled from the desert. Although the Tuareg exacted sizable tributes and plundered periodically, trade and learning continued to flourish in Timbuktu. By 1450, its population increased to about 100,000. The city's scholars, many of whom had studied in Mecca or in Egypt, numbered some 25,000.

In 1468 the city was conquered by the Songhai ruler Sonni 'Alī. He was generally ill-disposed to the city's Muslim scholars, but his successor—the first ruler of the new Askia dynasty, Muḥammad I Askia of Songhai (reigned 1493–1528)—used the scholarly elite as legal and moral counselors. During the Askia period (1493–1591) Timbuktu was at the height of its commercial and intellectual development. Merchants from Ghudāmis (Ghadames; now in Libya), Augila (now Awjidah, Libya), and numerous other cities of North Africa gathered there to buy gold and slaves in exchange for the Saharan salt of Taghaza and for North African cloth and horses.

After it was captured by Morocco in 1591, the city declined. In 1593, its scholars were ordered arrested on suspicion of disaffection; some were killed during a resulting struggle, while others were exiled to Morocco. Perhaps worse still, the small Moroccan garrisons placed in command of the city offered inadequate protection, and Timbuktu was repeatedly attacked and conquered by the Bambara, Fulani, and Tuareg.

European explorers reached Timbuktu in the early 19th century. The ill-fated Scottish explorer Gordon Laing was the first to arrive (1826), followed by the French explorer René-Auguste Caillié in 1828. Caillié, who had studied Islam and learned Arabic, reached Timbuktu disguised as an Arab. After two weeks he departed, becoming the first explorer to return to Europe with firsthand knowledge of the city (rumours of Timbuktu's wealth had reached Europe centuries before, owing to tales of Mūsā's 11th-century caravan to Mecca). In 1853 the German geographer Heinrich Barth reached the city during a five-year trek across Africa. He, too, survived the journey, later publishing a chronicle of his travels.

Timbuktu was captured by the French in 1894. They partly restored the city from the desolate condition in which they found it, but no connecting railway or hard-surfaced road was built. In 1960 it became part of the newly independent Republic of Mali. The modern city of Timbuktu is now an administrative centre of Mali. It was designated a UNESCO World Heritage site in 1988.

HAUSA STATES

Occasionally interconnected from the mid-14th century by loose alliances, the Hausa states lay above the confluence of the Niger and Benue rivers (in present-day northern Nigeria), between the Songhai empire in the west and that of the Kanem-Bornu, or Bornu, in the east. The seven true Hausa states, or Hausa Bakwai (Biram, Daura, Gobir, Kano, Katsina, Rano, and Zaria [Zazzau]), and their seven outlying satellites, or Banza Bakwai (Zamfara, Kebbi, Yauri, Gwari, Nupe, Kororofa [Jukun], and Yoruba), had no central authority, were never combined in wars of conquest, and were therefore frequently subject to domination from outside. Isolated until the 14th century, they were then introduced to Islam by missionaries from Mali. Conquered early in the 19th century by Fulani, in whose jihad, or "holy war," many Hausa peasants had voluntarily combined, they were organized into emirates. At the beginning of the 20th century, the British took over the administration of the former emirates, to which they attached Bornu to form the northern provinces (subsequently the Northern Region) of the Protectorate of Nigeria.

SONGHAI EMPIRE

The great West African trading empire of Songhai (Songhay) flourished during the 15th and 16th centuries. It centred on the middle reaches of the Niger River in what is now central Mali and eventually extended west to the Atlantic coast and east into Niger and Nigeria.

Though the Songhai people are said to have established themselves in the city of Gao about 800 CE, they did not regard it as their capital until the beginning of the 11th century during the reign of the *dia* (king) Kossoi, a Songhai convert to Islam. Gao so prospered and expanded during the next 300 years that from 1325 to 1375 the rulers of Mali added it to their empire. In about 1335 the *dia* line of rulers gave way to the *sunni*, or *shi*, one of whom, Sulaiman-Mar, is said to have won back Gao's independence. The century or so of vicissitudes that followed was ended by the accession in about 1464 of Sonni 'Alī, also known as 'Alī Ber (d. 1492). By repulsing a Mossi attack on Timbuktu, the second most important city of Songhai, and by defeating the Dogon and Fulani in the hills of Bandiagara, he had by 1468 rid the empire of any immediate danger. He later evicted the Tuareg from Timbuktu, which they had occupied since 1433, and, after a siege of seven years, took Jenne (Djenné) in 1473, and by 1476 had dominated the lakes region of the middle Niger to the west of Timbuktu. He repulsed a Mossi attack on Walata to the northwest in 1480 and subsequently discouraged raiding by all the inhabitants of the Niger valley's southern periphery. The civil policy of Sonni 'Alī was to conciliate the interests of his pagan pastoralist subjects with those of the Muslim city dwellers, on whose wealth and scholarship the Songhai empire depended. His son Sonni Baru (reigned 1493), who sided completely with the pastoralists, was deposed by the rebel Muḥammad ibn Abī Bakr Ture, also known as Muḥammad I Askia (reigned 1493–1528), who welded the central region of the western Sudan into a single empire. He too fought the Mossi of Yatenga, tackled Borgu, in what is now northwestern Nigeria (1505)—albeit with little success—and mounted successful campaigns against the Diara (1512), against the kingdom of Fouta-Toro in Senegal, and to the east against the Hausa states. In order to win control of the principal caravan markets to the north, he ordered his armies to found a colony in and around Agadez in Aïr. He was deposed by his eldest son, Musa, in 1528.

Throughout the dynastic squabbles of successive reigns (Askia Musa, 1528–31; Bengan Korei, also known as Askia Muḥammad II, 1531–37; Askia Ismail, 1537–39; Askia Issihak I, 1539–49), the Muslims in the towns continued to act as middlemen in the profitable gold trade with the states of Akan in central Guinea. The peace and prosperity of Askia Dāwūd's reign (1549–82) was followed by a raid initiated by Sultan Aḥmad al-Manṣūr of Morocco on the salt deposits of Taghaza. The situation, which continued to worsen under Muḥammad Bāni (1586–88), culminated disastrously for Songhai under Issihak II (1588–91) when Moroccan forces, using firearms, advanced into the Songhai empire to rout his forces, first at Tondibi and then at Timbuktu and Gao. Retaliatory guerrilla action of the pastoral Songhai failed to restore the empire, the economic and administrative centres of which remained in Moroccan hands.

KINGDOM OF BAGIRMI

The Kingdom of Bagirmi (Baguirmi) was founded in the 16th century in the region just southeast of Lake Chad. Europeans first learned about the existence of Bagirmi and the other powerful states of central Africa (e.g., Wadai and Bornu-Kanem) when Dixon Denham penetrated the Lake Chad region in 1823. Details became known particularly from written records of the later explorers Heinrich Barth and Gustav Nachtigal.

The Bagirmi dynasty appears to have been established in 1522. The Bagirmi king, called the *mbang*, ruled from the capital city of Massenya. The rulers as well as many of their followers accepted Islam during the reign of the fourth sultan, Abdullah (*c.* 1600). The 17th century brought prosperity as a result of the slave trade. Bagirmi became a pawn in the conflicts between the rival empires of Bornu to the west and Wadai to the east. A vassal of Bornu in the 17th and 18th centuries, it fell to Wadai early in the 19th century and was repeatedly sacked by and forced to pay tribute to both states. Drought and the persecution of Muslim teachers promoted substantial migration out of Bagirmi in the 19th century. Nonetheless, it was an important commercial and craft centre in the first half of the 19th century, exporting locally woven and dyed cloths and non-Muslim slaves. In 1894 Massenya was destroyed by the army of the adventurer Rābiḥ az-Zubayr. A series of treaties in the late 19th and early 20th centuries brought the territory under French control.

GORÉE ISLAND

Gorée Island, a rather barren volcanic rock of only 88 acres (36 hectares) located just south of Cape Verde Peninsula, Senegal, was the site of one of the earliest European settlements in Western Africa and long served as an outpost for slave and other trading.

The island was first visited (1444) by Portuguese sailors under Dinís Dias and occupied in subsequent years. The island's indigenous Lebu people were later displaced, and fortifications were erected. The town was active in the Atlantic slave trade from 1536 until 1848, when slavery was abolished in Senegal. The Slave House (now a museum) was constructed in 1786. Historians debate whether Gorée was a major centre for the trade or simply one of many centres from which Africans were taken to the Americas. Nevertheless, in 1978 Gorée Island was declared a UNESCO World Heritage site.

OYO EMPIRE

The Oyo empire was the most important and authoritative of all the early Yoruba principalities. Located north of Lagos, in present-day southwestern Nigeria, it dominated, during its apogee (1650–1750), most of the states between the Volta River in the west and the Niger River in the east.

According to traditions, Oyo derived from a great Yoruba ancestor and hero, Oduduwa, who came from the east to settle at Ile-Ife and whose son became the first *alafin*, or ruler, of Oyo. Linguistic evidence suggests that two waves of immigrants came into Yorubaland between 700 and 1000, the second settling at Oyo in the open country north of the Guinea forest. This second state became preeminent among all Yoruba states because of its favourable trading position, its natural resources, and the industry of its inhabitants.

Early in the 16th century Oyo was a minor state, powerless before its northern neighbours Borgu and Nupe—by whom it was conquered in 1550. The power of Oyo was already growing by the end of the century, however, thanks to the *alafin* Orompoto, who used the wealth derived from trade to establish a cavalry force and to maintain a trained army.

Oyo subjugated the kingdom of Dahomey in the west in two phases (1724–30, 1738–48) and traded with European merchants on the coast through the port of Ajase (Porto-Novo). As Oyo's wealth increased, so did its leaders' political options; some wished to concentrate on amassing wealth, while others advocated the use of wealth for territorial expansion. This difference was not resolved until the *alafin* Abiodun (reigned *c.* 1770–89) conquered his opponents in a bitter civil war and pursued a policy of economic development based primarily on the coastal trade with European merchants.

Abiodun's neglect of everything but the economy weakened the army, and thus the means by which the central government maintained control. His successor, the *alafin* Awole, inherited local revolts, an administration tenuously maintained by a complex system of public service, and a decline in the power of tributary chiefs. The decline was exacerbated by quarrels between the *alafin* and his advisers; it continued throughout the 18th century and into the 19th, when Oyo began to lose control of its trade routes to the coast. Oyo was invaded by the newly risen Fon of Dahomey, and soon after

1800 it was captured by militant Fulani Muslims from Hausaland in the northeast.

DJENNÉ

Like Timbuktu, Djenné (also spelled Jenne or Dienné) was a vital trading city and centre of Muslim scholarship. It is situated in southern Mali on the Bani River on floodlands between the Bani and Niger rivers, 220 miles (354 km) southwest of Timbuktu. Djenné was founded in the 13th century near the site of Djenné-Jeno, an ancient city then in decline, and grew into a transshipment centre between the traders of the central and western Sudan and those of Guinea's tropical forests. It was captured in 1468 (or 1473) by the Songhai emperor Sonni ʿAlī. The city benefited both from its direct connection by river with Timbuktu and from its situation at the head of the trade routes to the gold mines of Bitou (now in Côte d'Ivoire), to Lobé, and to Bouré; it was also an important entrepôt for salt. By the mid-17th century, Djenné was renowned as a centre of Muslim learning. The city was besieged after 1818 and subsequently subdued by the Fulani ruler of Macina, Shehu Aḥmadu Lobbo, who expelled those inhabitants practicing a form of Muslim worship that he disapproved of and allowed its mosque to fall into ruin.

Djenné was conquered by the Tukulor emperor ʿUmar Tal about 1861 and was occupied by the French in 1893. Thereafter its commercial functions were taken over by the town of Mopti, situated northeast of Djenné at the confluence of the Niger and Bani rivers. Djenné is now an agricultural trade centre, of diminished importance, though its mosque and other historic buildings were designated a World Heritage site in 1988.

ASANTE EMPIRE

The Asante (Ashanti) empire occupied what is now southern Ghana in the 18th and 19th centuries. Extending from the Comoé River in the west to the Togo Mountains in the east, it was active in the slave trade in the 18th century and unsuccessfully resisted British penetration in the 19th.

In their struggle against the suzerain state of Denkyera and lesser neighbouring states, the Asante people made little headway until the accession, probably in the 1670s, of Osei Tutu. After a series of campaigns that crushed all opposition, he was installed as Asantehene, or king of the new Asante state, whose capital was named Kumasi. His authority was symbolized by the Golden Stool, on which all subsequent kings were enthroned.

From the beginning of the 18th century, the Asante supplied slaves to British and Dutch traders on the coast; in return they received firearms with which to enforce their territorial expansion. After the death of Osei Tutu in either 1712 or 1717, a period of internal chaos and factional strife was ended with the accession of Opoku Ware (ruled c. 1720–50), under whom Asante reached its fullest extent in the interior of the country. Kings Osei Kwadwo (ruled c. 1764–77), Osei Kwame (1777–1801), and Osei Bonsu (c. 1801–24) established a strong centralized state, with an efficient, merit-based bureaucracy and a fine system of communications.

In 1807 Osei Bonsu occupied southern Fante territory—an enclave around British headquarters at Cape Coast; in the same year, Great Britain outlawed the slave trade. Declining trade relations and disputes over the Fante region caused friction over the following decade and led to warfare in the 1820s. The Asante defeated a British force in 1824 but made peace in 1831 and avoided conflict for the next 30 years.

In 1863, under Kwaku Dua (ruled 1834–67), the Asante again challenged the British by sending forces to occupy the coastal provinces. In 1869 the British took possession of Elmina (over which Asante claimed jurisdiction), and in 1874 an expeditionary force under Sir Garnet Wolseley marched on Kumasi. Though Wolseley managed to occupy the Asante capital for only one day, the Asante were shocked to realize the inferiority of their military and communications systems. The invasion, moreover, sparked numerous secessionary revolts in the northern provinces. The old southern provinces were formally constituted the Gold Coast colony by the British later in 1874. Asante's king Kofi Karikari was then deposed, and Mensa Bonsu (ruled 1874–83) assumed power. He attempted to adapt the agencies of Asante government to the changed situation. Although he reorganized the army, appointed some Europeans to senior posts, and increased Asante resources, he was prevented from restoring Asante imperial power by the British political agents, who supported the northern secessionist chiefs and the opponents of central government in Kumasi. The empire continued to decline under his successor, Prempeh I (acceded 1888), during whose reign, on Jan. 1, 1902, Asante was formally declared a British crown colony, the former northern provinces being on the same day separately constituted the Protectorate of the Northern Territories of the Gold Coast.

KAZEMBE

Kazembe (Cazembe) was the largest and most highly organized of the Lunda (Luba-Lunda) kingdoms in central Africa. At the height of its power (c. 1800), Kazembe occupied almost all of the territory now included in the Katanga region of Congo (Kinshasa) and in northern Zambia. Apparently created about 1740 by an exploring party from western Lunda, the kingdom rapidly increased in size and influence through the conquest and annexation of neighbouring states. After 1850, however, disputed succession led to civil war, and the kingdom was finally destroyed about 1890 by attacks from eastern tribes.

During the existence of Kazembe there were nine kings with the name Kazembe. The greatest of these was Kazembe II, known as Kaniembo (reigned c. 1740–60), who conquered most

of the territory that the kingdom eventually occupied, extending citizenship to those he conquered and establishing the complicated network of tribute and trade that held the vast kingdom together. His grandson, Kazembe IV, known as Kibangu Keleka (reigned 1805–50), encouraged contacts with Portuguese traders from Angola, and Kazembe became an important centre of trade between the peoples in the central African interior and the Portuguese and Arabs on the eastern coast.

FULANI EMPIRE

A Muslim theocracy, the Fulani empire of the Western Sudan flourished in the 19th century. The Fulani, a people of obscure origins, expanded eastward from Futa Toro in Lower Senegal in the 14th century. By the 16th century they had established themselves at Macina (upstream from the Niger Bend) and were proceeding eastward into Hausaland. Some settled in the 19th century at Adamawa (in the northern Cameroons). Many of the Fulani continued to pursue a pastoral life; some, however, particularly in Hausaland, gave up their nomadic pursuits, settled into existing urban communities, and were converted to Islam.

In the 1790s a Fulani divine, Usman dan Fodio (1754–1817), who lived in the northern Hausa state of Gobir (northeast of Sokoto) quarreled with its rulers. Accusing the Hausa kings of being little more than pagans, he encouraged

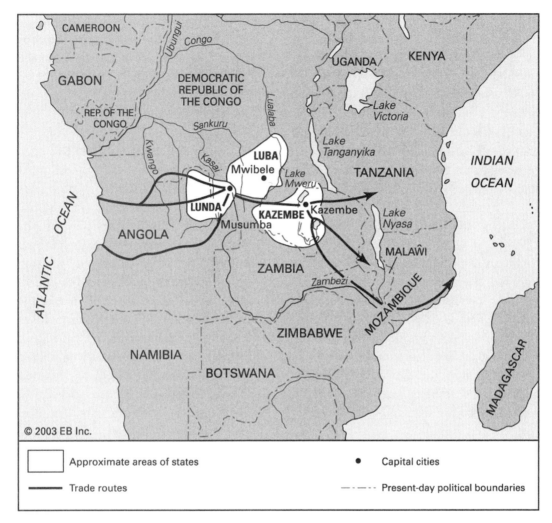

Luba and Lunda states—among the larger of the Bantu states in the 15th to 19th centuries—shown with neighbouring Kazembe and some of the major trade routes.

the Hausa people to revolt. Joined both by Hausa commoners and by Fulani pastoralists alike, the jihad, or "holy war," swept through Hausaland and, repulsed only by the eastern empire of Kanem-Bornu, engulfed Adamawa, Nupe, and Yorubaland to the south. After the invasion by the Fulani of the northern provinces of the Oyo, the emirate of Ilorin to the northeast became the base from which Islam was to spread among the Yoruba. Usman, who was more a scholar than a statesman, ceded the practical direction of the eastern part of the empire to his son Muḥammad Bello, who settled in Sokoto, and the western (with its capital at Gwandu) to his brother Abdullahi. All three continued the Fulani denunciation of Bornu. The empire reached its zenith under Muḥammad Bello, who, like Usman, administered it according to the principles of Muslim law. The decay of this system was to aid the establishment in the late 19th century of British rule over what was later to be known as Northern Nigeria.

LUNDA EMPIRE

The Bantu-speaking Lunda empire was founded in the 16th century in the region of the upper Kasai River (now in northeastern Angola and western Congo [Kinshasa]). Although the Lunda people had lived in the area from early times, their empire was founded by invaders coming west from Luba. Between 1600 and 1750, bands of Lunda adventurers established numerous satellites (e.g., Kasanje; Kazembe). The Lunda empire consisted of a centralized core, a ring of provinces closely tied to the capital, an outer ring of provinces that paid tribute but were otherwise autonomous, and a fringe of independent kingdoms that shared a common Lunda culture. The imperial boundaries were thus only loosely defined.

Lunda traded with both the Arabs on the Indian Ocean and, from about 1650, the Portuguese on the Atlantic. The leading exports were ivory and slaves; imports included cloth and guns. The empire reached the height of its power by the 1850s. Thereafter its might was eroded by the incursions of the neighbouring Chokwe. Portuguese troops arrived from Angola in the west in 1884 and Belgians from the Congo Free State in the northeast in 1898. Lunda was partitioned between them.

LUBA-LUNDA STATES

The Luba-Lunda complex of states flourished in Central Africa (in the present-day Democratic Republic of the Congo) from the late 15th to the late 19th century. The Luba state was situated east of the Kasai River around the headwaters of the Lualaba River, and the Lunda state east of the Kwango River around the headwaters of the Kasai River. A later state, Kazembe, was located to the southeast.

Lunda traditions record no large or powerful states until the late 15th century, when the warrior Kongolo entered the region, subdued several small chiefdoms, and founded a centralized state, with its capital at Mwibele. Around this central state a number of satellites proliferated; by the 17th century they had spread into the southern Congo Basin and to what are now parts of Angola and Zambia. The largest of these satellites was Lunda, to the south and west of the Luba state and surpassing it in territory. Its founder, known by the title of Mwata Yamvo (ruler), was a Luba nobleman who married a Lunda princess. The Lunda state expanded westward in the middle of the 18th century and imposed its rule on peoples living near the Kwango River.

Largest of all the Luba-Lunda states was Kazembe, which was founded early in the 18th century, when the last major expansion of the Luba-Lunda complex occurred; migrants from Lunda moved southeastward, establishing a capital in the Luapula River valley to the south of Lake Mweru (in present-day Zambia).

From the outset the Luba-Lunda states were indirectly connected with the Portuguese in Angola, who supplied cloth and other goods in return for slaves and ivory. The Kazembe Lunda, who established their state with the aid of Portuguese arms, soon were exchanging their ivory at the Portuguese trading stations on the Zambezi River. Kazembe continued to flourish until late in the 19th century, when it was colonized by the British.

The once-independent states now are part of the country of the Democratic Republic of the Congo, but the Lunda people continue to recognize a Lunda ruler with ceremonial authority. The last Luba ruler, Kasongo Nyembo, led the state from 1891 to 1917.

KASANJE

The kingdom of Kasanje was founded by the Imbangala about 1630 along the upper Cuango River (in present-day Angola). By the mid-17th century Kasanje had risen to become a dominant power along the Cuango, as it allied with the Portuguese in the area and often fought against the neighbouring kingdom of Matamba. By the end of the 17th century,

the kingdom had abandoned the commitment to rapine that was characteristic of Imbangala groups and had regularized marriage and child raising. The Portuguese established a controlled market, or *feira*, in Kasanje at this time, which served as a channel for the slave trade from states further in the interior, such as the Lunda empire. In the mid-19th century, Kasanje was able to repulse a Portuguese military expedition. However, this resolve was tested when commercially minded nobles, enriched by the commodity trade of the 19th century, subsequently challenged the power of the kings. The kingdom then had a number of civil wars, though it still managed to stave off Portuguese campaigns in the area in the 1890s. Kasanje was eventually conquered by Portugal and integrated into Angola about 1911.

MATAMBA

Located on the Cuango River northeast of present-day Luanda, Angola, the kingdom of Matamba was founded by Kimbundu-speaking people before the 16th century. It was loosely under the orbit of the Kongo kingdom until about 1550. The Matamba kingdom was noteworthy in that it was frequently ruled by women. In 1630–32 it was conquered by Njinga Mbande (often referred to simply as Njinga, also spelled Nzinga, Jinga, or Ginga; also known by her Christian name, Ana de Sousa), ruler of the neighbouring Ndongo kingdom, when she was expelled from some of her domains by rivals and their Portuguese allies. Matamba served as Njinga's main base in the long war with Portugal and her Ndongo rival, Ngola a Hari. A treaty in 1656 ended the war and established Matamba's boundary with the Portuguese colony of Angola. Njinga left no children, and, following a civil war in 1666, Matamba was ruled by the descendants of her general, João Guterres Ngola Kanini. Matamba wrestled with the neighbouring Kasanje kingdom for control of the Cuango River valley until Queen Verónica Guterres Ngola Kanini settled border issues and regularized the new kingdom. Matamba then enjoyed generally peaceful relations with Portugal that were only occasionally broken by war, as in 1744 when Portuguese troops invaded and defeated a Matamba army before withdrawing, resulting in the imposition of a nominal relationship of vassalage on Queen Ana II Guterres da Silva Ngola Kanini. In a succession dispute following the death of Ana III Guterres in 1767, the state was split in two by a rivalry between her nephew Francisco II Kaluete ka Mbandi and her daughter Kamana, but it was later reunited by Kamana's son.

During the 19th century—particularly after 1830—the Portuguese began to encroach on Matamba's western provinces with the goal of expanding their coffee plantations, leading to the establishment of a fort at Duque de Bragança (present-day Calandula) in 1838. Matamba participated in a number of wars to stop Portuguese expansion in the 1890s, but the kingdom became the focus of a Portuguese expedition in 1909 and ultimately was integrated into the Portuguese colony of Angola.

NDONGO

The original core of Ndongo, the kingdom of the Mbundu people, was in the highlands east of Luanda, Angola, between the Cuanza and Lucala rivers. At its height in the late 16th century, it stretched west to the Atlantic coast and south of the Cuanza.

According to early tradition, Ndongo was founded from the Kongo kingdom, probably in the late 15th or early 16th century. Ndongo's kings bore the title *ngola*, which later gave its name to the Portuguese colony of Angola. Portugal had intermittent relations with Ndongo from 1520, but it was only in 1575 that a Portuguese base was established—by Paulo Dias de Novais at Luanda Island. At first Dias de Novais cooperated with Ndongo, his forces serving as mercenaries in Ndongo's army, but in 1579 he and his forces were expelled from the capital and nearly driven from the kingdom. The Kongo kingdom intervened on Dias de Novais's behalf and rescued his forces, who then waged war against Ndongo. During this conflict, the Portuguese established an important inland fort on the Cuanza at Massangano, which served as a base for the capture of slaves for use in Brazil.

A military stalemate that had developed by the end of the 16th century was broken when the Portuguese governor, Luis Mendes de Vasconcelos, recruited Imbangala mercenaries and drove King Ngola Mbande from his capital to a refuge in the Cuanza River in a series of campaigns (1617–21). Ngola Mbande was able to negotiate a partially satisfactory peace agreement through his sister, Njinga Mbande (Njinga also spelled Nzinga, Jinga, or Ginga; also known by her Christian name, Ana de Sousa). After Ngola Mbande's death in 1624, Njinga took power in Ndongo—first as regent, then as queen. Her rival for the throne, Ngola a Hari, was supported by the Portuguese, and, in the civil war that followed, their combined forces had driven Njinga from Ndongo to Matamba by 1631. Ngola a Hari was then baptized Felipe I de Sousa and proclaimed king of Ndongo, ruling from his fortified mountain base at Pungo a Ndongo, although the war between Njinga and Felipe continued in the following years. When the region was invaded by the Dutch in 1641, Felipe allied Ndongo with the Portuguese against them in an indecisive war that ended with the 1648 ouster of the Dutch, led by Brazilian governor Salvador de Sá on behalf of the Portuguese. Years later, a peace treaty between Njinga and the Portuguese recognized Njinga as the ruler of Matamba, over protests from Felipe. Felipe's successor, his son, later revolted against the Portuguese: he was defeated in 1671, and his lands were integrated into the Portuguese colony of Angola.

KONGO

The kingdom of Kongo was located south of the Congo River (present-day Angola and Democratic Republic of the Congo). According to traditional accounts, the kingdom was founded by Lukeni lua Nimi about 1390. Originally, it was probably a loose federation of small polities, but, as the kingdom expanded, conquered territories were integrated as a royal patrimony. Soyo and Mbata were the two most powerful provinces of the original federation; other provinces included Nsundi, Mpangu, Mbamba, and Mpemba. The capital of the kingdom was Mbanza Kongo. The capital and its surrounding area were densely settled—more so than other towns in and near the kingdom. This allowed the *manikongo* (king of Kongo) to keep close at hand the manpower and supplies necessary to wield impressive power and centralize the state.

When Portuguese arrived in Kongo in 1483, Nzinga a Nkuwu was the *manikongo*. In 1491 both he and his son, Mvemba a Nzinga, were baptized and assumed Christian names—João I Nzinga a Nkuwu and Afonso I Mvemba a Nzinga, respectively. Afonso, who became *manikongo* c. 1509, extended Kongo's borders, centralized administration, and forged strong ties between Kongo and Portugal. He eventually faced problems with the Portuguese community that settled in Kongo regarding their handling of Atlantic trade—in particular, the slave trade. As a result, in 1526 Afonso organized the administration of the slave trade in an attempt to ensure that people were not illegally enslaved and exported.

Kongo's system of *manikongo* succession was often prone to disputes, frequently between sons or between sons and brothers of former kings, and at times the rivals would form factions, some of which were long-lived. Significant struggles over succession took place after Afonso's death in 1542 and many times after that. In 1568, possibly as a result of such a struggle, Kongo was temporary overrun by rival warriors from the east known as the Jagas, and Álvaro I Nimi a Lukeni (reigned 1568–87) was able to restore Kongo only with Portuguese assistance. In exchange, he allowed them to settle in at Luanda (a Kongo territory) and create the Portuguese colony that became Angola. Relations with Angola soon soured and then worsened when Angola's governor briefly invaded southern Kongo in 1622. Later, Garcia II Nkanga a Lukeni (reigned 1641–61) sided with the Dutch against Portugal when the former country seized portions of Angola from 1641 to 1648. Further disputes between Kongo and Portugal over joint claims in the region led to skirmishes in the small district of Mbwila, culminating in the Battle of Mbwila (or Ulanga) on Oct. 29, 1665. The Portuguese were victorious and killed the reigning *manikongo*,

António I Nvita a Nkanga, during the battle. Although Kongo continued to exist, from this point on it ceased to function as a unified kingdom.

After the Battle of Mbwila and the death of the *manikongo*, the Kimpanzu and Kinlaza—two rival factions that had formed earlier in Kongo's history—disputed the kingship. Unresolved, the civil war dragged on for most of the remainder of the 17th century, destroying the countryside and resulting in the enslavement and transport of thousands of Kongo subjects. These factions created several bases throughout the region, partitioning the kingdom among them. Pedro IV Agua Rosada Nsamu a Mvemba of Kibangu (reigned 1696–1718) engineered an agreement that recognized the integrity of the territorial bases while rotating kingship among them. During these negotiations, the abandoned capital of Mbanza Kongo (renamed São Salvador in the late 16th century) was taken by the Antonians (a religious movement, named after Saint Anthony, whose goal was to create a new Christian Kongo kingdom), led by Beatriz Kimpa Vita. Pedro subsequently tried and executed Beatriz as a heretic and then reoccupied the capital and restored the kingdom in 1709.

The rotational system of kingship worked moderately well in the 18th century, producing the long reign of Manuel II Nimi a Vuzi of the Kimpanzu (reigned 1718–43), followed by Garcia IV Nkanga a Mvandu of the Kinlaza (reigned 1743–52). Factional fighting continued on a smaller scale, and rotational succession was sometimes contested, as it was by José I Mpazi za Nkanga (reigned 1778–85), resulting in a weak monarchy. Portugal intervened in the succession dispute that followed the death of Henrique II Mpanzu a Nzindi (reigned 1842–57) and assisted Pedro V Agua Rosada Lelo (reigned 1859–91) in his installation. Eventually Pedro V ceded his territory to Portugal as a part of Angola in exchange for increased royal powers over outlying areas. A revolt against Portuguese rule and complicity of the kings led by Álvaro Buta in 1913–14 was suppressed but triggered the collapse of the Kongo kingdom, which was then fully integrated into the Portuguese colony of Angola.

SUMMARY

Many of these historic states were ultimately undone as a consequence of European colonialism, especially in the late 19th and early 20th centuries; however, as Lerone Bennett, Jr., wrote in *Before the Mayflower*, "The end of World War II marked the end of the European (white) expansion that began in the 15th century with the slave trade and the appropriation of the land and bodies of Africans and Asians. Now suddenly, after 500 years . . . all that was over, and peoples, especially European people, were forced to redefine themselves in a world without divine rights, without colonies, without natives."

CHAPTER 3

AFRICAN ROOTS: ART

No survey of historic African states and their legacy for African Americans would be complete without at least some consideration of the art created in those societies. Among the most important contributions by African Americans to the society and culture of the United States have been in the arts. In trying to understand the nature and breadth of those contributions, it is useful to consider the metaphoric conversation between the past and present, and between African and Western art forms. An examination of the African tradition in the visual arts in general and of some of the characteristic traditions of West African peoples in particular is a good starting place. Moreover, because many of the most profound creations of African Americans have been in literature and music, a look at African oral traditions may be even more instructive.

AFRICAN VISUAL ART: GENERAL CHARACTERISTICS, STYLE, TRIBE, AND ETHNIC IDENTITY

It is difficult to give a useful summary of the main characteristics of the art of sub-Saharan Africa. The variety of forms and practices is so great that the attempt to do so results in a series of statements that turn out to be just as true of, for example, Western art. Thus, some African art has value as entertainment; some has political or ideological significance;

some is instrumental in a ritual context; and some has aesthetic value in itself. More often than not, a work of African art combines several or all of these elements. Similarly, there are full-time and part-time artists; there are artists who figure in the political establishment and those who are ostracized and despised; further, some art forms can be made by anyone, while others demand the devotion of an expert. Claims of an underlying pan-African aesthetic must be viewed as highly contentious.

Some further general points can be made, however, in regard to the status of precolonial sub-Saharan art. First, in any African language, a concept of art as meaning something other than skill would be the exception rather than the rule. This is not because of any inherent limitation of African culture but because of the historical conditions under which European cultures arrived at their concept of art. The Western separation of fine art from the lowlier craft (i.e., useful skill) came out of a sequence of social, economic, and intellectual changes in Europe that did not occur in Africa before the colonial period at the very earliest. This separation, therefore, cannot be applied without qualification to African traditions of precolonial origin. Philosophers of art in the West might agree that works of art are simply artifacts made with the intention of possessing aesthetic value, and in that sense art, which would include craftwork as well as works of fine art, would indeed be found in all parts of Africa (as it is throughout human culture). But even in this case, African art must be understood through the investigation and understanding of local aesthetic values rather than through the imposition of categories of external origin.

The popular notion of African art in the West, however, is very different, for it is thought to comprise masks and very little else—except, perhaps, "local colour." This misconception has been enhanced by the aforementioned European concept of fine art, but it may have originated in a dependence, during the first period of Western interest in African art, upon collectible artifacts—some of which (pieces of sculpture, for instance) fitted neatly into the category of fine art, while others (such as textiles and pottery) were dismissed as craftwork. Painting in Africa was long presumed not to exist to any significant extent, largely because it was to be found on the skins of human bodies, on the walls of houses, and on rock faces—none of which were collectible. Clearly, the aesthetic field in Africa is not so limited.

Another misapprehension is that in the West art is created for art's sake, while in precolonial Africa art was solely functional. The motive for the creation of any work of art is inevitably complex, in Africa as elsewhere, and the fact that most of the sculpted artifacts known from Africa were made with some practical use in mind (whether for ritual or other purposes) does not mean that they could not simultaneously be valued as sources of aesthetic pleasure.

It is also often assumed that the African artist was constrained by tradition in a way contrasting with the freedom given to the Western artist. But there were also African traditions of precolonial origin that demanded a high level of inventive originality—for example, Asante silk weaving and Kuba raffia embroidery.

That being said, some general characteristics of African art may be identified. Among these were innovation of form—i.e., the concern on the part of the African artist with innovation and creativity; visual abstraction and conventionalization; a combination of balanced composition and asymmetry; the primacy of sculpture; the transformation and adornment of the human body; and a general multiplicity of meaning. It should also be noted that a primary component of traditional African art was performance and assemblage. The combination of music, dance, dress, and bodily ornamentation—as well as sculpture and masks—was frequently what imparted both significance and dynamism to individual art objects.

A commonplace of African art criticism has been to identify particular styles according to supposedly tribal names—for example, Asante, Kuba, or Nuba. The concept of tribe is problematic, however, and has generally been discarded. "Tribal" names, in fact, sometimes refer to the language spoken, sometimes to political entities, and sometimes to other kinds of groupings, yet the boundaries between peoples speaking different languages or acknowledging different chiefs did not necessarily coincide with their respective tribal boundaries. Moreover, the very idea of tribe is an attempt to impose identity from the outside. That this happened is understandable, given the demands of colonial administration, but this historical contingency cannot help in understanding the dynamic of stylistic variation in Africa. The sense of identity that individuals and groups undoubtedly had with others, which was misunderstood as "tribe" but which is better referred to as "ethnic identity," is something that derives from the relationship built up through many different networks: whom one could marry, one's language and religious affiliations, the chief whose authority one acknowledged, who one's ancestors were, the kind of work one did, and so forth. Sometimes African art played a part in this, as when a religious cult or a chief or a guild employed distinctive artifacts as a mark of uniqueness. Sometimes boundaries were based on linguistic differences, but this may have been coincidental.

As to differences of style, regularities of form and tradition did occur such that it is possible to attribute particular African art objects to particular places, regions, or periods. Four distinct variables make this kind of stylistic identification possible. The first is geography, in that, all other things being equal, people in different places tend to make or do things in different ways. The second is technology, in that in some areas differences of style depend on the material employed. The third is individuality, in that an expert can identify the works of individual artists; inability to do so usually derives from a lack of familiarity. The fourth is institution, in that the creation of works of art took place under the influence of the social and cultural institutions characteristic of any given location. But artifacts could be traded and then copied; artists themselves could travel; institutions, complete with associated artifacts, could move or spread from one area to another, sometimes because they were copied by a neighbouring people, sometimes because they were purchased, and sometimes as a result of conquest. The end result is a stylistic complexity in African art that defies easy classification. The names previously understood as referring to tribes can continue to be used, however, as convenient shorthand as long as it is realized that they do not all represent equivalent categories. One tribal name may refer to a group numbering no more than a few thousand; another may refer to the language that was spoken in a given area; yet another may describe an empire comprising peoples of distinct historical identities.

REPRESENTATIVE WESTERN AFRICAN TRADITIONS IN VISUAL ART

Fon

The Fon kingdom of Dahomey, with its capital at Abomey (now in Benin), was also founded in the early 17th century. Artists in Abomey were organized into guilds, as were the artists of the Asante in Kumasi, producing pavilions, canopies, umbrellas, and banners embellished with appliqué, as well as images of deities or symbols of state in iron and brass, and empowered sculptural objects known as *bo* (plural *bocio*). The exterior walls of the palace were ornamented with painted clay reliefs that celebrated the achievements of the king; royal *bocio* in the palace were sculptures combining animal and human characteristics that protected against harm and reinforced the king's power. A significant example is the sculpture of Gu, the god of iron and war, made from sheets of metal. The thrones of Fon kings are similar in form to Asante stools but are much taller and are preserved as the focus of reverence for ancestral kings. Small figures cast in brass, often in groups, are prestige items employed also to decorate royal tombs. Brightly coloured appliqué cloth is used on state umbrellas and chiefs' caps, as well as banners for the tourist market.

IFE AND YORUBA

The Yoruba peoples inhabit a large part of southwestern Nigeria. Their art traditions are of considerable antiquity. Excavations at Ife, in central Yorubaland (the site of the creation of the world in some Yoruba myths), have shown that naturalistic sculpture in brass and pottery was being produced sometime between 1100 and 1450 CE. The sculptures may represent royal figures and their attendants, and life-size portrait heads in brass were perhaps used as part of funerary effigies. During this time, Ife appears to have had widespread importance, and the naturalism of its art seems to have influenced the basic development of Yoruba sculptural style. Throughout Yorubaland, human figures were represented in a fundamentally naturalistic way, except for bulging eyes, flat, protruding, and usually parallel lips, and stylized ears. The evolution of these characteristics can be observed in a number of pottery sculptures at Ife, which, on stylistic grounds, are considered to be relatively late.

Within the basic canon of Yoruba sculpture, many local styles can be distinguished, down to the hand of the individual artist. Individual cults too have their own characteristic requirements of form and ethnography. Staffs for Shango, the thunder god, bear the symbol of a double ax. On his altars are placed carved mortars, for the pounding of food in a mortar sounds like thunder; on the wall behind hangs his leather bag, with a motif

Brass figure of an oni (king) of Ife, 14th–15th century; in the Museum of Ife Antiquities, Lagos, Nigeria. Height 46.7 cm. Frank Willett

based on the extensive gesture of a Shango dancer. Because Shango was king of Oyo, largest of the Yoruba kingdoms, his cult is mainly restricted to areas that were under Oyo domination.

Typical of Ekiti is the Epa cult, which is connected with both the ancestors and agriculture. The mask proper, roughly globular, has highly stylized features that vary little; but the superstructure, which may be 4 feet (120 cm) or more in height, is often of very great complexity—for example, a king on horseback, surrounded by two tiers of attendant warriors and musicians. The most widely distributed cult was of twins—*ibeji*—whose birth among the Yoruba is unusually frequent. Their effigies, made on the instructions of the oracle, are among the most numerous of all classes of African sculpture. Carved doors and house posts are found in shrines and palaces and in the houses of important men. Fulfilling purely secular functions were bowls for kola nuts, offered in welcoming a guest; *ayo* boards for the game, known also as *wari*, played with seeds or pebbles in two rows of cup-like depressions; and stools, spoons, combs, and heddle pulleys.

To the north is Esie, where about 800 sculptures in soapstone were found by the local Yoruba population some centuries ago. Their origin is obscure; they are by no means certainly Yoruba. The city of Owo, to the southeast of Yorubaland near the frontier with the Edo-speaking peoples, developed an art style—indeed, a whole culture—that was a blend of Yoruba

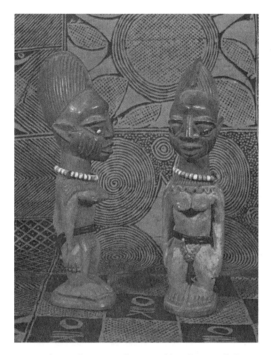

Pair of Yoruba twin figures (ibeji), wood, from Efon Alaye, Nigeria. Height 11 inches (27.6 cm). The starch-resist dyed cloth is also Yoruba; in the Frank Willett Collection. Frank Willett

and Benin traditions. Ivory carving was especially important, and wooden heads of rams and of humans with rams' horns were used on ancestral altars. Excavations in 1971 revealed a large number of pottery sculptures that are clearly related to those of Ife but with some Benin features. The site was dated by carbon-14 to about the 15th century CE.

IGBO

Traditionally the Igbo lived in small and often isolated settlements scattered through the forest. In Igbo society there was strong social pressure toward individual distinction, and men could move upward through successive grades by demonstrating their achievements and their generosity. One of the traditional representations of this was the *ikenga*, that part of oneself enabling personal achievement, with cult figures representing the attributes of distinction.

The lack of overall centralization among the Igbo-speaking people was conducive to the development of a great variety of art styles and cultural practices. The earliest-known sculpture from Igboland is from the village of Igbo Ukwu, where the grave of a man of distinction and a ritual store dating from the 9th century CE contained both chased copper objects and elaborate castings of leaded bronze. The earliest artistic castings from sub-Saharan Africa, these pieces consist of ritual vessels and other ceremonial objects with intricate surface decoration, often small animals and insects represented in the round.

A very great variety of masks have been found among the Igbo. The masks, of wood or fabric, were employed in a variety of dramas: social satires, sacred rituals (for ancestors and invocation of the gods), initiation, second burials, and public festivals. Some masks appeared at only one festival, but the majority appeared at many or all. Best known were those of the Northern Igbo Mmo society, which represented the spirits of deceased maidens and their mothers with masks

Leaded bronze ceremonial object, thought to have been the head of a staff, decorated with coloured beads of glass and stone, 9th century, from Igbo Ukwu, Nigeria; in the Nigerian Museum, Lagos. Height 6.5 inches (16.8 cm).
Frank Willett

symbolizing beauty. Among the Southern Igbo, the Ekpe society, introduced from the Cross River area, used contrasting masks to represent the maiden spirit and the elephant spirit, the latter representing ugliness and aggression and the former representing beauty and peacefulness. A similar contrast is found in their Okorosia masks, which correspond to the Mmo of the Northern Igbo. The Eastern Igbo were best known for masquerades associated with the Iko *okochi* harvest festival, in which the forms of the masks were determined by tradition, though the content of the play varied from year to year. Stock characters include Mbeke, the

European; Mkpi, the he-goat; and Mba, which appeared in pairs, one representing a boy dressed as a girl mimicking the behaviour of a girl, the other representing the girl being satirized.

Most impressive are the *ijele* masks of the Northern Igbo, which are 12 feet (366 cm) high. Consisting of platforms 6 feet (183 cm) in diameter, supporting tiers of figures made of coloured cloth and representing everyday scenes, they honoured the dead to ensure the continuity and well-being of the community.

Wooden figures were carved for ancestors of both sexes, varying from less than 1 to more than 5 feet (less than 30 to more than 150 cm) in height. Those

Maiden spirit mask symbolizing beauty and peacefulness, painted wood, Southern Igbo Ekpe society, Nigeria; in the Nigerian Museum, Lagos. Height 8 inches (21.3 cm).
Frank Willett

representing founders of the village were kept in a central shrine and sometimes became patrons of the market. A great many other decorative wooden objects were made, including musical instruments, doors, stools, mirror frames, trays for offering kola nuts to guests, dolls, and a variety of small figures used in divination. Shrines called *mbari*, which contain elaborate tableaux of painted unfired earth, were made in honour of the earth spirit in villages near Owerri in southern Nigeria. In Igbo communities to the west of the Niger, elaborate pottery groups representing a man and his family were made for the yam cult. There seems to be no tradition of pottery sculpture in other Igbo groups.

FULANI

The Fulani were nomadic pastoralists. They were particularly known for their body decoration and for their engraved milk gourds. In addition, settled groups of Fulani artists worked as goldsmiths, leatherworkers, blacksmiths, weavers, and potters.

NUPE

The Nupe have been Muslim for some centuries and are best known for their weaving, embroidery, beadmaking, wood carving, and sheet metalwork. They have produced many doors carved in low relief in a blend of decorative designs. Carved and painted masks are made for the *elo*, a purely secular performance intended only to entertain. The *elo* mask has a human face with a motif (sometimes a human figure) rising above it, flanked with stylized horns. The *gugu* masquerader wore a cloth mask decorated with cowrie shells, but sometimes Yoruba masks were used. The *ndako gboya* appears to be indigenous; a spirit that affords protection from witches, it is controlled by a small secret society that cleanses communities by invitation. The mask consists of a tall tube of white cotton supported inside on a bamboo pole about 12 feet (366 cm) long.

That Nupe art should have been influenced by the Yoruba is not surprising. Yoruba live among the Nupe, and there are bronzes in the Nupe villages of Tada and Jebba—one of them apparently an Ife work and another in a more recent Yoruba style. Others of this group, which include the largest castings ever made in sub-Saharan Africa, share features with Benin sculpture and have other elements that are widely distributed in time and space on the lower Niger. Nupe tradition says these sculptures were taken from Idah, the Igala capital, in the early 16th century. Many were probably already ancient, but nothing is known of ancient Igala bronze casting.

ORAL TRADITIONS

To see the accomplishments of African Americans in literature and music within the context of African oral traditions is to glimpse continuities of form and influence across the centuries. The nature of storytelling and the important social role played by the griot (storyteller), for example, set the stage for trickster tales that were an important element in early African American literature. Beyond that, they point all the way to the pivotal role of the rapper in hip-hop culture, and not just to the centrality of the rapper as a presenter of "real" news (Public Enemy's Chuck D. famously called rap the black version of the Cable News Network), but also to the braggadocio that is the operative conceit for many of hip-hop's biggest stars.

The Nature of Storytelling

The African storyteller speaks, time collapses, and the members of the audience are in the presence of history. It is a time of masks. Reality, the present, is here, but with explosive emotional images giving it a context. This is the art not only of the African storyteller but of any storyteller: to mask the past, making it mysterious and seemingly inaccessible. In truth, it is inaccessible only to one's present intellect; it is always available to one's heart and soul—one's emotions. The best storyteller combines the audience's present waking state and its past condition of semiconsciousness, and so the audience walks again in history, joining its forebears. And history, always more than an academic subject, becomes for the audience a collapsing of time. History becomes the audience's memory of and a means of reliving an indeterminate and deeply obscure past.

Storytelling is a sensory union of image and idea, a process of re-creating the past in terms of the present; the storyteller uses realistic images to describe the present and fantasy images to evoke and embody the substance of a culture's experience of the past. These ancient fantasy images are a culture's heritage and the storyteller's bounty: they contain the emotional history of the culture, its most deeply felt yearnings and fears, and they therefore have the capacity to elicit strong emotional responses. In an African context, these universals are rooted in and shaped by the specificities of the African experience. During a performance, these envelop contemporary images—the most unstable parts of the oral tradition, because they are by their nature always in a state of flux—and thereby visit the past on the present.

It was, and always will be, the task of the storyteller to forge the fantasy images of the past into masks of the realistic images of the present, enabling the performer to pitch the present to the past, to visualize the present within a context of—and therefore in terms of—the past. Flowing through this potent emotional grid is a variety of ideas that have the look of antiquity and ancestral sanction. Story occurs under the mesmerizing influence of performance—the body of the performer, the music of her voice, the complex relationship between her and her audience. It is a world unto itself, whole, with its own set of laws. Images that are unlike are juxtaposed, and then the storyteller reveals—to the delight and

GRIOT

The griot profession is hereditary and has long been a part of western African culture. The griots' role has traditionally been to preserve the genealogies, historical narratives, and oral traditions of their people; praise songs are also part of the griot's repertoire. Many griots play the kora, a long-necked harp lute with 21 strings. In addition to serving as the primary storytellers of their people, griots have also served as advisers and diplomats. Over the centuries their advisory and diplomatic roles have diminished somewhat, and their entertainment appeal has become more widespread.

instruction of the members of the audience—the linkages between them that render them homologous. In this way the past and the present are blended; ideas are thereby generated, forming a conception of the present. Performance gives the images their context and ensures the audience a ritual experience that bridges past and present and shapes contemporary life.

Storytelling is alive, ever in transition, never hardened in time. Stories are not meant to be temporally frozen; they are always responding to contemporary realities, but in a timeless fashion. Storytelling is therefore not a memorized art. The necessity for this continual transformation of the story has to do with the regular fusing of fantasy and images of the real, contemporary world. It is inevitable, if not essential, that performers take images from the present and wed them to the past, and in that way the past regularly shapes any audience's experience of the present. Storytellers reveal connections between humans—within the world, within a society, within a tribe,

within a family—emphasizing an interdependence and the disaster that occurs when obligations to one's fellows are forsaken. The artist makes the linkages, the storyteller forges the bonds, tying past and present, joining humans to their gods, to their leaders, to their families, to those they love, to their deepest fears and hopes, and to the essential core of their societies and beliefs. This is a central aspect of African oral tradition.

The language of storytelling includes, on the one hand, image, the patterning of image, and the manipulation of the body and voice of the storyteller and, on the other, the memory and present state of the audience. A storytelling performance involves memory: the recollection of each member of the audience of his experiences with respect to the story being performed, the memory of his real-life experiences, and the similar memories of the storyteller. It is the rhythm of storytelling that welds these disparate experiences, yearnings, and thoughts into the images of the story. And the images are known, familiar to the audience. That familiarity is a crucial part of storytelling. The storyteller does not craft a story out of whole cloth: she re-creates the ancient story within the context of the real, contemporary, known world. It is the metaphorical relationship between these memories of the past and the known images of the world of the present that constitutes the essence of storytelling. The story is never history; it is built of the shards of history. Images are removed from historical contexts, then reconstituted within the demanding and authoritative frame of the story. And it is always a sensory experience, an experience of the emotions. Storytellers know that the way to the mind is by way of the heart. The interpretative effects of the storytelling experience give the members of the audience a refreshed sense of reality, a context for their experiences that has no existence in reality. It is only when images of contemporary life are woven into the ancient familiar images that metaphor is born and experience becomes meaningful.

Stories deal with change: mythic transformations of the cosmos, heroic transformations of the culture, transformations of the lives of everyman. The storytelling experience was and remains always ritual, always a rite of passage; one relives the past and, by so doing, comes to insight about present life. Myth is both a story and a fundamental structural device used by storytellers. As a story, it reveals change at the beginning of time, with gods as the central characters. As a storytelling tool for the creation

of metaphor, it is both material and method. The heroic epic unfolds within the context of myth, as does the tale. At the heart of each of these genres is metaphor, and at the core of metaphor is riddle with its associate, proverb. Each of these oral forms is characterized by a metaphorical process, the result of patterned imagery. That these forms can be found in all cultures, African and otherwise, points to the universal, timeless aspects of storytelling that allow a line to be drawn between trickster tales and hip-hop culture. But these forms also have distinct African inflections, which are considered below.

THE RIDDLE

A pot without an opening. (An egg.)
The silly man who drags his intestines. (A needle and thread.)

In the riddle, two unlike (and sometimes unlikely) things are compared. The obvious thing that happens during this comparison is that a problem is set, then solved. But there is something more important here, involving the riddle as a figurative form: the riddle is composed of two sets, and, during the process of riddling, the aspects of each of the sets are transferred to the other. On the surface it appears that the riddle is largely an intellectual rather than a poetic activity. But through its imagery and the tension between the two sets, the imagination of the audience is also engaged. As they seek to solve the riddle, the audience itself becomes a part of the images and therefore—and most significantly—of the metaphorical transformation.

This may not seem a very complex activity on the level of the riddle, but in this deceptively simple activity can be found the essential core of all storytelling, including the interaction of imagery in lyric poetry, the tale, and the epic. In the same way as those oral forms, the riddle works in both a literal figurative mode. During the process of riddling, the literal mode interacts with the figurative in a vigorous and creative way. It is that play between the literal and the figurative, between reality and fantasy, that characterizes the riddle: in that relationship can be found metaphor, which explains why it is that the riddle underlies other oral forms. The images in metaphor by their nature evoke emotion; the dynamics of metaphor trap those emotions in the images, and meaning is caught up in that activity. So meaning, even in such seemingly simple operations as riddling, is more complex than it may appear.

THE LYRIC

People were those who
Broke for me the string.
Therefore,
The place became like this to me,
On account of it,
Because the string was that which
broke for me.
Therefore,
The place does not feel to me,

As the place used to feel to me,
On account of it.
For,
The place feels as if it stood open
before me,
Because the string has broken for
me.
Therefore,
The place does not feel pleasant
to me,
On account of it.
(San poem, from W.H.I. Bleek and
L.C. Lloyd, *Specimens of Bushman Folklore* [1911])

The images in African lyric interact in dynamic fashion, establishing metaphorical relationships within the poem, and so it is that riddling is the motor of the lyric. And, as in riddles, so also in lyric: metaphor frequently involves and invokes paradox. In the lyric, it is as if the singer were stitching a set of riddles into a single richly textured poem, the series of riddling connections responsible for the ultimate experience of the poem. The singer organizes and controls the emotions of the audience as he systematically works his way through the levels of the poem, carefully establishing the connective threads that bring the separate metaphorical sets into the poem's totality. None of the separate riddling relationships exists divorced from those others that compose the poem. As these riddling relationships interact and interweave, the poet brings the audience to a close, intense sense of the meaning of the poem. Each riddling relationship provides an emotional clue to the overall design of the poem. Further clues to meaning are discovered by the audience in the rhythmical aspects of the poem, the way the poet organizes the images, the riddling organization itself, and the sound of the singer's voice as well as the movement of the singer's body. As in the riddle, everything in the lyric is directed to the revelation of metaphor.

THE PROVERB

Work the clay while it is fresh.
Wisdom killed the wise man.

The African proverb seems initially to be a hackneyed expression, a trite leftover repeated until it loses all force. But proverb is also performance, it is also metaphor, and it is in its performance and metaphorical aspects that it achieves its power. In one sense, the experience of a proverb is similar to that of a riddle and a lyric poem: different images are brought into a relationship that is novel, that provides insight. When one experiences proverbs in appropriate contexts, rather than in isolation, they come to life. In the riddle the poser provides the two sides of the metaphor. In lyric poetry the two sides are present in the poem but in a complex way; the members of the audience derive their aesthetic experience from comprehending that complexity. The words of the proverb are by themselves only one part of the metaphorical experience. The other side of the riddle is not to be found in the same way it is in

the riddle and the lyric. The proverb establishes ties with its metaphorical equivalent in the real life of the members of the audience or with the wisdom of the past. The words of the proverb are a riddle waiting to happen. And when it happens, the African proverb ceases to be a grouping of tired words.

THE TALE

The riddle, lyric, and proverb are the materials that are at the dynamic centre of the tale. The riddle contains within it the possibilities of metaphor; and the proverb elaborates the metaphorical possibilities when the images of the tale are made lyrical—that is, when they are rhythmically organized. Such images are drawn chiefly from two repertories: from the contemporary world (these are the realistic images) and from the ancient tradition (these are the fantasy images). These diverse images are brought together during a storytelling performance by their rhythmic organization. Because the fantasy images have the capacity to elicit strong emotional reactions from members of the audience, these emotions are the raw material that is woven into the image organization by the patterning. The audience thereby becomes an integral part of the story by becoming a part of the metaphorical process that moves to meaning. And meaning, therefore, is much more complex than an obvious homily that may be readily available on the surface of the tale.

This patterning of imagery is the main instrument that shapes a tale. In the simplest of tales, a model is established, and then it is repeated in an almost identical way. With little more than a brief introduction and a quick close, the storyteller can develop a tale. There may be an uninterrupted linear movement of a realistic single character fleeing from a fantasy ogre or some other supernatural being—from a conflict to a resolution. But that fantasy and that reality are controlled by the lyrical centre of the tale, and that seemingly simple mechanism provides the core for complexity. That linear movement, even in the simplest stories, is subverted by a cyclical movement—the song, for instance—and that is the engine of metaphor. It is the cyclical movement of the tale that makes it possible to experience linear details and images in such a way that they become equated one with the other. So it is that the simplest tale becomes a model for more-complex narratives. That lyrical centre gives the tale a potential for development.

In a more complex tale, the storyteller moves two characters through three worlds, each of those worlds seemingly different. But by means of that lyrical pulse, the rhythmical ordering of those worlds brings them into such alignment that the members of the audience experience them as the same. It is this discernment of different images as identical that results in complex structures, characters, events, and meanings. And what brings those different images into this alignment is poetry—more specifically, the metaphorical character of the lyrical poem. The very composition of tales makes it possible to link them and to order them metaphorically. The possibilities of epic are visible in the simplest of tales, and so also are the possibilities of the novel.

The trickster tale, as it does with so much of the oral tradition, provides insights into this matter of the construction of stories. Masks are the weapons of the trickster: he creates illusions, bringing the real world and the world of illusion into temporary, shimmering proximity, convincing his dupe of the reality of metaphor. That trickster and his antic activities are another way of describing the metaphorical motor of storytelling.

While Hare is a common trickster of northern, eastern, and southern Africa, the tricksters of West Africa are Spider (Ghana, Liberia, Sierra Leone) or Tortoise (the Igbo and Yoruba people of Nigeria). Many African cultures also have tales about human tricksters (e.g., the stories of Yo in Benin). In African traditions, particularly those involving the spider Anansi, the trickster often appears as a mythological figure and a rival of the sky god, tricking the god in one way or another. In this function Anansi shows some similarity with the Yoruba trickster god Eshu, who constantly opposes the other gods and thwarts their intentions.

HEROIC POETRY

Hero who surpasses other heroes!
Swallow that disappears in the

clouds,
Others disappearing into the
heavens!
Son of Menzi!
Viper of Ndaba!
Erect, ready to strike,
It strikes the shields of men!
Father of the cock!
Why did it disappear over the
mountains?
It annihilated men!
That is Shaka,
Son of Senzangakhona,
Of whom it is said, Bayede!
You are an elephant!
(From a heroic poem dedicated to
the Zulu chief Shaka)

It is in heroic poetry, or panegyric, that lyric and image come into their most obvious union. As in the tale and as in the lyric, riddle, and proverb, the essence of panegyric is metaphor, although the metaphorical connections are sometimes somewhat obscure. History is more clearly evident in panegyric, but it remains fragmented history, rejoined according to the poetic intentions of the bard. Obvious metaphorical connections are frequently made between historical personages or events and images of animals, for example. The fantasy aspects of this kind of poetry are to be found in its construction, in the merging of the real and the animal in metaphorical ways. It is within this metaphorical context that the hero is described and assessed. As in other forms of oral tradition, emotions associated with both historical and nonhistorical images are at the heart of meaning in panegyric. It is the lyrical rhythm of panegyric that works such emotions into form. In the process, history is reprocessed and given new meaning within the context of contemporary experience. It is a dual activity: history is thereby redefined at the same time that it shapes experiences of the present.

Among the Tuareg of western Africa, a stringed instrument often accompanies the creation of such poetry, and the main composers are women. The Songhai have *mabe,* the professional bards; they are present at all rites of passage, celebrating, accompanying, and cushioning the transformation being experienced. In Mauritania it is the *iggiw* (plural *iggawen*) who creates heroic poetry and who plays the lute while singing the songs of the warriors. The *diare* (plural *diarou*) is the bard among the Soninke. He goes to battle with the soldiers, urging them, placing their martial activities within the context of history, building their acts within the genealogies of their family. Drums and trumpets sometimes accompany the *maroka* among the Hausa. When a king is praised, the accompaniment becomes orchestral. Yoruba bards chant the *ijala,* singing of lineage, and, with the *oriki,* saluting the notable. Among the Hima of Uganda, the bard is the *omwevugi.* In the evenings, he sings of the *omugabe,* the king, and of men in battle and of the cattle. The *mbongi wa ku pfusha* is the bard among the Tonga of Mozambique. He too sings of the glories of the past, creating poetry about chiefs and kings.

The images vary, their main organizing implement being the subject of the poem. It is the metrical ordering of images, including sound and motion, that holds the poem together, not the narrative of history.

THE EPIC

In the epic can be found the merging of various frequently unrelated tales, the metaphorical apparatus, the controlling mechanism found in the riddle and lyric, the proverb, and heroic poetry to form a larger narrative. All of this centres on the character of the hero and a gradual revelation of his frailty, uncertainties, and torments; he often dies, or is deeply troubled, in the process of bringing the culture into a new dispensation often prefigured in his resurrection or his coming into knowledge. The mythical transformation caused by the creator gods and culture heroes is reproduced precisely in the acts and the cyclical, tortured movements of the hero.

An epic may be built around a genealogical system, with parts of it developed and embellished into a story. The epic, like the heroic poem, contains historical references such as place-names and events; in the heroic poem these are not greatly developed. When they are developed in an epic, they are built not around history but around a fictional tale. The fictional tale ties the historical episode, person, or place-name to the cultural history of the people. In an oral society, oral genres include history (the heroic poem) and imaginative story (the tale). The epic combines the two, linking the historical episode to the imaginative tale. Sometimes, myth is also a part of epic, with emphasis on origins. The tale, the heroic poem, history, and myth are combined in the epic. In an echo of the tale—where the emphasis is commonly on a central but always nonhistorical character—a single historical or nonhistorical character is the centre of the epic. And at the core of the epic is that same engine composed of the riddle, the lyric, and the proverb.

Much is frequently made of the psychology of this central character when he appears in the epic. He is given greater detail than the tale character, given deeper dimension. The epic performer remembers the great events and turning points of cultural history. These events change the culture. In the epic these elements are tied to the ancient images of the culture (in the form of tale and myth), an act that thereby gives these events cultural sanction. The tale and myth lend to the epic (and, by inference, to history) a magical, supernatural atmosphere: all of nature is touched in the Malagasy epic *Ibonia*; in the West African epic *Sunjata*, magic keeps Sumanguru in charge and enables Sunjata to take over. It is a time of momentous change in the society. In *Ibonia* there are major alterations in the relationship between men and women; in *Sunjata* and in the epic *Mwindo* of the Nyanga people of Congo there are major political changes.

But, in *Mwindo*, why was Mwindo such a trickster? He was, after all, a great hero. And why must he be taught by the gods after he has established his heroic credentials? Central to this question is the notion of the transitional phase—of the betwixt and between, of the someone or something that crosses yet exists between boundaries. There is a paradox in Mwindo's vulnerability—how, after all, can a hero be vulnerable?—but more important is his nonmoral energy during a period of change. Mwindo is a liminal hero-trickster: he is liminal while he seeks his father, and then he becomes liminal again at the hands of the gods. "Out there" is where the learning, the transformation, occurs. The trickster energy befits and mirrors this in-between period, as no laws are in existence. There is change and transformation, but it is guided by a vision: in the myths, it is god's vision for the cosmos; in the tales, it is the society's vision for completeness; in the epics, it is the hero's vision for a new social dispensation.

The heroic epic is a grand blending of tale and myth, heroic poetry and history. These separate genres are combined in the epic, and separate epics contain a greater or lesser degree of each—history (and, to a lesser extent, poetry) is dominant in *Sunjata*, heroic poetry and tale in *Ibonia*, and tale and myth (and, to a lesser extent, poetry) in *Mwindo*. Oral societies have these separate categories: history, the imaginative tale, heroic poetry, myth, and epic. Epic, therefore, is not simply history. History exists as a separate genre.

The essential characteristic of epic is not that it is history but that it combines history and tale, fact and fancy, and worlds of reality and fantasy. The epic becomes the grand summation of the culture because it takes major turning points in history (always with towering historical or nonhistorical figures who symbolize these turning points) and links them to tradition, giving the changes their sanction. The epic hero may be revolutionary, but he does not signal a total break with the past. Continuity is stressed in epic—in fact, it is as if the shift in the direction of the society is a return to the paradigm envisioned by ancient cultural wisdom. The effect of the epic is to mythologize history, to bring history to the essence of the culture, to give history the resonance of the ancient roots of the culture as these are expressed in myth, imaginative tale (and motif), and metaphor. In heroic poetry, history is fragmented, made discontinuous. In epic these discontinuous images are given a new form, that of the imaginative tale. And the etiological aspects of history (that is, the historical alteration of the society) are tied to the etiology of mythology—in other words, the acts of the mortal hero are tied to acts of the immortals.

History is not the significant genre involved in the epic. It is instead tale and myth that organize the images of history and give those images their meaning. History by itself has no significance: it achieves significance when it is juxtaposed to the images of a tradition grounded in tales and myths. This suggests the great value that oral societies place on the imaginative traditions: they are entertaining, certainly, but they are also major organizing devices. As the tales take routine, everyday experiences of reality and—by placing them in the fanciful context of conflict and resolution with the emotion-evoking motifs of the past—give them a meaning and a completeness that they do not actually have, so in epic is history given a form and a meaning that it does not possess. This imaginative environment revises history, takes historical experiences and places them into the context of the culture, and gives them cultural meaning. The epic is a blending, then, of the ancient culture as it is represented through imaginative tradition with historical events and personages. The divine trickster links heaven and earth, god and human; the epic hero does the same but also links fantasy and reality, myth and history, and cultural continuity and historical disjunction.

What is graphically clear in the epics *Ibonia* and *Sunjata* is that heroic poetry, in the form of the praise name, provides a context for the evolution of a heroic story. In both of those epics, the panegyric forms a pattern, the effect of which is to tie the epic hero decisively and at the same time to history and to the gods. Those epics, as well as *Mwindo*, dramatize the rite of passage of a society or a culture: the hero's movement through the familiar stages of the ritual becomes a poetic metaphor for a like movement of the society itself. The tale at the centre of the epic may be as straightforward as any tale in the oral tradition. But that tale is linked to a complex of other tales, the whole given an illusion of poetic unity by the heroic poetry, which in turn provides a lyrical rhythm.

Storytelling is the mythos of a society: at the same time that it is conservative, at the heart of nationalism, it is the propelling mechanism for change. The struggle between the individual and the group, between the traditions that support and defend the rights of the group and the sense of freedom that argues for undefined horizons of the individual—this is the contest that characterizes the hero's dilemma, and the hero in turn is the personification of the quandary of the society itself and of its individual members.

PRAISE SONG

A praise song is one of the most widely used poetic forms in Africa; a series of laudatory epithets applied to gods, men, animals, plants, and towns that capture the essence of the object being praised. Professional bards, who may be both praise singers to a chief and court historians of their tribe, chant praise songs such as these of the great Zulu chieftain Shaka:

> He is Shaka the unshakeable,
> Thunderer-while-sitting, son of Menzi.
> He is the bird that preys on other birds,
> The battle-axe that excels over other battle-axes.

He is the long-strided pursuer, son of Ndaba,
Who pursued the sun and the moon.
He is the great hubbub like the rocks of Nkandla
Where elephants take shelter
When the heavens frown...
(Trans. by Ezekiel Mphahlele)

Although he is expected to know all of the traditional phrases handed down by word of mouth in his tribe, the bard is also free to make additions to existing poems. Thus the praise songs of Shango, the Yoruba god of thunder and lightning, might contain a modern comparison of the god to the power and noise of a railway.

Among some Bantu-speaking peoples, the praise song is an important form of oral literature. The Sotho of Lesotho required all boys undergoing initiation to compose praises for themselves that set forth the ideals of action or manhood. Sotho bards also composed traditional praises of chiefs and warriors, and even a very young man was allowed to create praises of himself if he had performed feats of great courage.

These praise songs were recited as follows: the reciter stood in an open space, visible to all assembled. He then began reciting in a high voice, punctuating his victories in war by stabbing the ground with his spear, until he had set forth not only his lineage and the battles in which he had fought but his entire life history. Sotho praises are telegraphic, leaving much to the listener's imagination; their language is poetic, and the sequence of events not necessarily logical. Metaphor is a key device for suggesting worth (a reciter might call himself a ferocious animal), and poetic license is granted for coining new words.

To the subjects used by the Sotho, the Tswana of Botswana add women, tribal groups, domestic animals (especially cattle) and wild animals, trees, crops, various features of the landscape, and divining bones. Their praise songs consist of a succession of loose stanzas with an irregular number of lines and a balanced metrical form. Experiences such as going abroad to work for Europeans have become a subject of recent praise poems, and recitation has been extended from tribal meetings and ritual occasions such as weddings to the beer hall and labour camp.

In western Africa, also, praise songs have been adapted to the times, and a modern praise singer often serves as an entertainer hired to flatter the rich and socially prominent or to act as a master of ceremonies for paramount chiefs at state functions—e.g., among the Hausa and Manding peoples. Thus praise-song poems, though still embodying and preserving a tribe's history, have also been adapted to an increasingly urbanized and Westernized African society.

CHAPTER 4

RACE AND RACISM

A ny study of African American history must include a discussion of race, a concept that not only has divided people typologically but also has driven the deepest wedges imaginable between people, as characteristics such as skin colour and physical features allowed one group to treat another as property. The concept of race is at the centre of American history, but many believe it is just that, a concept. Genetic studies in the late 20th century, such as the Human Genome Project, refuted the existence of biogenetically distinct races, and scholars now argue that "races" are cultural interventions reflecting specific attitudes and beliefs that were imposed on different populations in the wake of western European conquests beginning in the 15th century. It can be argued then, simply, that before there could be race there had to be racism. This chapter explores the development of the notion of race and its far-reaching consequences for human and especially American history.

THE MANY MEANINGS OF "RACE"

The modern meaning of the term *race* with reference to humans began to emerge in the late 16th century. Since then it has had a variety of meanings in the languages of the Western world. What most definitions have in common is an attempt to categorize peoples primarily by their physical differences. In the United States, for example, the term *race* generally refers to a group of people who have in common some visible physical traits such as skin colour, hair texture, facial features, and eye formation. Such distinctive features are associated with large, geographically separated populations, and these continental aggregates are also designated as races, as the "African race," the "European race," and the "Asian race." Many people think of race as reflective of any visible physical (phenotypic) variations among human groups, regardless of the cultural context and even in the absence of fixed racial categories.

The term race has also been applied to linguistic groups (the "Arab race" or the "Latin race"), to religious groups (the "Jewish race"), and even to political, national, or ethnic groups with few or no physical traits that distinguish them from their neighbours (the "Irish race," the "French race," the "Spanish race," the "Slavic race," the "Chinese race," etc.).

For much of the 20th century, scientists in the Western world attempted to identify, describe, and classify human races, and to document their differences and the relationships among them. Some scientists used the term race for subspecies: subdivisions of the human species that were presumed sufficiently different biologically that they might later evolve into separate species.

At no point—from the first rudimentary attempts at classifying human populations in the 17th and 18th centuries to the present day—have scientists agreed on the number of races of humankind, the features to be used in the identification of races, or even the meaning of race itself. Experts have suggested a range of different races varying from three to more than 60, based on what they have considered distinctive differences in physical characteristics alone (these include hair type, head shape, skin colour, height, and so on). The lack of concurrence on the meaning and identification of races continued into the 21st century, and contemporary scientists are no closer to agreement than their forebears. Thus, race has never in the history of its use had a precise meaning.

Although most people continue to think of races as physically distinct populations, scientific advances in the 20th century demonstrated that human physical variations do not fit a "racial" model. Instead, human physical variations tend to overlap. There are no genes that can identify distinct groups that accord with the conventional race categories. In fact, DNA analyses have proved that all humans have much more in common, genetically, than they have differences. The genetic difference between any two humans is less than 1 percent. Moreover, geographically widely separated populations vary from one another in only about 6 to 8 percent of their genes. Because of the overlapping of traits that bear no relationship to one another (such as skin colour and hair texture) and the inability of scientists to cluster peoples into discrete racial packages, modern researchers have concluded that the concept of race has no biological validity.

Many scholars in other disciplines now accept this relatively new scientific understanding of biological diversity in the human species. Moreover, they have long understood that the concept of race as relating solely to phenotypic traits encompasses neither the social reality of race nor the phenomenon of "racism." Prompted by advances in other fields, particularly anthropology and history, scholars began to examine race as a social and cultural, rather than biological, phenomenon, and have determined that race is a social invention of relatively recent origin. It derives its most salient characteristics from the social consequences of its classificatory use. The idea of "race" began to evolve in the late 17th century, after the beginning of European exploration and colonization, as a folk ideology about human differences associated with the different populations—Europeans, native Americans, and Africans— that came together in the New World. In the 19th century, after the abolition of slavery, the ideology fully emerged as a new mechanism of social division and stratification.

"RACE" AS MECHANISM OF SOCIAL DIVISION IN NORTH AMERICA

Racial classifications appeared in North America, and in many other parts of the world, as a form of social division predicated on what were thought to be natural differences between human groups. Analysis of the folk beliefs, social policies, and practices of North Americans regarding race from the 18th to the 20th century reveals the development of a unique and fundamental ideology about human differences. This ideology or "racial worldview" is a systematic, institutionalized set of beliefs and attitudes that includes the following components:

- All the world's peoples can be divided into biologically separate, discrete, and exclusive populations called races. A person can belong to only one race.
- Phenotypic features, or visible physical differences, are markers or symbols of race identity and status. Because an individual may belong to a racial category and not have any or all of the associated physical features, racial scientists early in the 20th century invented an invisible internal element, "racial essence," to explain such anomalies.
- Each race has distinct qualities of temperament, morality, disposition, and intellectual ability. Consequently, in the popular imagination each race has distinct behavioral traits that are linked to its phenotype.
- Races are unequal. They can, and should, be ranked on a gradient of inferiority and superiority. As the 19th-century biologist Louis Agassiz observed, since races exist,

we must "settle the relative rank among [them]."

- The behavioral and physical attributes of each race are inherited and innate—therefore fixed, permanent, and unalterable.
- Distinct races should be segregated and allowed to develop their own institutions, communities, and lifestyles, separate from those of other races.

These are the beliefs that wax and wane but never entirely disappear from the core of the American version of differences among the races. From its inception, racial ideology accorded inferior social status to people of African or Native American ancestry. This ideology was institutionalized in law and social practice, and social mechanisms were developed for enforcing the status differences.

THE DIFFERENCE BETWEEN RACISM AND ETHNOCENTRISM

Although they are easily and often confused, race and racism must be distinguished from ethnicity and ethnocentrism. While extreme ethnocentrism may take the same offensive form and may have the same dire consequences as extreme racism, there are significant differences between the two concepts. Ethnicity, which relates to culturally contingent features, characterizes all human groups. It refers to a sense of identity and

membership in a group that shares common language, cultural traits (values, beliefs, religion, food habits, customs, etc.), and a sense of a common history. All humans are members of some cultural (ethnic) group, sometimes more than one. Most such groups feel—to varying degrees of intensity—that their way of life, their foods, dress, habits, beliefs, values, and so forth, are superior to those of other groups.

The most significant quality of ethnicity is the fact that it is unrelated to biology and can be flexible and transformable. People everywhere can change or enhance their ethnicity by learning about or assimilating into another culture. American society well illustrates these facts, consisting as it does of groups of people from hundreds of different world cultures who have acquired some aspects of American culture and now participate in a common sense of ethnic identity with other Americans.

Ethnic identity is acquired, and ethnic features are learned forms of behaviour. Race, on the other hand, is a form of identity that is perceived as innate and unalterable. Ethnicity may be transient and even superficial. Race is thought to be profound and grounded in biological realities. Ethnocentrism is based upon a belief in the superiority of one's own culture over others, and it too may be transient and superficial. Racism is the belief in and promotion of the racial worldview described above. Ethnocentrism holds skin colour and other physical features to be irrelevant as long as one is a member of the same culture, or becomes so. The racial worldview holds that, regardless of behaviour or cultural similarities, a member of an inferior race (who is usually perceived to be so by means of physical features) can never be accepted. Race is an invented, fictional form of identity; ethnicity is based on the reality of cultural similarities and differences and the interests that they represent. That race is a social invention can be demonstrated by an examination of the history of the idea of race as experienced in the English colonies.

THE HISTORY OF THE IDEA OF RACE

Race as a categorizing term referring to human beings was first used in the English language in the late 16th century. Until the 18th century it had a generalized meaning similar to other classifying terms such as *type, sort,* or *kind.* Occasional literature of Shakespeare's time referred to a "race of saints" or "a race of bishops." By the 18th century, race was widely used for sorting and ranking the peoples in the English colonies—Europeans who saw themselves as free people, Amerindians who had been conquered, and Africans who were being brought in as slave labour— and this usage continues today.

The peoples conquered and enslaved were physically different from western and northern Europeans, but such differences were not the sole cause for the construction of racial categories. The English had a long history of separating themselves from others and treating foreigners, such as the Irish, as alien "others." By the 17th century their policies and practices in Ireland had led to an image of the Irish as "savages" who were incapable of being civilized. Proposals to conquer the Irish, take over their lands, and use them as forced labour failed largely because of Irish resistance. It was then that many Englishmen turned to the idea of colonizing the New World. Their attitudes toward the Irish set precedents for how they were to treat the New World Indians and, later, Africans.

THE PROBLEM OF LABOUR IN THE NEW WORLD

One of the greatest problems faced by settlers in the New World, particularly in the southern colonies, was the shortage of labour. Within a few decades after the settlement of Jamestown, planters had established indentured servitude as the main form of labour. Under this system, young men (and some women) worked for masters, to whom they were indebted for their transportation, normally for a period of four to seven years. They were paid no wages, received only minimal upkeep, and often were treated brutally.

By the mid-17th century a wealthy few had encumbered virtually all lands not under Indian control and were attempting to work these lands using indentured servants. The working poor and those eventually freed from servitude had little on which to survive, and their dissatisfaction with the inequities of colonial society led to riots and numerous threats of revolt. After 1619 this group of poor servants included many Africans and their descendants, some of whom had experience in the Spanish and Portuguese colonies, where slave labour was widely used.

The social position of Africans in the early colonies has been a source of considerable debate. Some scholars have argued that they were separated from European servants and treated differently from the beginning. Later historians, however, have shown that there was no such uniformity in the treatment of Africans. Records indicate that many Africans and their descendants were set free after their periods of servitude. They were able to purchase land and even bought servants and slaves of their own. Some African men became wealthy tradesmen, craftsmen, or farmers, and their skills were widely recognized. They voted, appeared in courts, engaged in business and commercial dealings, and exercised all the civil rights of other free men. Some free Africans intermarried, and their children suffered little or no special discrimination. Other Africans were poor and lived with other poor men and women; blacks and whites worked together, drank together, ate together, played together, and frequently ran away together. Moreover, the poor of all colours protested together against the policies of the government (at least 25 percent of the rebels in Bacon's Rebellion

East African slave market in the port of Zanzibar, engraving from Harper's Weekly. The city was infamous for its trade in slaves, having some 7,000 slaves sold annually by the 1860s. Encyclopædia Britannica, Inc.

[1676] were blacks, both servants and freedmen). The social position of Africans and their descendants for the first six or seven decades of colonial history seems to have been open and fluid and not initially overcast with an ideology of inequality or inferiority.

Toward the end of the 17th century, labour from England began to diminish, and the colonies were faced with two major dilemmas. One was how to maintain control over the restless poor and the freedmen who seemed intent on the violent overthrow of the colony's leaders. There had been several incidents that threatened the leadership of the fragile colonies. The aforementioned rebellion led by Nathaniel Bacon in Virginia was a high point in the caustic relations between the planters and leaders of the colony and the impoverished workers. Although that rebellion failed, discontent continued to be expressed in riots, destruction of property, and other forms of social violence.

The second dilemma was how to obtain a controllable labour force as cheaply as possible. Tobacco was the chief source of wealth, and its production was labour-intensive. The colonial leaders found a solution to both problems: by the 1690s they had divided the restless poor into categories reflecting their origins, homogenizing all Europeans into a "white" category and instituting a system of permanent slavery for Africans, the most vulnerable members of the population.

THE ENSLAVEMENT AND RACIALIZATION OF AFRICANS

Between 1660 and 1690, leaders of the Virginia colony began to pass laws and establish practices that provided or sanctioned differential treatment for freed servants whose origins were in Europe. They conscripted poor whites, with whom they had never had interests in common, into the category of free men and made land, tools, animals, and other resources available to them. African Americans and Africans, mulattoes, and American Indians, regardless of their cultural similarities or differences, were forced into categories separate from whites. Historical records show that the Virginia Assembly went to great extremes not only to purposely separate Europeans from Indians and Africans but to promote contempt on the part of whites against blacks. Recognizing the vulnerability of African labour, colonial leaders passed laws that increasingly bound Africans and their children permanently as servants and, eventually, as slaves. White servants had the protection of English laws, and their mistreatment was criticized abroad. Africans, however, had no such recourse. By 1723 even free African Americans, descendants of several generations then of free people, were prohibited from voting and exercising their civil rights. Colonial leaders thus began using the physical differences among the population to structure an inegalitarian society. In the island colonies of Barbados and Jamaica, the numbers of Irish and Indian slaves had also declined, and planters turned increasingly to Africans. Southern planters, who were in regular communication with these island communities, brought in large numbers of Africans during the 18th century and systematically developed their slave practices and laws. Christianity provided an early rationalization for permanent enslavement: Africans were heathens and slaves in their own lands; under English slavery, their souls would be saved.

The underlying reality was that their labour was needed to produce wealth for the colonies and for England's upper classes. During the early decades of the 17th century, many Englishmen considered the Africans to be civilized. Unlike the Indians, whom they called "savages" and who were largely nomadic hunter-gatherers, the English knew the Africans in the colonies as sophisticated cultivators who understood how to grow foods and other crops in tropical soils. In this they surpassed the Irish who had been enslaved on plantations in the Caribbean; with no tradition of agriculture in tropical habitats, the Irish failed as producers of necessary goods. Some Africans were skilled metalworkers, knowledgeable about smelting, blacksmithing, and toolmaking. Many others were skilled in woodworking, weaving, pottery production, rope making, leatherwork, brick making, thatching, and other crafts.

Two additional factors made Africans more desirable as slaves: Africans were immune to Old World diseases, which caused Indians to sicken and die, and, most important, Africans had nowhere to run, unlike the Indians, who could escape from slavery into their own familiar territory. The Irish, who were also in an alien land, were perceived as unruly and violent. When they escaped, they often joined their fellow Catholics, the Spanish and the French, in conspiracies against the English.

Thus, Africans became the preferred slaves—not because of their physical differences, although such differences became increasingly important—but because they had the knowledge and skills that made it possible to put them to work immediately to develop the colonies. They were not Christian, they were vulnerable, with no legal or moral opposition to their enslavement, and, once transported to the New World, they had few options. Moreover, the supply of Africans increased as the costs of transporting them fell, and English merchants became directly involved in the slave trade.

HUMAN RIGHTS VERSUS PROPERTY RIGHTS

Chattel slavery was not established without its critics. From the beginning, many Englishmen condemned the presence of slavery in English territories. They argued that theirs was a society of free men and of democratic institutions and that it was committed to the preservation of human rights, justice, and equality. For several hundred years, trends in English culture had been toward the expansion of human rights and the recognition of individual liberty. Slavery, many argued, was antithetical to a free society and subversive of Christian values.

Throughout the 18th century, however, another powerful value in English culture, the sanctity of property and property rights, came to dominate colonial concerns. When faced with growing anti-slavery arguments, planters in the southern colonies and Caribbean islands, where slavery was bringing great wealth, turned to the argument that slaves were property and that the rights of slave owners to their property were by law unquestionable and inviolable. The laws and court decisions reflected the belief that the property rights of slave owners should take precedence over the human rights of slaves.

Historians concur that the emphasis on the slave as property was a requisite for dehumanizing the Africans. Says the historian Philip D. Morgan, "The only effective way to justify slavery was to exclude its victims from the community of man." Attitudes and beliefs about all Africans began to harden as slavery became more deeply entrenched in the colonies. A focus on the physical differences of Africans expanded as new justifications for slavery were needed, especially during the Revolutionary War period, when the rallying cry of freedom from oppression seemed particularly hypocritical. Many learned men on both sides of the Atlantic disputed the moral rightness of slavery. Opponents argued that a society of free men working for wages would be better producers of goods and services. But pro-slavery forces, which included some of the wealthiest men in America and England, soon posed what they came to believe was an unassailable argument for keeping blacks enslaved: the idea of black inferiority.

BUILDING THE MYTH OF BLACK INFERIORITY

A number of 18th-century political and intellectual leaders began publicly to assert that Africans were naturally inferior and that they were indeed best suited for slavery. A few intellectuals revived an older image of all living things, the *scala naturae* (Latin: "scale of nature"), or Great Chain of Being, to demonstrate that nature or God had made men unequal. This ancient hierarchical paradigm—encompassing all living creatures, starting with the simplest organisms and reaching to humans, angels, and ultimately to God—became for the advocates of slavery a perfect reflection of the realities of inequality that they had created. The physical differences of blacks and Indians became the symbols or markers of their status. It was during these times that the term *race* became widely used to denote the ranking and inequality of these peoples—in other words, their placement on the Chain of Being.

Beginning in the late 18th century, differences between the races became magnified and exaggerated in the public mind. Hundreds of battles with Indians had pushed these populations westward to the frontiers or relegated them increasingly to reservation lands. A widely accepted stereotype had grown that the Indian race was weak and would succumb to the advances of white civilization so that these native peoples would no longer be much of a problem. Their deaths from disease and warfare were seen as a testament to the inevitable demise of the Indian.

Racial stereotyping of Africans was magnified by the Haitian rebellion of 1791. This event heightened the American fear of slave revolts and retaliation, causing greater restrictions and ever harsher and more degrading treatment. Grotesque descriptions of the low-status races, blacks and Indians, were widely publicized, and they helped foster fear and loathing. This negative stereotyping of low-status racial populations was ever present in the public consciousness, and it affected relations among all people.

By the mid-19th century, race in the popular mind had taken on a meaning equivalent to species-level distinctions, at least for differences between blacks and whites. The ideology of separateness that this proclaimed difference implied was soon transformed into social policy. Although legal slavery in the United States ended in 1865 with the passage of the Thirteenth Amendment to the Constitution, the ideology of race continued as a new and major form of social differentiation in both American and British society. The black codes of the 1860s and the Jim Crow laws of the 1890s were passed in the United States to legitimate the social philosophy of racism. More laws were enacted to prevent intermarriage and intermating, and the segregation of public facilities was established by law, especially in the South. The country's low-paying, dirty, and demeaning jobs were relegated to "the Negro," as he was seen fit for only such tasks. Supreme Court decisions, such as the Dred Scott case of 1857, made clear that Negroes were not and could not be citizens of the United States. They were to be excluded from the social community of whites but not from the production of their wealth. The Supreme Court decision in *Plessy* v. *Ferguson* (1896), which permitted "separate but equal" facilities, guaranteed that the racial worldview, with its elements of separateness and exaggerated difference, would continue to flourish.

ENLIGHTENMENT PHILOSOPHERS AND SYSTEMATISTS

The development of the idea and ideology of race coincided with the rise of science in American and European cultures. Much of the inspiration for the growth of science has been credited to the period known as the Enlightenment that spanned most of the 18th century. Many early Enlightenment writers believed in the power of education and fostered very liberal ideals about the potentiality of all peoples, even "savages," for human progress. Yet, later in the century, some of the earliest assertions about the natural inferiority of Africans were published. Major proponents of the ideology of race inequality were the German philosopher Immanuel Kant, the French philosopher Voltaire, the Scottish philosopher and historian David Hume, and the influential American political philosopher Thomas Jefferson. These writers expressed negative opinions about Africans and other "primitives" based on purely subjective impressions or materials gained from secondary sources, such as travelers, missionaries, and explorers. These philosophers expressed the common attitudes of this period; most also had investments in the slave trade or slavery.

During the same period, influenced by taxonomic activities of botanists and biologists that had begun in the 17th century, other European scholars and scientists were involved in the serious work of identifying the different kinds of human groups increasingly discovered around the world. The work of the naturalists and systematists brought attention to the significance of classifying all peoples into "natural" groupings, as had been done with flora and fauna. Eighteenth-century naturalists had greater information and knowledge about the world's peoples than their predecessors, and a number of scholars attempted to organize all this material into some logical scheme. Although many learned men were involved in this enterprise, it was the classifications developed by the Swedish botanist Carolus Linnaeus and the German physiologist Johann Friedrich Blumenbach that provided the models and terms for modern racial classifications.

SCIENTIFIC CLASSIFICATIONS OF RACE

In publications issued from 1735 to 1759, Linnaeus classified all the then-known animal forms. He included humans with the primates and established the use of both genus and species terms for identification of all animals. For the human species, he introduced the still-current scientific name *Homo sapiens*. He listed four major subdivisions of this species, *H. americanus*, *H. africanus*, *H. europaeus*, and *H. asiaticus*. Such was the nature of knowledge at the time that Linnaeus also included the categories *H. monstrosus* (which included many exotic peoples) and *H. ferus* ("wild man"), an indication that some of his categories were based on tall tales and travelers' myths.

Blumenbach divided humankind into five "varieties" and noted that clear lines of distinction could not be drawn between them, as they tended to blend "insensibly" into one another. His five categories included American, Malay, Ethiopian, Mongolian, and Caucasian. (He chose the term Caucasian to represent the

Europeans because a skull from the Caucasus Mountains of Russia was in his opinion the most beautiful.) These terms were still commonly used by many scientists in the early 20th century, and most continue today as major designations of the world's peoples.

These classifications not only rendered human groups as part of nature but also gave them concreteness, rigidity, and permanence. Moreover, some descriptions, especially those of Linnaeus, included statements about the temperament and customs of various peoples that had nothing to do with biophysical features but were forms of learned behaviour that are now known as "culture." That cultural behaviour and physical characteristics were conflated by these 18th-century writers reflects both their ethnocentrism and the limited scientific knowledge of the time.

THE INSTITUTIONALIZING OF RACE

Slavery always creates social distance between masters and slaves, and intellectuals are commonly called upon to affirm and justify such distinctions. As learned men began to write a great deal about the "racial" populations of the New World, Indians and Negroes were increasingly projected as alien. In this way did some Enlightenment thinkers help pro-slavery interests place responsibility for slavery in the "inferior" victims themselves.

Would-be "scientific" writings about the distinctiveness of blacks and Indians commenced late in the 18th century in tandem with exaggerated popular beliefs, and writings of this type continued on into the 20th century. The European world sought to justify not only the institution of slavery but also its increasingly brutal marginalization of all non-European peoples, slave or free. Science became the vehicle through which the delineation of races was confirmed, and scientists in Europe and America provided the arguments and evidence to document the inferiority of non-Europeans.

About the turn of the 19th century, some scholars advanced the idea that the Negro (and perhaps the Indian) was a separate species from "normal" men (white and Christian), an idea that had been introduced and occasionally expressed in the 18th century but that had drawn little attention. This revived notion held that the "inferior races" had been created at a different time than Adam and Eve, who were the progenitors of the white race. Although multiple creations contradicted both the well-known definition of species in terms of reproductively isolated populations and the biblical description of creation, it is clear that in the public mind the transformation from race to species-level difference had already evolved. In the courts, statehouses, assemblies, and churches and throughout American institutions, race became institutionalized as the premier source, and the causal agent, of all human differences.

TRANSFORMING "RACE" INTO "SPECIES"

One of those whose direct experience of African slaves and assessment of them was given great weight was Edward Long (1734–1813), a former plantation owner and jurist in Jamaica. In a book titled *The History of Jamaica* (1774), Long asserted that "the Negro" was "void of genius" and "incapable" of civilization; indeed, he was so far inferior as to constitute a separate species of mankind. Long's work was published as a defense of slavery during a period of rising antislavery sentiment. Its greatest influence came during and after the American Revolutionary War (1775–83), when some southern Americans started freeing their slaves and moving north. Long's writings, published in popular magazines, were widely read in the United States during the last decade of the 18th century.

In 1799 Charles White, a Manchester physician, published the earliest proper "scientific" study of human races. He described each racial category in physical terms, identifying what he thought were differences in the head, feet, arms, complexion, skin colour, hair texture, and susceptibility to disease. White actually measured the body parts of a group of blacks and whites, lending the semblance of hard science to his conclusions. He not only advocated a gradation of the races, but he provided support for the speculation that the Negro, the American Indian, some Asiatic tribes, and Europeans were of different species. His explanation for the presumed savagery of Africans was that they had degenerated from the pure and idyllic circumstances provided in the Garden of Eden while Europeans had made advances toward civilization.

Such works as those of Long and White initiated a debate among scholars and scientists that had long-range implications for European attitudes toward human differences. The issue, as expressed by mid-19th-century scientists, was "the Negro's place in nature"—that is, whether "the Negro" was human like Europeans or a separate species nearer to the ape.

Samuel Morton, a Philadelphia physician and founder of the field of craniometry, collected skulls from around the world and developed techniques for measuring them. He thought he could identify racial differences among these skulls. After developing techniques for measuring the internal capacity of the skull, he concluded that blacks had smaller brains than whites, with Indian brains intermediate between the two. Because brain size had long been correlated with intelligence in both the popular mind and science, Morton's findings seemed to confirm that blacks were also less intelligent than whites. In publications of 1839 and 1844, he produced his results, identifying the Native Americans as a separate race from Asians and arguing from his Egyptian materials that these ancient peoples were not Negroes. His findings magnified and exaggerated the differences between racial populations, imposing meaning on the differences that led to the conclusion that they were separate species.

Morton soon became the centre of a network of scholars and scientists who advocated multiple creations (polygeny) and thus contradicted the long-established biblical view of one single creation from which all humans descended (monogeny). The most influential of the scientists involved in this debate was Louis Agassiz, who accepted a position at Harvard University and revolutionized the field of natural science. Agassiz converted from monogenism to polygenism after moving to the United States from Switzerland in 1846. It was then that he saw blacks for the first time. He was also impressed with Morton's work with skulls, and eventually he became the most important advocate of polygenism, conveying it in public lectures and to generations of students, many of whom took leading intellectual roles in American society.

One result of the mid-19th-century concern with documenting racial distinctions by means of body measurements was the establishment of the "scientific" enterprise of anthropometry. During the Civil War the U.S. Sanitary Commission and the provost marshall general's office collected data on the physical condition of military conscripts and volunteers in the army, navy, and marines. Using

anthropometric techniques, they produced massive tables of quantitative measurements of the body dimensions of tens of thousands of whites, blacks, mulattoes, and Indians. Scientists interpreted the data in a way that strengthened the argument that races were fundamentally distinct and that confirmed that blacks, Indians, and mulattoes were inferior to whites. Anthropometry flourished as a major scientific method for demonstrating race differences well into the 20th century.

THE FALSE ASSUMPTIONS OF ANTHROPOMETRY

For the first half of the 20th century, scholars continued to debate "the Negro's place in nature." But the debate over multiple or single origins receded after 1859, when the publication of Charles Darwin's theory of evolution led to a more dynamic understanding of human diversity. Evolution produced a new perspective on the causes of blacks' (supposedly) innate condition; the central issue became whether they evolved before or after whites. By the 1860s black primitiveness was assumed without question. "The Negro," in fact, had become the new savage, displacing Indians and Irishmen, and the ideology proclaimed that his savagery was intrinsic and immutable.

The use of metrical descriptions, while they seemed objective and scientific, fostered typological conceptions of human group differences. From massive quantitative measurements, experts computed averages, means, and standard deviations from which they developed statistical profiles of each racial population. These profiles were thought to represent the type characteristics of each race expressed in what seemed to be impeccable scientific language. When statistical profiles of one group were compared with those of others, one could theoretically determine the degree of their racial differences.

The activities of typologists carried a number of false assumptions about the physical characteristics of races. One was that racial characteristics did not change from one generation to another, meaning that averages of measurements such as body height would remain the same in the next generations. Another false assumption was that statistical averages could accurately represent huge populations, when the averaging itself obliterated all the variability within those populations.

Expressed alongside existing myths and popular racial stereotypes, these measurements inevitably strengthened the assumption that some races were "pure" and some not so pure. Scholars argued that all the major races were originally pure and that some races represented the historical mixing of two or more races in the past. "Racial types" were conceived as representing populations with certain inherited morphological features that were originally characteristic of the race; every member of a race thus retained such traits. These beliefs attempted to validate the image of races as internally homogeneous and biologically discrete, having no overlapping features with other races.

THE INFLUENCE OF FRANZ BOAS

Typological thinking about race, however, was soon contradicted by the works of some early 20th-century anthropologists. Franz Boas, for example, published studies that showed that morphological characteristics varied from generation to generation in the same population, that skeletal material such as the cranium was malleable and subject to external influences, and that metrical averages in a given population changed in succeeding generations.

Boas and the early anthropologists trained in the United States recognized that the popular conception of race linked, and thus confused, biology with language and culture. They began to advocate the separation of "race," as purely a biological phenomenon, from behaviour and language, denying a relationship between physical traits and the languages and cultures that people carry.

Though their arguments had little impact on the public at the time, these scholars initiated a new way of thinking about human differences. The separation of culture and language, which are learned behaviours, from biological traits that are physically inherited became a major tenet of anthropology. As the discipline grew and spread by means of scholarship and academic training, public understanding and recognition of this fundamental truth increased. Yet the idea of a hereditary basis for human behaviour remained a stubborn element of both popular and scientific thought.

MENDELIAN HEREDITY AND THE DEVELOPMENT OF BLOOD GROUP SYSTEMS

In 1900, after the rediscovery of Austrian botanist Gregor Mendel's experiments dealing with heredity, scientists began to focus greater attention on genes and chromosomes. Their objective was to ascertain the hereditary basis for numerous physical traits. Once the ABO blood group system was discovered and was shown to follow the pattern of Mendelian heredity, other systems—the MNSs system, the Rhesus or Rh system, and many others—soon followed. Experts thought that at last they had found genetic features that, because they are inherited and not susceptible to environmental influences, could be used to identify races. By the 1960s and '70s, scientists were writing about racial groups as populations that differed from one another not in absolute features but in the frequencies of expression of genes that all populations share. It was expected that each race, and each population within each race, would have frequencies of certain ascertainable genes that would mark them off from other races.

Information on blood groups was taken from large numbers of populations, but, when scientists tried to show a correlation of blood group patterns with the conventional races, they found none. While populations differed in their blood group patterns, in such features as the frequencies of A, B, and O types, no evidence was found to document race distinctions. As knowledge of human heredity expanded, other genetic markers of difference were sought, but these also failed to neatly separate humanity into races. Most differences are expressed in subtle gradations over wide geographic space, not in abrupt changes from one "race" to another. Moreover, not all groups within a large "geographic race" share the same patterns of genetic features. The internal variations within races have proved to be greater than those between races. Most important, physical, or phenotypic, features assumed to be determined by DNA are inherited independently of one another, further frustrating attempts to describe race differences in genetic terms.

"RACE" AND INTELLIGENCE

Anthropometric measurements did not provide any direct data to prove group superiority or inferiority. As various fields of study emerged in the late 19th century, some scholars began to focus on mental traits as a means to examine and describe human differences. Psychology as a growing field began developing its own programmatic interests in discovering race differences.

In the 1890s the psychologist Alfred Binet began testing the mental abilities of French schoolchildren to ascertain how children learned and to help those who had trouble learning. Binet did not call his test an intelligence test, and its purpose was not to divide French schoolchildren into hierarchical groups. But with these tests a new mechanism was born that would provide powerful support to those who held beliefs in racial differences in intelligence.

Psychologists in the United States very quickly adopted Binet's tests and modified them for American use. More than that, they reinterpreted the results to be clear evidence of innate intelligence. Lewis Terman and his colleagues at Stanford University developed the Stanford-Binet IQ (intelligence quotient) test, which set the standard for similar tests produced by other American psychologists.

IQ tests began to be administered in large numbers during the second decade of the 20th century. The influences of hereditarian beliefs and the power of the racial worldview had conditioned Americans to believe that intelligence was inherited and permanent and that no external influences could affect it. Indeed, heredity was thought to determine a person's or a people's place in life and success or failure. Americans came to employ IQ tests more than any other nation. A major reason for this was that the tests tended to confirm the expectations of white Americans; on average,

blacks did less well than whites on IQ tests. But the tests also revealed that the disadvantaged people of all races do worse on IQ tests than do the privileged. Such findings were compatible with the beliefs of large numbers of Americans who had come to accept unqualified biological determinism.

Opponents of IQ tests and their interpretations argued that intelligence had not been clearly defined, that experts did not agree on its definition, and that there were many different types of intelligence that cannot be measured. They also called attention to the many discrepancies and contradictions of the tests. One of the first examples of empirical evidence against the "innate intelligence" arguments was the revelation by psychologist Otto Klineberg in the 1930s that blacks in four Northern states did better on average than whites in the four Southern states where expenditures on education were lowest. Klineberg's analysis pointed to a direct correlation between income and social class and performance on IQ tests. Further evidence indicated that students with the best primary education and greater cultural experiences always did better on such tests. Experts thus argued that such tests are culture-bound; that is, they reflect and measure the cultural experiences and knowledge of those who take the tests and their levels of education and training. Few would deny that African Americans and Native Americans have long had a much more restricted experience of American culture and a far inferior education.

EUROPEAN CONSTRUCTIONS OF RACE AND THEIR LEGACY IN AMERICA

Inheritance as the basis of individual social position is an ancient tenet of human history, extending to some point after the beginnings of agriculture (about 10,000 BCE). Expressions of it are found throughout the world in kinship-based societies where genealogical links determine an individual's status, rights, and obligations. Wills and testaments capture this principle, and caste systems, such as that of India, reflect the expression of another form of this principle, buttressed by religious beliefs. Arguments for the divine right of kings and succession laws in European societies mirrored deep values of hereditary status.

But many trends in European cultural history over the 18th and 19th centuries contradicted the idea of social placement by kinship fiat. Ever since the enclosure movement in England in the 15th century, the transformation to wage labour, the rise of merchant capitalism, and the entry into public consciousness of the significance of private property, Europeans have been conditioned to the values of individualism and of progress through prosperity. Wage labour strengthened ideas of individual freedom and advancement. The philosophy of autonomous individualism took root in western European societies, beginning first in England, and became the engine of social mobility in these rapidly changing areas. For their descendants in America, the limitations of hereditary status were antithetical to the values of individual freedom, at least freedom for those of European descent.

Reflecting and promoting these values were the works of some of the Enlightenment writers and philosophers, including Voltaire, Jean-Jacques Rousseau, John Locke, and Montesquieu. Their writings had a greater impact on Americans than on the writers' own compatriots. Their advocacy of human freedom and the minimal intrusion of government was uniquely interpreted by Americans.

THE GERMANIC MYTH AND ENGLISH CONSTRUCTIONS OF AN ANGLO-SAXON PAST

In England, from the time that Henry VIII broke with the Roman Catholic Church and Protestant sects emerged on the horizon, historians, politicians, and philosophers had been wrestling with the creation of a new English identity. Indeed, European powers were soon to be caught up in the ethnic rivalries, extreme chauvinism, and intolerance out of which all the nation-states of Europe would be created. The English sought their new identity in the myths and heroics of the past, striving to fashion an image of antiquity that would rival those of other great civilizations. They eventually created a myth of an Anglo-Saxon people, distinguished from the Vikings, Picts, Celts, Romans, Normans, and others who had inhabited English territory.

In their histories the Anglo-Saxons were a freedom-loving people who had advanced political institutions, an early form of representative government, and a pure religion long before the Norman Conquest. Although in part the English were concerned about the identification and preservation of ancient institutions to justify the distinctiveness of their political and ecclesiastical structures, they also wanted to establish and glorify a distinguished ancestry. The English too turned toward the German tribes and a "racial" ideology on which to base their claims of superiority.

GOBINEAU'S ESSAY ON THE INEQUALITY OF HUMAN RACES

The most important promoter of racial ideology in Europe during the mid-19th century was Joseph-Arthur, comte de Gobineau, who had an almost incalculable effect on late 19th-century social theory. Published in 1853–55, his *Essay on the Inequality of Human Races* was widely read, embellished, and publicized by many different kinds of writers. He imported some of his arguments from the polygenists, especially the American Samuel Morton. Gobineau claimed that the civilizations established by the three major races of the world (white, black, and yellow) were all products of the white races and that no civilization could emerge without their cooperation. The purest of the white races were the Aryans. When Aryans diluted their blood by intermarriage with lower races, they helped to bring about the decline of their civilization.

Americans of this period were among Gobineau's greatest admirers. So were many Germans. The latter saw in his works a formula for unifying the German peoples and ultimately proclaiming their superiority. Many proponents of German nationalism became activists and organized political societies to advance their goals. They developed a new dogma of "Aryanism" that was to expand and become the foundation for Nazi race theories in the 20th century.

Fueled by rising anti-Semitism in Europe, race ideology facilitated the manufacture of an image of Jews as a distinct and inferior population. Chamberlain's publications were widely disseminated in Germany during the turn of the 20th century.

GALTON AND SPENCER

Hereditarian ideology also flourished in late 19th-century England. Two major writers and proselytizers of the idea of the innate racial superiority of the upper classes were Francis Galton and Herbert Spencer. Galton wrote books with titles such as *Hereditary Genius* (1869), in which he showed that a disproportionate number of the great men of England—the military leaders, philosophers, scientists, and artists—came from the small upper-class stratum. Spencer incorporated the themes of biological evolution and social progress into a grand universal scheme. Antedating Darwin, Spencer introduced the ideas of competition, the struggle for existence, and the survival of the fittest. His "fittest" were the socially and economically most successful not only among groups but within societies. The "savage" or inferior races of men were clearly the unfit and would soon die out. For this reason, Spencer advocated that governments eschew policies that helped the poor; he was against all charities, child labour laws, women's rights, and education for the poor and uncivilized. Such actions, he claimed, interfered with the laws of natural evolution; these beliefs became known as social Darwinism.

The hereditarian ideologies of European writers in general found a ready market for such ideas among all those nations involved in empire building. In the United States these ideas paralleled and strengthened the racial ideology then deeply embedded in American values and thought. They had a synergistic effect on ideas of hereditary determinism in many aspects of American life and furthered the acceptance and implementation of IQ tests as an accurate measure of innate human ability.

CONQUEST AND THE CLASSIFICATION OF THE CONQUERED

As they were constructing their own racial identities internally, western European nations were also colonizing most of what has been called, in recent times, the Third World, in Asia and Africa. Since all the colonized and subordinated peoples differed physically from Europeans, the colonizers automatically applied racial categories to them, initiating a long history of discussions about how such populations should be classified. There is a very wide range of physical characteristics among Third World peoples, and subjective impressions generated much scientific debate, particularly about which features were most useful for racial classification. Experts never reached agreement on such classifications, and some questions, such as how to classify indigenous Australians, were subjects of endless, unresolved debate.

Race and race ideology had become so deeply entrenched in American and European thought by the end of the 19th century that scholars and other learned people came to believe that the idea of race was universal. They searched for examples of race ideology among indigenous populations and reinterpreted the histories of these peoples in terms of Western conceptions of racial causation for all human achievements or lack thereof.

"RACE" AND THE REALITY OF HUMAN PHYSICAL VARIATION

Scientists have known for many decades that there is little correlation between "race," used in its popular sense, and actual physical variations in the human species. In the United States, for example, the people identified as African Americans do not share a common set of physical characteristics. There is a greater range of skin colours, hair colours and textures, facial features, body sizes, and other physical traits in this category than in any other human aggregate identified as a single race. Features of African Americans vary from light skins, blue or gray eyes, and blond hair to dark skins, black eyes, and crinkly hair, and include every range and combination of characteristics in between. American custom has long classified any person with known African ancestry as black, a social mandate often called the "one-drop rule." This principle not only attests to the arbitrary nature of black racial identity, but was also presumed to keep those classified as racially "white" pure and untainted by the "blood" of low-status and inferior races. This rule has not applied to other "racial" mixtures, such as children born of white and Asian parents, although some of these children have suffered discrimination because of physical similarities to their "lower-status" parent. All this gives clear evidence of the socially arbitrary nature of race categories in North America.

Since World War II, travel and immigration have greatly increased the contact of Westerners with a wide variety of peoples throughout the world. Contact with peoples of the South Pacific and Southeast Asia, as well as with those from several areas of Africa and the Middle East, has shown that most of these people do not neatly fit into existing racial stereotypes. Many Americans are recognizing that the social categories of race as evolved in the United States are inadequate for encompassing such peoples who, indeed, do not share the social history of racial minorities in the United States. "Race" is indeed in the eye of the beholder.

Clearly, physical features are insufficient clues to a person's ethnic identity. They reveal nothing about a person's culture, language, religion, and values. Sixth-generation Chinese Americans have American ethnicity; many know little or nothing about traditional Chinese culture, just as European Americans and African Americans may know little or nothing about the cultures of their ancestors. Moreover, all cultures change, and they do so independently of the biogenetic features of their carriers.

MODERN SCIENTIFIC EXPLANATIONS OF HUMAN BIOLOGICAL VARIATION

Contemporary scientists hold that human physical variations, especially in those traits that are normally used to classify people racially—skin colour, hair texture, facial features, and to some extent bodily structure—must be understood in terms of evolutionary processes and the long-range adaptation of human groups to differing environments. Other features may simply reflect accidental mutations or functionally neutral changes in the genetic code.

In any given habitat, natural forces operate on all of the living forms, including human groups. The necessary interaction with these forces will affect the survival and reproduction of the members of these societies. Such groups already have a wide and complex range of hereditary physical characteristics; indeed, human hereditary variability is a product of human sexual reproduction, whereby every individual receives half of his or her genetic endowment from each parent and no two individuals (except for identical twins) inherit the same combination of genetic features.

The global distribution of skin colour is the best example of adaptation, and the consequences of this process have long been well known. Skin colour clines (gradations) in indigenous populations worldwide correlate with latitude and amounts of sunlight. Indigenous populations within a broad band known as the tropics (the regions falling in latitude between the Tropics of Cancer and Capricorn) have darker skin colours than indigenous populations outside of these regions.

Within the tropics, skin colours vary from light tan to very dark brown or black, both among populations and among individuals within groups. The darkest skin colours are found in those populations long residing in regions where intense ultraviolet sunlight is greatest and there is little natural forest cover. The bluish black skins of some peoples—such as some of the Dravidians of South India, the peoples of Sri Lanka and Bangladesh, and those of the eastern Sudan zone, including Nubia, and the grasslands of Africa—are examples of the extremes of dark skin colour. Medium brown to dark brown peoples are found in the rest of tropical Africa and India and throughout Australia, Melanesia, and other parts of Southeast Asia.

Peoples with light skin colours evolved over thousands of years in northern temperate climates. Human groups intermittently migrating into Europe and the northern parts of the Eurasian landmass over the past 25,000 to 50,000 years experienced a gradual loss of skin pigmentation. The changes were both physiological and genetic; that is, there were systemic changes in individuals and long-range genetic changes as a result of natural selection and, possibly, mutations. Those individuals with the lightest skin colours, with lowest amounts of melanin, survived and reproduced in larger numbers, thus passing on their genes for lighter skin. Over time, entire populations living in northern climates evolved lighter skin tones than those individuals living in areas with higher levels of sunlight. Between populations with light skin and those with the darkest coloration are populations with various shades of light tan to brown. The cline in skin colours shows variation by infinite degrees; any attempts to place boundaries along this cline represent purely arbitrary decisions.

Scientists at the turn of the 21st century understood why these superficial visible differences developed. Melanin, a substance that makes the skin dark, has been shown to confer protection from sunburn and skin cancers in those very areas where ultraviolet sunlight is strongest. Dark skin, which tends to be thicker than light skin, may have other protective functions in tropical environments where biting insects and other vectors of disease are constant threats to human survival. But humans also need vitamin D, which is synthesized by sunlight from sterols (chemical compounds) present in the skin. Vitamin D affects bone growth, and, without a sufficient amount, the disease known as rickets would have been devastating to early human groups trying to survive in the cold, wintry weather of the north. As these groups adapted to northern climates with limited sunlight, natural selection brought about the gradual loss of melanin in favour of skin tones that enabled some individuals to better synthesize vitamin D.

Other physical characteristics indicate adaptations to cold or hot climates, to variations in elevation from sea level, to rain forests with high levels of rainfall, and to hot deserts. Body structure and the amount of body fat have also been explained by evolutionists in terms of human adaptation to differing environments. Long, linear body builds seem to be highly correlated with hot, dry climates. Such people inhabit the Sahara and the desiccated areas of the Sudan in Africa. Short, stocky body builds with stubby fingers and toes are correlated with cold, wet climates, such as are found in Arctic areas. People adapted to cold climates have acquired genetic traits that provide them extra layers of body fat, which accounts for the epicanthic

fold over their eyes. People who live in areas of high elevation, as in the mountains of Peru, tend to have an adaptive feature not found among peoples who live at sea level; they have larger lungs and chest cavities. In an atmosphere where the oxygen supply is low, larger lungs are clearly adaptive.

Some adaptive variations are not obviously visible or measurable. Many peoples adapted to cold climates, for example, have protective physiological reactions in their blood supply. Their blood vessels either constrict the flow to extremities to keep the inner body warm while their surface skin may be very cold (vasoconstriction) or dilate to increase the blood flow to the hands, feet, and head to warm the outer surfaces (vasodilation).

The prevalence of diseases has been another major factor in the evolution of human diversity, and some of the most important of human genetic variations reflect differences in immunities to diseases. The sickle cell trait (hemoglobin S), for example, is found chiefly in those regions of the tropical world where malaria is endemic. Hemoglobin S in its heterozygous form (inherited from one parent only) confers some immunity to those people who carry it, although it brings a deadly disease (sickle cell anemia) in its homozygous form (inherited from both parents).

In the last decades of the 20th century, scientists began to understand human physical variability in clinal terms and to recognize that it reflects much more complex gradations and combinations than they had anticipated. To comprehend the full expression of a feature's genetic variability, it must be studied separately over geographic space and often in terms of its adaptive value. Many features are now known to relate to the environmental conditions of the populations that carry them.

THE SCIENTIFIC DEBATE OVER "RACE"

Although their numbers are dwindling, there remain some scientists who continue to believe that it is possible to divide *Homo sapiens* into discrete populations called races. These scientists believe that the physical differences manifest in wide geographic regions are more than superficial—that they reflect innate intellectual, moral, emotional, and other behavioral differences between human groups. They deny that social circumstances and the cultural realities of racism have any effect on behaviour or the performance of children and adults on IQ tests. Those scientists who advocate the continued acceptance of race and racial differences have been labeled "splitters." Among the highly popularized reflections of this point of view was *The Bell Curve: Intelligence and Class Structure in American Life* (1994) by Richard Herrnstein and Charles Murray. This work is a representation of social Darwinism in that the authors argue not only that minority or low-status races have innate deficiencies but that poor people of all races, including whites, are genetically inferior.

Those who deny the biological salience of race or argue against the use of the term have been labeled "lumpers." This group sees their position as being buttressed and confirmed by ongoing genetic and other research. They emphasize the failure of science to establish exclusive boundaries around populations or lines of rigid distinctions that the term *race* conveys. They also point to the evidence demonstrating that all people—regardless of their physical variations—are capable of learning any kind of cultural behaviour. They argue that genes and cultural conditioning work in tandem, together contributing to the formation of individual personalities.

An increasing number of scholars and other educated people now believe that the concept of race has outlived its usefulness. Social scientists, biologists, historians, and philosophers now point out that increasing migration and changes in attitudes toward human differences have brought about extensive intermingling of peoples to the extent that a growing number of people have ancestors originating in three or more continents. Such "mixed" people are not easily placed into a single "racial" category. As a result, many scholars perceive that "race" is becoming more and more irrelevant and may eventually be eliminated as people increasingly are recognized in terms of their ethnic or cultural identities, occupations, education, and local affiliations.

A contradictory trend also seems to be occurring among some writers who find it difficult to relinquish some elements of race ideology. Instead, they "biologize" ethnic identity and interpret peoples' cultures and behaviour as if such features stem from genetic heredity. Should this trend expand, society may continue to manifest the broad elements of race ideology, though perhaps in diminished intensity or in a different form.

SUMMARY

This chapter has argued the fallacy and intentions at the heart of the concept of race, but the term *race* remains pivotal to the discussion of African American history (no small amount of clarity would be lost, for example, if the term *race riot* were replaced with *ethnic riot* later in this volume) and to the understanding of the way that all Americans relate to one another in the early 21st century. Politicians and civic leaders often call for national and personal dialogues on race, the benefit of which is hard to argue against; however, these discussions (like the rest of this book) must be grounded in an appreciation of what really is meant by the topic of race and the terms *race* and *racial*; that is, that race should be understood as a social construct rather than as a genetic reality.

CHAPTER 5

SLAVERY, ABOLITIONISM, AND RECONSTRUCTION

SLAVERY

The previous chapter considered the "peculiar institution" of slavery in the context of the concept of race. This chapter takes a closer look at slavery as it relates to American history: the nature of slavery, its implementation, the defense of it, opposition to it, and its eradication. It also considers the era of Reconstruction and the efforts to redress the wrongs of slavery by conferring the rights of full citizenship not just on freedmen but on all African Americans.

ORIGINS OF SLAVERY IN THE UNITED STATES

Slaves were first brought to North America—to Virginia—in 1619. Subsequently, Africans were transshipped to North America from the Caribbean in increasing numbers, and by the 17th century African slaves had replaced English indentured labourers. As a result of the invention of the cotton gin by Eli Whitney in 1793, sugar and cotton replaced tobacco as the principal crop in Chesapeake. Cotton culture created a huge demand for slaves, especially after the opening of Alabama, Mississippi, Louisiana, and Texas. By 1850, nearly two-thirds of the plantation slaves were engaged in the production of cotton. During the reign of

"King Cotton," about 40 percent of the Southern population consisted of black slaves; the percentage of slaves rose as high 55 percent in Mississippi in 1810 and 1860. The South was totally transformed by the presence of slavery, which generated significant profits; it would take the Civil War to end it.

THE LAW AND NATURE OF AMERICAN SLAVERY

Throughout history slave owning and slave societies borrowed some of their laws about slavery from the religious texts of their respective civilizations; in a number of cases these laws prescribed that slaves be freed after a given period of time. In Christian slave societies such as the American South, however, the principle that the tenure of slavery should be limited was almost completely ignored.

Because English law did not address slavery, the English colonies in the New World were free to create their own laws. Beginning with Virginia in the l660s, each North American colony established its own ex post facto law. This process continued after the creation of the United States and until the Civil War. Indeed, slavery was mentioned only three times and referred to at most 10 times (and then only indirectly) in the antebellum U.S. Constitution. Except for a handful of measures on fugitives, there was no federal slave law. The Tenth Amendment of 1791, the reserved powers clause, provided the basic protection for the institution of slavery by leaving the issue of slavery and other matters to the states.

At the centre of slave law was the master-slave relationship, yet the law often said very little about it. In many parts of the American South before 1830 an owner had the right to kill his slave with impunity. On the other hand, the Louisiana Black Code of 1806 made cruel punishment of slaves a crime. Brutality and sadistic murder of slaves by their owners were rarely condoned because it was believed by some that such episodes demoralized other slaves and made them rebellious; however, few slave owners were actually punished for maltreating their slaves. In the American South before 1830 the owner's control over his slave was total. The law said little or nothing about how long a slave could be worked or whether he or she had a right to food and clothing, though there were exceptions. The Alabama Slave Code of 1852, for example, required owners to provide slaves sufficient healthy food, clothing, attention during illness, and necessities in old age.

Because the master owned not only his slave's body but everything that body might accumulate, the slave could *possess* property but could not *own* it. The master also automatically had sexual access to his slaves. Slave marriages were not legally recognized, and slaves generally had considerably fewer rights to their offspring than to their spouses. Slave owners did not hesitate to split up both the conjugal unit and the nuclear family.

Still, slaves formed what they considered marriages and had children. Some pragmatic Southern slave owners recognized both slave marriages and their offspring, because not to have done so would have interfered with production.

The American South was a major exception to the rule that most slave societies slaves rarely reproduced themselves, generally a consequence of many more men than women being imported as slaves. That slaves in the South began to procreate in significant numbers in the mid-18th century helped the slave owners survive the cutting off of imports that was first enforced in 1808. Between the censuses of 1790 and 1860, the slave population of the South expanded enormously—from some 650,000 to 3.8 million—one of the fastest rates of population growth ever recorded prior to the spread of modern medicine. The Southern slave regime was one of the most dehumanizing ever recorded, but because its nutritional and general living environments were conducive to explosive population growth, it thrived demographically. Indeed, between the early 1800s and 1860, without significant imports, the slave population of the South increased fourfold.

SLAVE PROTEST

Slaves protested their condition in many different ways, including alcoholism, flight, suicide, arson, murder of their owners, and mass rebellion. It may have been that the most frequent individual response to enslavement was sluggishness and passivity. Slaves were stereotypically thought be mendacious and lazy—dull brutes who had to be whipped or kicked. In all likelihood three mutually reinforcing factors came into play: an unconscious response to over-control in the absence of freedom, a conscious effort to sabotage the master's desires, and a conditioned response to the expectation of stereotypical behaviour. A minority of owners responded by introducing incentives or by implementing strict regimentation, such as the gang system.

Some slaves—such as those known to have jumped overboard during the transatlantic Middle Passage, fearing that they were being taken to witches to be eaten—chose suicide over enslavement. A more hopeful form of protest against enslavement was flight, either individually or in groups. The rates of flight usually depended more on the likelihood of success than on individual slave-owner relations. The brutality of an overseer or master or a lapse of supervision might precipitate slave flight, but willingness to flee was limited in the South by the fact that the refuge of freedom was often very far away. Nevertheless, during the American Revolution, when the slave owners were immersed in fighting the British, fugitive slaves numbered in the tens of thousands.

FUGITIVE SLAVE ACTS

Congress played its part in curbing slave flight by passing legislation that provided for the seizure and return of runaway slaves who escaped from one state into another or into a federal territory. Two such Fugitive Slave Acts were enacted, the first in 1793 and the second in 1850. The 1793 law enforced Article IV, Section 2, of the U.S. Constitution in authorizing any federal district judge or circuit court judge, or any state magistrate, to decide finally and without a jury trial the status of an alleged fugitive slave.

In the North, the measure met with strong opposition, and some states enacted personal-liberty laws that hampered the execution of the federal law. For example, Indiana and Connecticut, in 1824 and 1828, respectively, enacted laws making jury trials for escaped slaves possible upon appeal. In 1840 Vermont and New York granted fugitives the right of jury trial and provided them with attorneys. After 1842, when the U.S. Supreme Court ruled that enforcement of the Fugitive Slave Act was a federal function, some Northern state governments passed laws forbidding state authorities to cooperate in the capture and return of fugitives. As early as 1810 individual dissatisfaction with the Fugitive Slave Act of 1793 had taken the form of systematic assistance rendered to black slaves escaping from the South to New England or Canada—via the Underground Railroad.

SLAVE REVOLTS

Often, direct attacks on slave owners were a function of the nature of the slave regime they imposed. When owners exercised automatic sexual access to female slaves, both these women and their "husbands" were inclined to assault the owners. Where slaves were driven, assault on the drivers (such as the overseers in the Mississippi Valley who carried arms because they feared for their lives) was not an uncommon response.

Nothing enraged and terrified slaveholders as much as outright rebellion; however, there were noticeably few slave revolts in North America and most of these involved only a handful of participants. Among them were the New York revolt of 1712, the Stono rebellion of South Carolina (1739), and the Gabriel plot in Richmond, Va. (1800). Because of the absolute certainty that they would be brutally repressed, Southern slave uprisings were especially uncommon and small. Three slave rebellions stand out among all others: the Denmark Vesey conspiracy in Charleston, S.C. (1822), Nat Turner's uprising in Jerusalem, Va. (1831), and the *Amistad* mutiny (1839), which occurred at sea.

DENMARK VESEY CONSPIRACY

In 1800 Denmark Vesey, a self-educated slave, was permitted to purchase his freedom with the prize money he had won in a street lottery. While working as a carpenter he read antislavery literature, and thus became familiar with the Haitian slave revolt of the 1790s led by Toussaint Louverture. Disenchanted with his second-class status as a freedman and desirous of relieving the far more

UNDERGROUND RAILROAD

Though neither underground nor a railroad, the system by which escaped slaves from the South were secretly helped by sympathetic Northerners to reach places of safety in the North or in Canada, was thus named because its activities had to be carried out in secret, using darkness or disguise, and because railway terms were used in reference to the conduct of the system. Various routes were lines, stopping places were called stations, those who aided along the way were conductors, and their charges were known as packages or freight. The network of routes extended in all directions throughout 14 Northern states and "the promised land" of Canada, which was beyond the reach of fugitive-slave hunters. Those who most actively assisted slaves to escape by way of the "railroad" were members of the free black community (including such former slaves as Harriet Tubman),

Harriet Tubman. Library of Congress, Washington, D.C. (neg. no LC USZ 62 7816)

Northern abolitionists, philanthropists, and such church leaders as Quaker Thomas Garrett. Harriet Beecher Stowe, the author of Uncle Tom's Cabin *(1852), gained firsthand knowledge of fugitive slaves through her contact with the Underground Railroad in Cincinnati, Ohio.*

Estimates of the number of black people who reached freedom vary greatly, from 40,000 to 100,000. Although only a small minority of Northerners participated in the Underground Railroad, its existence did much to arouse Northern sympathy for the lot of the slave in the antebellum period, at the same time convincing many Southerners that the North as a whole would never peaceably allow the institution of slavery to remain unchallenged.

The demand from the South for more effective legislation resulted in enactment of a second Fugitive Slave Act in 1850. Under this law fugitives could not testify on their own behalf, nor were they permitted a trial by jury. Heavy penalties were imposed upon federal marshals who refused to enforce the law or from whom a fugitive escaped; penalties were also imposed on individuals who helped slaves to escape. Finally, under the 1850 act, special commissioners were to have concurrent jurisdiction with the U.S. courts in enforcing the law. The severity of the 1850 measure led to abuses and defeated its purpose. The number of abolitionists increased, the operations of the Underground Railroad became more efficient, and in many Northern states new personal-liberty laws were enacted that provided further guarantees of jury trial, authorized severe punishment for illegal seizure and perjury against alleged fugitives, and forbade state authorities to recognize claims to fugitives. Attempts to carry into effect the law of 1850 aroused much bitterness and probably had as much to do with inciting sectional hostility as did the controversy over slavery in the territories.

oppressive conditions of slaves he knew, Vesey organized an uprising of city and plantation blacks. Reportedly, his plan, which may have involved as many as 9,000 blacks (some scholars dispute this figure), called for the rebels to attack guardhouses and arsenals, seize their arms, kill all whites, burn and destroy the city, and free the slaves.

Because they were warned by a house servant, white authorities made massive military preparations, thereby forestalling the insurrection. Over the course of two months some 130 blacks were arrested. Sixty-seven of them were tried and convicted of trying to raise an insurrection, with Vesey and 34 others being hanged; the remaining 32 were condemned to exile. Four white men were fined and imprisoned for encouraging the plot.

NAT TURNER'S REBELLION

Nat Turner was born the property of a prosperous small-plantation owner in a remote area of Virginia. His mother was an African native who transmitted a passionate hatred of slavery to her son. He learned to read from one of his master's sons, and he eagerly absorbed intensive religious training. In the early 1820s he was sold to a neighbouring farmer of small means. During the following decade his religious ardour tended to approach fanaticism, and he saw himself called upon by God to lead his people out of bondage. He began to exert a powerful influence on many of the nearby slaves, who called him "the Prophet."

Nat Turner. Library of Congress, Washington, D.C.

In 1831, shortly after he had been sold again—this time to a craftsman named Joseph Travis—a sign in the form of an eclipse of the sun caused Turner to believe that the hour to strike was near. His plan was to take over the armoury at the county seat, Jerusalem, to gather recruits, and then to proceed to the Dismal Swamp, 30 miles to the east, where it would be difficult to capture his force. On the night of August 21, along with seven fellow slaves, Turner launched a campaign of total annihilation, murdering Travis and his family in their sleep and then setting forth on a violent march toward Jerusalem. In the course of two days and nights about 60 white people were slain. Handicapped by a lack of discipline and by the fact that only 75 blacks rallied to its cause, Turner's insurrection was doomed from the start. A total force of 3,000 armed men (made up of local whites and the state militia) provided the final crushing blow. The insurgents were either killed or captured within only a few miles of the county seat. Many innocent slaves were massacred in the hysteria that followed. For six weeks Turner eluded his pursuers. After his capture, he was tried and hanged.

Despite its defeat, Nat Turner's rebellion ended the white Southern myth that slaves were uninterested in or unable to mount an armed revolt. In Southampton County black people began marking time from "Old Nat's War." Moreover, for many years in African American churches across the United States, the name Jerusalem came to refer not only to the Bible but also covertly to the place where Nat Turner had met his death.

THE *AMISTAD* MUTINY

On July 2, 1839, the Spanish schooner *Amistad* was sailing from Havana to Puerto Príncipe, Cuba, when the ship's passengers, 53 recently enslaved Africans, revolted under the leadership of Joseph Cinqué. They killed the captain and the cook but spared the navigator, whom they instructed to sail them home to Sierra Leone. Instead he sailed the *Amistad* generally northward, until, two months later, it was seized by the U.S. Navy off Long Island, N.Y., and then conveyed to Connecticut, a state where slavery was still legal. (Slavery had been legally abolished in New York state in 1827.) The mutineers were jailed in New Haven.

Spain's demand for the return of the Africans to Cuba led to a trial in a federal court in Hartford, Connecticut, in 1840. Lewis Tappan, a New England abolitionist, stirred public sympathy for the captives; the U.S. government took the proslavery side. U.S. Pres. Martin Van Buren, who was running for reelection that year, anticipated a ruling against the Africans and hoped to gain proslavery votes by removing the defendants before abolitionists could appeal the case to a higher court. He ordered a navy vessel to take the Africans to Cuba immediately following the trial.

Prosecutors argued that because the mutineers were slaves they were subject to the laws governing conduct between slaves and their masters. However, during the course of the trial it was determined that while slavery was legal in Cuba, importation of slaves from Africa was illegal. As a result, the judge ruled that the Africans were victims of kidnapping (not merchandise) and had the right to try to escape their captors. The next year, Congressman and former president John Quincy Adams argued eloquently for the *Amistad* rebels when the case came before the U.S. Supreme Court, which upheld the lower court's ruling. Private and missionary society donations helped the 35 surviving Africans secure passage home. They arrived in Sierra Leone in January 1842, along with five missionaries and teachers who intended to found a Christian mission.

Spain continued to insist that the United States pay indemnification for the Cuban vessel. The U.S. Congress intermittently debated the *Amistad* case, without resolution, for more than two decades, until the Civil War began in 1861.

ABOLITIONISM

Despite its brutality and inhumanity, the slave system aroused little protest until the 18th century, when rationalist thinkers of the Enlightenment began to criticize it for its violation of the rights of man, and Quaker and other evangelical religious groups condemned it for its un-Christian qualities. By the late 18th century, moral disapproval of slavery was widespread, and antislavery reformers won a number of deceptively easy victories during this period. In Britain, English scholar and philanthropist Granville Sharp secured a legal decision in 1772 that West Indian planters could not hold slaves in Britain, since slavery was contrary to English law. In the United States, all of the states north of Maryland abolished slavery between 1777 and 1827. But antislavery sentiments had little effect on the great plantations of the Deep South and the West Indies. Turning their attention to these areas, British and American abolitionists began working in the late 18th century to prohibit the importation of African slaves into the British colonies and the United States. Under the leadership of British abolitionists William Wilberforce and Thomas Clarkson, these forces succeeded in getting the slave trade to the British colonies abolished in 1807. The United States prohibited the importation of slaves that same year, though widespread smuggling continued until about 1862.

Antislavery forces then concentrated on winning the emancipation of those populations already in slavery. They were triumphant when slavery was abolished in the British West Indies by 1838 and in French possessions 10 years later.

The situation in the United States was more complex because slavery was a domestic rather than a colonial phenomenon, being the social and economic base of the plantations of no fewer than 11 Southern states. Moreover, as has already been noted, slavery had gained new vitality when an extremely profitable cotton-based agriculture developed in the South in the early 19th century. Reacting to abolitionist attacks that branded its "peculiar institution" as brutal and immoral, the South had intensified its system of slave control, particularly after Nat Turner's Rebellion in 1831. By that time, American abolitionists realized the failure of gradualism and persuasion, and subsequently turned to a more militant policy, demanding immediate abolition by law.

Probably the best-known abolitionist was the aggressive agitator William Lloyd Garrison, founder of the American Anti-Slavery Society (1833–70) and the editor of *The Liberator*, the most influential antislavery periodical in the pre-Civil War period. Other prominent abolitionists, drawn from the ranks of the clergy, included Theodore Dwight Weld and Theodore Parker; from the world of letters, John Greenleaf Whittier, James Russell Lowell, and Lydia Maria Child; and, from the free-black community, such articulate former slaves as Frederick Douglass and William Wells Brown. Yet another influential abolitionist was David Walker, a freeborn African American whose pamphlet *Appeal...to the Colored Citizens of the World...* (1829), urging slaves to fight for their freedom, was one of the most radical documents of the antislavery movement.

American abolitionism laboured under the handicap that it threatened the harmony of North and South in the Union. And, as has already been shown, it also ran counter to the U.S. Constitution, which left the question of slavery to the individual states. Consequently, the Northern public remained unwilling to adopt abolitionist policy and was distrustful

Abolitionist Wendell Phillips speaking against the Fugitive Slave Act of 1850 at an antislavery meeting in Boston. In the rigorous moral climate of New England, slavery was anathema, and much of the fire and righteousness of the abolitionist movement originated there. Library of Congress, Washington, D.C.

THE LIBERATOR

Although The Liberator, *published weekly in Boston for 35 years, could claim a paid circulation of only 3,000, it reached a much wider audience with its uncompromising advocacy of immediate emancipation for the millions of African Americans held in bondage throughout the South. In the North, Garrison's message of moral suasion challenged moderate reformers to apply the principles of the Declaration of Independence to all people, regardless of colour. Fearful slaveholders in the South, erroneously assuming that* The Liberator *represented the majority opinion of Northerners, reacted militantly by defending slavery as a "positive good" and by legislating ever more stringent measures to suppress all possible opposition to it. Garrison's publication further altered the course of the American antislavery movement by insisting that abolition, rather than African colonization, was the answer to the problem of slavery.*

of abolitionist extremism. But a number of factors combined to give the movement increased momentum. Chief among these was the question of permitting or outlawing slavery in new Western territories, with Northerners and Southerners taking increasingly adamant stands on opposite sides of that issue throughout the 1840s and '50s. There was also revulsion at the ruthlessness of slave hunters under the Fugitive Slave Law (1850). The far-reaching emotional response to Harriet Beecher Stowe's antislavery novel *Uncle Tom's Cabin* as well as indignation at the U.S. Supreme Court's decision in the Dred Scott case (1857) further strengthened the abolitionist cause.

Jolted by the raid led by the abolitionist extremist John Brown on Harpers Ferry, Va. (now in West Virginia), in 1859, the South became convinced that its entire way of life, based on the cheap labour provided by slaves, was irretrievably threatened by the election to the presidency of Abraham Lincoln (November 1860), who was opposed to the spread of slavery into the Western territories. The ensuing secession of the Southern states led to the Civil War (1861–65). The war, which began as a sectional power struggle to preserve the Union, in turn led Lincoln (who had never been an abolitionist) to issue the Emancipation Proclamation, which freed only those slaves held in the Confederate States of America. In depriving the South of its greatest economic resource—abundant free human labour—Lincoln's proclamation was intended primarily as an instrument of military strategy; only when emancipation was universally proposed through the Thirteenth Amendment in 1865 did it become national policy. Moreover, the legality of abolition by presidential edict was questionable.

Although the words *slavery* and *slave* are never mentioned in the Constitution,

DRED SCOTT DECISION

Dred Scott was a slave who was owned by Dr. John Emerson of Missouri. In 1834 Emerson undertook a series of moves as part of his service in the U.S. military. He took Scott from Missouri (a slave state) to Illinois (a free state) and finally into the Wisconsin Territory (a free territory under the provisions of the Missouri Compromise). During this period, Scott met and married Harriet Robinson, who became part of the Emerson household. In the early 1840s the Emersons (Dr. Emerson had married in 1838) and the Scotts returned to Missouri, where Dr. Emerson died in 1843.

Dred Scott reportedly attempted to purchase his freedom from Emerson's widow, who refused the sale. In 1846, with the help of antislavery lawyers, Harriet and Dred Scott filed individual lawsuits for their freedom in the Missouri state courts on the grounds that their residence in a free state and a free territory had freed them from the bonds of slavery. It was later agreed that only Dred's case would move forward; the decision in that case would apply to Harriet's as well. Although the case was long thought to have been unusual, historians have demonstrated that several hundred suits for freedom were filed by or on behalf of slaves in the decades before the Civil War.

Dred Scott v. Irene Emerson took years to reach a definitive decision. The case was initially filed in the Saint Louis Circuit Court. In 1850 a lower court declared Scott free, but the verdict was overturned in 1852 by the Missouri Supreme Court. Mrs. Emerson soon left Missouri and gave control of her late husband's estate to her brother, John F.A. Sanford, a resident of New York (his last name was incorrectly spelled Sandford on court documents). Because Sanford was not subject to suit in Missouri, Scott's lawyers filed a suit against him in the U.S. federal courts. The case eventually reached the U.S. Supreme Court, which announced its decision on March 6, 1857, just two days after the inauguration of Pres. James Buchanan.

Though each justice wrote a separate opinion, Chief Justice Roger B. Taney's opinion is most often cited on account of its far-reaching implications for the sectional crisis. As one of the seven justices denying Scott his freedom (two dissented), Taney declared that an African American could not be entitled to rights as a U.S. citizen, such as the right to sue in federal courts. In fact, Taney wrote, African Americans had "no rights which any white man was bound to respect." The decision might have ended there, with the dismissal of Scott's appeal. But Taney and the other justices in the majority went on to declare that the Missouri Compromise of 1820 (which had forbidden slavery in that part of the Louisiana Purchase north of the latitude 36°30', except for Missouri) was unconstitutional because Congress had no power to prohibit slavery in the territories. Slaves were property, and masters were guaranteed their property rights under the Fifth Amendment. Neither Congress nor a territorial legislature could deprive a citizen of his property without due process of law. As for Scott's temporary residence in a free state, Illinois, the majority said that Scott had still been subject then to Missouri law.

The decision—only the second time in the country's history that the Supreme Court declared an act of Congress unconstitutional—was a clear victory for the slaveholding South. Southerners had argued that both Congress and the territorial legislature were powerless to exclude slavery from a territory, maintaining that only a state could exclude slavery. This seemed a mortal blow to the newly created Republican Party, formed to halt the extension of slavery into the Western territories. It also forced Stephen A. Douglas, advocate of popular sovereignty, to come up with a method (the "Freeport Doctrine") whereby settlers could actually ban slavery from their midst. Pres. Buchanan, the South, and the majority of the Supreme Court hoped that the Dred Scott decision would mark the end of antislavery agitation. Instead, the decision increased antislavery sentiment in the North, strengthened the Republican Party, and fed the sectional antagonism that burst into war in 1861.

Newspaper notice for a pamphlet on the U.S. Supreme Court's Dred Scott decision. Library of Congress, ng. No. LC-USZ62-132561 the Thirteenth Amendment abrogated those sections of the Constitution which had tacitly codified the "peculiar institution": Article I, Section 2, regarding apportionment of representation in the House of Representatives, which had been "determined by adding to the whole Number of free Persons, including those bound to Service for a Term of Years, and excluding Indians not taxed, three fifths of all other Persons provided for the appointment," with "all other persons" meaning slaves; Article I, Section 9, which had established 1807 as the end date for the importation of slaves, referred to in this case as "such Persons as any of the States now existing shall think proper to admit"; and Article IV, Section 2, which mandated the return to their owners of fugitive slaves, here defined as persons "held to Service or Labour in one State, under the Laws thereof, escaping into another."

The full text of the amendment is:

Neither slavery nor involuntary servitude, except as a punishment for crime whereof the party shall have been duly convicted, shall exist within the United States, or any place subject to their jurisdiction. Congress shall have power to enforce this article by appropriate legislation.

The amendment was passed by the Senate on April 8, 1864, but did not pass in the House until Jan. 31, 1865. The joint resolution of both bodies that submitted the amendment to the states for approval was signed by Lincoln on Feb. 1, 1865; however, he did not live to see its ratification. Assassinated by John Wilkes Booth, he died on April 15, 1865, and the amendment was not ratified by the required number of states until December 6 of that year. (The war had effectively ended with the surrender of the Army of Virginia by Gen. Robert E. Lee to Gen. Ulysses S. Grant at Appomattox Courthouse, on April 9, 1865, though the last, remote Confederate forces did not surrender until the summer.)

With the passage of the Thirteenth Amendment and the eradication of slavery, some abolitionists believed their mission had been accomplished. For others the hard work of securing for African Americans citizenship, suffrage, equal protection under the law, and full participation in American economic, political, and social life was just beginning.

RECONSTRUCTION

As early as 1862, Lincoln had appointed provisional military governors for Louisiana, Tennessee, and North Carolina. The following year, initial steps were taken to reestablish governments in newly occupied states in which at least 10 percent of the voting population had taken the prescribed oath of allegiance. Aware that the presidential plan omitted any provision for social or economic reconstruction, the Radical Republicans in Congress resented such a lenient political arrangement under solely executive jurisdiction. As a result, the stricter

ABRAHAM LINCOLN'S LETTER EXTOLLING EMANCIPATION AS A MILITARY MEASURE

In June 1863 "Copperhead" Democrats, feeding on the war-weariness in the North, held a huge rally in Springfield, Illinois, to protest Pres. Abraham Lincoln's policies. Republican leaders, heartened by the victories of Gettysburg and Vicksburg, decided to hold a counter-rally in support of the administration. They asked Lincoln to attend, but the president was unable to leave Washington and instead sent the following letter to James C. Conkling, an old friend, on Aug. 26, 1863, asking him to read the letter at the rally. Source: Complete Works of Abraham Lincoln, John G. Nicolay and John Hay, eds., New York, 1905, Vol. IX, pp. 95–102.

My Dear Sir:

Your letter inviting me to attend a mass meeting of unconditional Union men, to be held at the capital of Illinois on the 3rd day of September has been received. It would be very agreeable to me to thus meet my old friends at my own home, but I cannot just now be absent from here so long as a visit there would require.

The meeting is to be of all those who maintain unconditional devotion to the Union; and I am sure my old political friends will thank me for tendering, as I do, the nation's gratitude to those and other noble men whom no partisan malice or partisan hope can make false to the nation's life.

There are those who are dissatisfied with me. To such I would say: "You desire peace; and you blame me that we do not have it." But how can we attain it? There are but three conceivable ways. First, to suppress the rebellion by force of arms. This I am trying to do. Are you for it? If you are, so far we are agreed. If you are not for it, a second way is to give up the Union. I am against this. Are you for it? If you are, you should say so plainly. If you are not for force nor yet for dissolution, there only remains some imaginable compromise. I do not believe any compromise embracing the maintenance of the Union is now possible. All I learn leads to a directly opposite belief.

The strength of the rebellion is its military — its army. That army dominates all the country and all the people within its range. Any offer of terms made by any man or men within that range in opposition to that army is simply nothing for the present; because such man or men have no power whatever to enforce their side of a compromise if one were made with them.

To illustrate, suppose refugees from the South and peace men of the North get together in convention and frame and proclaim a compromise embracing a restoration of the Union. In what way can that compromise be used to keep Lee's army out of Pennsylvania? Meade's army can keep Lee's army out of Pennsylvania and, I think, can ultimately drive it out of existence. But no paper compromise to which the controllers of Lee's army are not agreed can at all affect that army. In an effort at such compromise we should waste time, which the enemy would improve to our disadvantage; and that would be all. A compromise to be effective must be made either with those who control the Rebel army or with the people first liberated from the domination of that army by the success of our own army.

Now, allow me to assure you that no word or intimation from that Rebel army, or from any of the men controlling it, in relation to any peace compromise has ever come to my knowledge or belief. All charges and insinuations to the contrary are deceptive and groundless. And I promise you that if any such proposition shall hereafter come, it shall not be rejected and kept a secret from you. I freely acknowledge myself the servant of the people according to the bond of service — the United States Constitution — and that, as such, I am responsible to them.

But to be plain, you are dissatisfied with me about the Negro. Quite likely there is a difference of opinion between you and myself upon that subject. I certainly wish that all men could be free, while I suppose you do not. Yet I have neither adopted nor proposed any measure which is not consistent with even your view, provided you are for the Union. I suggested compensated emancipation; to which you replied you wished not to be taxed to buy Negroes. But I had not asked you to be taxed to buy Negroes, except in such way as to save you from greater taxation to save the Union exclusively by other means.

You dislike the Emancipation Proclamation and, perhaps, would have it retracted. You say it is unconstitutional — I think differently. I think the Constitution invests its commander in chief with the law of war in time of war. The most that can be said, if so much, is that slaves are property. Is there — has there ever been — any question that by the law of war, property, both of enemies and friends, may be taken when needed? And is it not needed whenever taking it helps us or hurts the enemy? Armies the world over destroy the enemy's property when they cannot use it and even destroy their own to keep it from the enemy. Civilized belligerents do all in their power to help themselves or hurt the enemy, except a few things regarded as barbarous or cruel. Among the exceptions are the massacre of vanquished foes and noncombatants, male and female.

But the proclamation, as law, either is valid or is not valid. If it is not valid, it needs no retraction. If it is valid, it cannot be retracted, any more than the dead can be brought to life. Some of you profess to think its retraction would operate favorably for the Union. Why better after the retraction than before the issue? There was more than a year and a half of trial to suppress the rebellion before the proclamation issued, the last 100 days of which passed under an explicit notice that it was coming unless averted by those in revolt returning to their allegiance. The war has certainly progressed as favorably for us since the issue of the proclamation as before.

[I know, as fully as one can know the opinions of others, that some of the commanders of our armies in the field who have given us our most important successes believe the emancipation policy and the use of the colored troops constitute the heaviest blow yet dealt to the rebellion, and that at least one of these important successes could not have been achieved when it was but for the aid of black soldiers. Among the commanders holding these views are some who have never had any affinity with what is called Abolitionism or with the Republican Party politics, but who hold them purely as military opinions. I submit these opinions as being entitled to some weight against the objections often urged that emancipation and arming the blacks are unwise as military measures and were not adopted as such in good faith.] This paragraph, which has

been placed between brackets to distinguish it, was not included in the letter as first sent but was forwarded in a separate letter with instructions on Aug. 31, 1863.

You say you will not fight to free Negroes. Some of them seem willing to fight for you; but, no matter. Fight you, then, exclusively to save the Union. I issued the proclamation on purpose to aid you in saving the Union. Whenever you shall have conquered all resistance to the Union, if I shall urge you to continue fighting, it will be an apt time, then, for you to declare you will not fight to free Negroes.

I thought that in your struggle for the Union, to whatever extent the Negroes should cease helping the enemy, to that extent it weakened the enemy in his resistance to you. Do you think differently? I thought that whatever Negroes can be got to do as soldiers leaves just so much less for white soldiers to do in saving the Union. Does it appear otherwise to you? But Negroes, like other people, act upon motives. Why should they do anything for us if we will do nothing for them? If they stake their lives for us, they must be prompted by the strongest motive — even the promise of freedom. And the promise, being made, must be kept.

The signs look better. The Father of Waters again goes unvexed to the sea. Thanks to the great Northwest for it. Nor yet wholly to them. Three hundred miles up, they met New England, Empire, Keystone, and Jersey, hewing their way right and left. The sunny South, too, in more colors than one, also lent a hand. On the spot, their part of the history was jotted down in black and white. The job was a great national one; and let none be banned who bore an honorable part in it. And while those who have cleared the great river may well be proud, even that is not all. It is hard to say that anything has been more bravely and well done than at Antietam, Murfreesboro, Gettysburg, and on many fields of lesser note. Nor must Uncle Sam's webfeet be forgotten. At all the watery margins they have been present. Not only on the deep sea, the broad bay, and the rapid river, but also up the narrow, muddy bayou, and wherever the ground was a little damp, they have been and made their tracks. Thanks to all — for the great republic; for the principle it lives by and keeps alive; for man's vast future — thanks to all.

Peace does not appear so distant as it did. I hope it will come soon, and come to stay; and so come as to be worth the keeping in all future time. It will then have been proved that among freemen there can be no successful appeal from the ballot to the bullet; and that they who take such appeal are sure to lose their case and pay the cost. And then there will be some black men who can remember that with silent tongue, and clenched teeth, and steady eye, and well-poised bayonet, they have helped mankind on to this great consummation; while, I fear, there will be some white ones unable to forget that with malignant heart and deceitful speech they strove to hinder it.

Still, let us not be oversanguine of a speedy final triumph. Let us be quite sober. Let us diligently apply the means, never doubting that a just God, in His own good time, will give us the rightful result.

Wade–Davis Bill was passed in 1864 but pocket vetoed by the president.

After Lincoln's assassination, the former vice president and new president, Andrew Johnson, further alienated Congress by continuing Lincoln's moderate policies. Passed by Congress in 1866, the Fourteenth Amendment, called the Reconstruction Amendment, granted citizenship and equal civil and legal rights to African Americans and slaves who had been emancipated after the Civil War, including them under the umbrella phrase "all persons born or naturalized in the United States." Specifically, it prohibited the states from depriving any person of "life, liberty, or property, without due process of law" and from denying anyone within a state's jurisdiction equal protection under the law. Nullified by the Thirteenth Amendment, the section of the Constitution apportioning representation in the House of Representatives based on a formula that counted each slave as three-fifths of a person was replaced by a clause in the Fourteenth Amendment specifying that representatives be "apportioned among the several states according to their respective numbers, counting the whole number of persons in each state, excluding Indians not taxed." The amendment also prohibited former civil and military office holders who had supported the Confederacy from again holding any state or federal office—with the proviso that this prohibition could be removed from individuals by a two-thirds vote in both Houses of Congress.

In response to Johnson's intemperate outbursts against the opposition as well as to several reactionary developments in the South, the North gave a smashing victory to the Radical Republicans in the 1866 congressional election. On July 28, 1868, the Fourteenth Amendment was ratified, despite rejection by most Southern states. However, its attempt to guarantee civil rights was circumvented for many decades by black codes, Jim Crow laws, and the "separate but equal" ruling of *Plessy* v. *Ferguson* (1896).

The 1866 election victory launched the era of congressional Reconstruction (usually called Radical Reconstruction), which lasted 10 years starting with the Reconstruction Acts of 1867. Under that legislation, the 10 remaining Southern states (Tennessee had been readmitted to the Union in 1866) were divided into five military districts; and, under supervision of the U.S. Army, all were readmitted between 1868 and 1870. Each state had to accept the Fourteenth or, if readmitted after its passage, the Fifteenth Constitutional Amendment, which guaranteed that the right to vote could not be denied based on "race, color, or previous condition of servitude." The passage of the amendment and its subsequent ratification (Feb. 3, 1870) effectively enfranchised African American men (though the Constitution continued to deny that right to women of all colours). A series of four acts, usually referred to as the Force Acts, was also passed by Republican Reconstruction supporters in

FREEDMEN'S BUREAU

The U.S. Bureau of Refugees, Freedmen, and Abandoned Lands, better known as the Freedmen's Bureau, was established by Congress 1865 to provide practical aid to 4,000,000 newly freed African Americans in their transition from slavery to freedom. Headed by Maj. Gen. Oliver O. Howard, the Freedmen's Bureau might be termed the first federal welfare agency. Despite handicaps of inadequate funds and poorly trained personnel, the bureau built hospitals for, and gave direct medical assistance to, more than 1,000,000 freedmen. More than 21,000,000 rations were distributed to impoverished blacks as well as whites.

Its greatest accomplishments were in education: more than 1,000 black schools were built and over $400,000 spent to establish teacher-training institutions. All major black colleges were either founded by, or received aid from, the bureau. Less success was achieved in civil rights, for the bureau's own courts were poorly organized and short-lived, and only the barest forms of due process of law for freedmen could be sustained in the civil courts. Its most notable failure concerned the land itself. Thwarted by Pres. Andrew Johnson's restoration of abandoned lands to pardoned Southerners and by the adamant refusal of Congress to consider any form of land redistribution, the bureau was forced to oversee sharecropping arrangements that inevitably became oppressive. Congress, preoccupied with other national interests and responding to the continued hostility of white Southerners, terminated the bureau in July 1872.

A group of freedmen, Richmond, Va. Library of Congress, Washington, D.C.

By about 1900, many U.S. historians were espousing a theory of racial inferiority of blacks. The Reconstruction governments were viewed as an abyss of corruption resulting from Northern vindictiveness and the desire for political and economic domination. Later, revisionist historians noted that public and private dishonesty was widespread in all regions of the country at that time, but they were also quick to champion Reconstruction's legacy of successes: courts were reorganized, judicial procedures improved, public-school systems established, and more feasible methods of taxation devised. Many provisions of the state constitutions adopted during the postwar years have continued in existence.

The Reconstruction experience led to an increase in sectional bitterness, an intensification of the racial confrontation, and the development of one-party politics in the South. Scholarship has suggested that the most fundamental failure of Reconstruction was in not effecting a distribution of land in the South that would have offered an economic base to support the newly won political rights of African American citizens.

the Congress between May 31, 1870, and March 1, 1875, to protect the constitutional rights guaranteed to African Americans by the Fourteenth and Fifteenth Amendments. The major provisions of the acts authorized federal authorities to enforce penalties upon anyone interfering with the registration, voting, office holding, or jury service of blacks; provided for federal election supervisors; and empowered the president to use military forces to make summary arrests. Under the act of April 20, 1871, nine South Carolina counties were placed under martial law in October 1871. This act and earlier statutes resulted in more than 5,000 indictments and 1,250 convictions throughout the South.

The newly created state governments were generally Republican in character and were governed by political coalitions of blacks, carpetbaggers (Northerners who had gone into the South), and scalawags (Southerners who collaborated with the blacks and carpetbaggers). The Republican governments of the former Confederate states were seen by most Southern whites as artificial creations imposed from without, and the conservative element in the region remained hostile to them. Southerners particularly resented the activities of the Freedmen's Bureau, which Congress had established to feed, protect, and help educate the newly emancipated blacks. Southern resentment led to formation of secret terroristic organizations such as the Ku Klux Klan and the Knights of the White Camelia. The use of fraud, violence, and intimidation helped Southern conservatives regain control of their state governments, and by the time the last Federal troops had been withdrawn in 1877, the Democratic Party was back in power. By the 1890s efforts by several states to enact such measures as poll taxes, literacy tests, and grandfather clauses—in addition to widespread threats and violence—had completely reversed Reconstruction's landmark attempts to guarantee civil rights. For many decades to come black codes, Jim Crow laws, and the "separate but equal" ruling of the aforementioned *Plessy* v. *Ferguson* would deny African Americans rights that for a short while had been in their grasp.

CHAPTER 6

LAW AND SOCIETY

For much of the post-Civil War period, the Supreme Court held that the Fourteenth and Fifteenth amendments had but one purpose: to guarantee "the freedom of the slave race ... and the protection of the newly made freeman and citizen from the oppressions of those who had formerly exercised unlimited domination over him." Thus, the equal protection clause of the Fourteenth Amendment was applied minimally—except in some cases of racial discrimination, such as the invalidation of literacy tests and grandfather clauses for voting. As the high hopes and grand schemes of Reconstruction faded with most Northerners' diminished interest in their realization, the retrenchment of the rights of African Americans in the South intensified through violence, intimidation, and new codes, laws, and court decisions that all but reestablished the old order, putting African Americans "back in their place"—or as close to it as the law and its enforcement would allow. The Supreme Court's *Plessy* v. *Ferguson* ruling (1896) sanctioned racial segregation, and with its decisions creating the doctrine of state action—thereby limiting the enforcement of national civil rights legislation—the court diminished the equal protections envisioned by the Radical Republicans. Indeed, for nearly 80 years after the adoption of the Fourteenth Amendment, the intent of the equal protection clause was effectively circumvented.

For many African Americans in the South, where the vast majority of black Americans lived, the alternative to lives of diminishing expectations was to relocate to the cities of the North and West. The massive stream of European emigration to the United States, which had begun in the late 19th century and waned during World War I, slowed to a trickle with immigration reform in the 1920s. As a result, urban industries were faced with labour shortages. A huge internal population shift among African Americans addressed these shortfalls, particularly during World War I, when defense industries required more unskilled labour. (Although this Great Migration slowed during the Great Depression, it surged again after World War II, when rates of migration were high for several decades.)

In addition to the oppression in the form of Jim Crow laws, the "push" factors for the exodus included the poor economic conditions in the South—exacerbated by the limitations of sharecropping, farm failures, and crop damage from the boll weevil. "Pull" factors included encouraging reports of good wages and living conditions that spread by word of mouth and appeared in African American newspapers. Among the cities that absorbed large numbers of migrants were Chicago, Detroit, Cleveland, and New York City. Seeking better civil and economic opportunities, many African Americans were not wholly able to escape racism by migrating to the North. There they were segregated into ghettos, and faced new and alien obstacles of urban life.

OPPRESSION AND OPPRESSORS

Covering a period from the immediate aftermath of the Civil War until the first decades of the 20th century, the following entries provide a close-up look at forces that deprived African Americans of their rights and freedom, as well as at events reflecting the precariousness of their condition. The series of riots described here serve as a reminder to 21st-century Americans more familiar with urban conflagrations of the 1960s that for most of American history, "race" riots were occasions of unbridled violence against African Americans by whites.

BLACK CODES

Numerous black codes were enacted in the states of the former Confederacy after the Civil War, all of which were intended to assure the continuance of white supremacy. Enacted in 1865 and 1866, the laws were designed to replace the social controls of slavery that had been removed by the Emancipation Proclamation and the Thirteenth Amendment.

The black codes had their roots in the former slave codes that, in their many loosely defined forms, were seen as effective tools against slave unrest, particularly as a hedge against uprisings and runaways. Enforcement of slave codes also varied, but corporal punishment was widely and harshly employed.

Though varying from state to state, the black codes were all intended to secure a steady supply of cheap labour, and all continued to assume the inferiority of freed slaves. There were vagrancy laws that declared an African American to be vagrant if unemployed and without permanent residence; a person so defined could be arrested, fined, and bound out for a term of labour if unable to pay the fine. Apprentice laws provided for the "hiring out" of orphans and other young dependents to whites, who often turned out to be their former owners. Some states limited the type of property African Americans could own; in other states African Americans were excluded from certain businesses or from the skilled trades. Former slaves were forbidden to carry firearms or to testify in court, except in cases concerning other blacks. Legal marriage between African Americans was provided for, but interracial marriage was prohibited.

It was Northern reaction to the black codes (as well as to the bloody antiblack riots in Memphis, Tennessee, and New Orleans, Louisiana, in 1866) that helped produce Radical Reconstruction and the Fourteenth and Fifteenth amendments to the U.S. Constitution. Reconstruction did away with the black codes, but, after Reconstruction ended in 1877, many of their provisions were reenacted in the Jim Crow laws .

Memphis Race Riot

In May 1866 members of the white majority of Memphis, Tenn., attacked black residents of that city, illustrating Southern intransigence in the face of defeat and indicating unwillingness to share civil or social rights with the newly freed African Americans. In the attack, which occurred just over a year after the Confederate surrender, 46 African Americans (most of them Union veterans) were murdered, more than 70 wounded, 5 black women raped, and 12 churches and 4 schools burned. This unprovoked violence aroused sympathy in the U.S. Congress for the freedmen, drawing attention to the need for legal safeguards on their behalf.

New Orleans Race Riot

Another of the events that was influential in focusing Northern public opinion on the necessity of taking firmer measures to govern the South during Reconstruction was the New Orleans Race Riot of July 1866. With the compliance of local civilian authorities and police, whites in late July killed 35 New Orleans black citizens and wounded more than 100.

Ku Klux Klan

The Ku Klux Klan is actually two distinct hate organizations that have employed terror in pursuit of their white supremacist agenda. One group was founded immediately after the Civil War and lasted until the 1870s; the other began in 1915 and has continued to the present.

The 19th-century Klan was originally organized as a social club by Confederate veterans in Pulaski, Tenn., in 1866. They apparently derived the name from the Greek word *kyklos*, from which comes the English "circle"; "Klan" was added for the sake of alliteration and Ku Klux Klan emerged. The organization quickly became a vehicle for Southern white underground resistance to Radical Reconstruction. Klan members sought the restoration of white supremacy through intimidation and violence aimed at the newly enfranchised black freedmen. A similar organization, the Knights of the White Camelia, began in Louisiana in 1867.

In the summer of 1867, the Klan was structured into the "Invisible Empire of the South" at a convention in Nashville, Tenn., attended by delegates from former Confederate states. The group was presided over by a grand wizard (Confederate cavalry general Nathan Bedford Forrest is believed to have been the first grand wizard) and a descending hierarchy of grand dragons, grand titans, and grand cyclopses. Dressed in robes and sheets designed to frighten superstitious blacks and to prevent identification by the occupying federal troops, Klansmen whipped and killed freedmen and their white supporters in nighttime raids.

The 19th-century Klan reached its peak between 1868 and 1870. A potent force, it was largely responsible for the restoration of white rule in North Carolina, Tennessee, and Georgia. But Forrest ordered it disbanded in 1869, largely as a result of the group's excessive violence. Local branches remained active for a time, however, prompting Congress to pass the Force Act in 1870 and the Ku Klux Act in 1871.

These bills authorized the president to suspend the writ of habeas corpus, suppress disturbances by force, and impose heavy penalties upon terrorist organizations. President Grant was lax in utilizing this authority, although he did send federal troops to some areas, suspend habeas corpus in nine South Carolina counties, and appoint commissioners who arrested hundreds of Southerners for conspiracy. In *United States* v. *Harris* in 1882, the Supreme Court declared the Ku Klux Act unconstitutional, but by that time the Klan had practically disappeared. It disappeared because its original objective—the restoration of white supremacy throughout the South—had been largely achieved during the 1870s. The need for a secret antiblack organization diminished accordingly.

The 20th-century Klan had its roots more directly in the American nativist tradition. It was organized in 1915 near Atlanta, Ga., by Col. William J. Simmons, a preacher and promoter of fraternal orders who had been inspired by Thomas Dixon's racially incendiary book *The Clansman* (1905) and D.W. Griffith's film *The Birth of a Nation* (1915), based upon Dixon's book. The new organization remained small until Edward Y. Clarke and Elizabeth Tyler brought to it their talents as publicity agents and fundraisers. The revived Klan was fueled partly by patriotism and partly by a romantic nostalgia for the old South, but, more important, it expressed the defensive reaction of white Protestants in small-town America who felt threatened by the Bolshevik revolution in Russia and the large-scale immigration of the previous decades that had changed the ethnic character of American society.

This second Klan peaked in the 1920s, when its membership exceeded 4,000,000 nationally, and profits rolled in from the sale of its memberships, regalia, costumes, publications, and rituals. A burning cross became the symbol of the new organization, and white-robed Klansmen participated in marches, parades, and nighttime cross burnings all over the country. To the old Klan's hostility toward blacks the new Klan—which was strong in the Midwest as well as in the South—added bias against Roman Catholics, Jews, foreigners, and organized labour. The Klan enjoyed a last spurt of growth in 1928, when Alfred E. Smith, a Catholic, received the Democratic presidential nomination.

During the Great Depression of the 1930s the Klan's membership dropped drastically, and the last remnants of the organization temporarily disbanded in 1944, but it returned to the field during the civil rights movement of the 1960s, as civil rights workers attempted to force Southern communities' compliance with the Civil Rights Act of 1964. There were numerous instances of bombings, whippings, and shootings in Southern communities, carried out in secret but apparently the work of Klansmen. Pres. Lyndon B. Johnson publicly denounced the organization in a nationwide television address announcing the arrest of four Klansmen in connection with the slaying of a civil rights worker, a white woman, in Alabama.

The Klan was unable to stem the growth of a new racial tolerance in the South in the years that followed. Though the organization continued some of its surreptitious activities into the late 20th century, cases of Klanviolence became more isolated, and its membership had declined to a few thousand. The Klan became a chronically fragmented mélange made up of several separate and competing groups, some of which occasionally entered into alliances with neo-Nazi and other right-wing extremist groups.

LYNCHING

It is difficult to imagine an act of racist violence more horrifying than lynching, which was employed over and over again against African Americans by white supremacists in the South following the Civil War—especially during the Jim Crow era.

By definition, lynching is a form of violence in which a mob, under the pretext of administering justice without trial, executes a presumed offender, often after inflicting torture and corporal mutilation. The term *lynch law* refers to a self-constituted court that imposes sentence on a person without due process of law. Both terms are derived from the name of Charles Lynch (1736–96), a Virginia planter and justice of the peace who, during the American Revolution, headed an irregular court formed to punish loyalists.

Historically, the secrect tribunals of medieval Germany known as *fehmic* courts had imposed some punishments that involved lynching, as did England's Halifax gibbet law (execution by hanging of those guilty of theft valued over a specific amount—a gibbet is a gallows) as well as what was called Cowper justice (trial *after* execution). Resembling these cases were the Santa Hermandad constabulary in medieval Spain and pogroms directed against Jews in Russia and Poland, although in these cases there was support from legally constituted authorities.

Vigilante justice has been practiced in many countries under unsettled conditions whenever informally organized groups have attempted to supplement or replace legal procedure or to fill the void where institutional justice did not yet exist. Such conditions commonly give rise to acts of genocide. Statistics of reported lynching in the United States indicate that, between 1882 and 1951, 4,730 persons were lynched, of whom 1,293 were white and 3,437 were black. Perhaps the most outspoken antilynching crusader was journalist Ida B. Wells-Barnett.

JIM CROW LAWS

Jim Crow laws were the laws that enforced racial segregation in the South between the end of the formal Reconstruction period in 1877 and the beginning of a strong civil rights movement in the 1950s. *Jim Crow* was the name of a minstrel routine (actually *Jump Jim Crow*) performed beginning in 1828 by its creator, Thomas Dartmouth ("Daddy") Rice (a white man appearing in blackface), and by many imitators, including actor Joseph Jefferson (also white). The term *Jim Crow* came to be a derogatory epithet for African Americans and a designation for their segregated life.

From the late 1870s, Southern state legislatures, no longer controlled by carpetbaggers and freedmen, passed laws requiring the separation of whites from "persons of colour" in public transportation and schools. Generally, anyone of ascertainable or strongly suspected African American ancestry in any degree was for this purpose a "person of colour"; the pre-Civil War distinction favouring those whose ancestry was known to be mixed—particularly the half-French "free persons of colour" in Louisiana—was abandoned. The segregation principle was extended to parks, cemeteries, theatres, and restaurants in an effort to prevent any contact between blacks and whites as equals. It was codified on local and state levels and most famously with the "separate but equal" decision of the U.S. Supreme Court in *Plessy* v. *Ferguson* .

GRANDFATHER CLAUSE

Enacted by seven Southern states between 1895 and 1910, the grandfather clause was a statutory or constitutional device that was used to deny suffrage to African Americans; it provided that those who had enjoyed the right to vote prior to 1866 or 1867, or their lineal descendants, would be exempt from educational, property, or tax requirements for voting. Because the former slaves had not been granted the franchise until the adoption of the Fifteenth Amendment in 1870, these clauses worked effectively to exclude African Americans from the vote—but assured the franchise to many impoverished and illiterate whites. In 1915 the Supreme Court declared the grandfather clause unconstitutional because it violated equal voting rights guaranteed by the Fifteenth Amendment.

PLESSY V. FERGUSON

On May 18, 1896, in the *Plessy* v. *Ferguson* decision, the U.S. Supreme Court, by an eight-to-one majority, advanced the controversial "separate but equal" doctrine for assessing the constitutionality of racial segregation laws. Decided nearly 30 years after the passage of the Fourteenth Amendment to the Constitution of the United States, which had granted full and equal citizenship rights to African Americans, the *Plessy* case was the first major inquiry into the meaning of the amendment's equal-protection clause. In

upholding a Louisiana law that required the segregation of passengers on railroad cars, the court reasoned that equal protection is not violated as long as reasonably equal accommodations are provided to each racial group. Despite a series of civil rights advances in subsequent years, the ruling served as a controlling judicial precedent until its reversal in the case of *Brown* v. *Board of Education of Topeka* (1954).

BROWNSVILLE AFFAIR

The racial incident that became known as the Brownsville Affair grew out of tensions between whites in Brownsville, Tex., and African American soldiers stationed at nearby Fort Brown. About midnight, Aug. 13–14, 1906, rifle shots on a street in Brownsville killed one white man and wounded another. White commanders at Fort Brown believed all the African American infantrymen were in their barracks at the time of the shooting; but the city's mayor and other whites asserted that they had seen black soldiers on the street firing indiscriminately, and they produced spent shells from army rifles to support their statements. Despite evidence that the shells had been planted as part of a frame-up, investigators accepted the statements of the mayor and the white citizens.

When the African American soldiers insisted that they had no knowledge of the shooting, Pres. Theodore Roosevelt ordered 167 black infantrymen dishonourably discharged because of their conspiracy of silence. His action caused much resentment among African Americans and drew some criticism from whites, but a U.S. Senate committee, which investigated the episode in 1907–08, upheld Roosevelt's action.

The Brownsville Affair has ever since been a matter of controversy, and with the rise of the civil rights movement it became a matter of embarrassment to the army. After the publication in 1970 of John D. Weaver's *The Brownsville Raid*, which argued that the discharged soldiers had been innocent, the army conducted a new investigation and, in 1972, reversed the order of 1906.

SPRINGFIELD RACE RIOT

Occurring in August 1908, the Springfield Race Riot was a brutal two-day assault by several thousand white citizens on the black community of the capital of Illinois. Triggered by the transfer of an African American prisoner charged with rape (an accusation later withdrawn), the riot was symptomatic of white fears in the North and South alike of the consequences of the implementation of equal protection. Almost the entire Illinois state militia was required to quell the frenzy of the mob, which shot innocent people, burned homes, looted stores, and mutilated and lynched two elderly African Americans.

Afterward, the population seemed to show no remorse, and some persons even advocated the Southern political strategy of disenfranchisement as a means of keeping African Americans "in their place." In a moving account of the riot called "Race War in the North" that appeared in the *Independent* on Sept. 3, 1908, Southern white journalist William English Walling called for a revival of the abolitionist spirit to stem the tide of such shocking occurrences. Fearing further degeneration in race relations, white liberals were inspired by the article to join with African Americans in launching the National Association for the Advancement of Colored People.

EAST SAINT LOUIS RACE RIOT OF 1917

Stemming specifically from the employment of African American workers in a factory holding government contracts, a bloody riot occurred in East Saint Louis, Ill., on July 2, 1917. It was the worst of many violent incidents of antagonism in the United States during World War I that were directed especially toward African Americans newly employed in war industries. In the riot, whites turned on blacks, indiscriminately stabbing, clubbing, and hanging them and driving 6,000 from their homes; 40 African Americans and 8 whites were killed.

On July 28 the National Association for the Advancement of Colored People (NAACP) staged a silent parade down Fifth Avenue in New York City, protesting the riot and other acts of violence toward black Americans. German propaganda magnified these incidents in an attempt to arouse antiwar sentiment in the African American community, and Pres. Woodrow Wilson publicly denounced mob violence and lynchings, of which there had been 54 in 1916 and 38 in 1917.

CHICAGO RACE RIOT OF 1919

The Chicago Race Riot of 1919 was the most severe of approximately 25 race riots that occurred throughout the United States in the "Red Summer" (meaning "bloody") following the end of World War I. Those outbreaks of violence were a manifestation of racial frictions intensified by the Great Migration of rural African Americans from the South to cities in the North, by industrial labour competition, by overcrowding in urban ghettos, and by greater militancy among African American war veterans who had fought "to preserve democracy" and now sought the realization of the promise of democracy in their own lives. In the South, revived Ku Klux Klan activities resulted in 64 lynchings in 1918 and 83 in 1919; race riots broke out in Washington, D.C.; Knoxville, Tenn.; Longview, Texas; and Phillips County, Ark. In the North the worst race riots erupted in Chicago and in Omaha, Neb.

Racial tension in Chicago, concentrated on the city's South Side, was particularly exacerbated by the pressure for adequate housing: the African American population had increased from 44,000 in 1910 to more than 109,000 in 1920. The riot was triggered by the death of an African American youth on July 27. He had been swimming in Lake Michigan and had drifted into an area tacitly reserved for whites; he was pelted with stones, and he shortly drowned. When police refused to arrest the white man whom black observers held responsible for the incident, indignant crowds began to gather on the beach, and the disturbance began. Distorted rumours swept the city as sporadic fighting broke out between gangs and mobs of both races. Violence escalated with each incident, and for 13 days Chicago was without law and order despite the fact that the state militia had been called out on the fourth day. By the end, 38 Chicagoans were dead (23 blacks, 15 whites), 537 injured, and 1,000 African American families made homeless.

The horror of the Chicago Race Riot helped shock the country out of indifference to its growing racial conflict. President Wilson castigated the "white race" as "the aggressor" in both the Chicago and Washington riots, and efforts were launched to promote racial harmony through voluntary organizations and ameliorative legislation in Congress. The period also marked a new willingness on the part of African Americans to fight for their rights in the face of injustice and oppression.

SCOTTSBORO CASE

One of the most significant civil rights controversies of the 1930s, the Scottsboro case involved the prosecution in Scottsboro, Ala., of nine African American youths charged with the rape of two white women. The nine, after nearly being lynched, were brought to trial in Scottsboro in April 1931 just three weeks after their arrest. Not until the first day of the trial were the defendants provided with the services of two volunteer lawyers.

Despite testimony by doctors who had examined the women that no rape had occurred, the all-white jury convicted the nine, and all but the youngest, who was 12 years old, were sentenced to death. The announcement of the verdict and sentences brought a storm of charges from outside the South that a gross miscarriage of justice had occurred in Scottsboro. The cause of the "Scottsboro Boys" was championed, and in some cases exploited, by Northern liberal and radical groups, notably the Communist Party of the U.S.A.

In 1932 the U.S. Supreme Court overturned the convictions (*Powell* v. *Alabama*) on the grounds that the defendants had not received adequate legal counsel in a capital case. The state of Alabama then retried one of the accused and again convicted him. In a 1935 decision (*Norris* v. *Alabama*), the U.S. Supreme Court overturned this conviction, ruling that the state had systematically excluded blacks from juries.

Alabama again tried and convicted another of the group, Haywood Patterson, this time sentencing him to 75 years in prison. Further trials of the rest of the defendants resulted in more reconvictions and successful appeals until, after persistent pressure from citizens' groups, the state freed the four youngest (who had already served six years in jail) and later paroled all but Patterson. Patterson escaped in 1948 and fled to Michigan, where, three years later, he was convicted of manslaughter in a barroom stabbing death. In 1952 he died of cancer in prison.

The last known surviving member of the group, Clarence Norris, who had fled North after his parole in 1946, was granted a full pardon by the governor of Alabama, George C. Wallace, in 1976.

SUMMARY

It is perhaps telling that this section ends beyond the historical scope of this volume, with a mention of George C. Wallace, the one time presidential candidate who led the South's fight against federally ordered integration in the 1960s, for it is a reminder that the oppression and injustice described in these passages would continue largely unabated for decade upon decade to come.

ORGANIZING AND ORGANIZATIONS

In 1963 in his famous letter from the Birmingham jail, civil rights crusader Martin Luther King, Jr., another individual whose moment on the stage of history falls beyond the limits of this volume, wrote, "We know through painful experience that freedom is never voluntarily given by the oppressor; it must be demanded by the oppressed." The previous section considered those who oppressed African Americans in the 19th and early 20th centuries and their tools of oppression; this section presents portraits of the organizing efforts and organizations that steadfastly met that oppression with demands for freedom.

UNION LEAGUE

One of the earliest of these organizations, the Union League (also called the Loyal League) was a group of associations originally organized in the North to inspire loyalty to the Union cause during the Civil War. During Reconstruction, these associations spread to the South to ensure Republicans of support among newly enfranchised African Americans. Though their agenda may have been self-serving, it nevertheless largely benefitted the cause of black American freedom.

Ohio Republicans established the first Union League of America in 1862 to counteract such antiwar groups as the Copperheads and to stem the tide of Democratic political victories resulting from too many Northern defeats on the battleground. Attempting to rouse enthusiasm for the war effort and to infuse new vitality into the Republican Party, the leagues quickly spread throughout the North, serving as a social as well as a political force.

As the Federal armies swept southward toward the end of the war, the leagues followed. Under Radical Reconstruction, societies became the main vehicle for propagandizing the Republican cause among the emancipated African Americans.

Unwilling to share political power, Southern whites countered by organizing their own secret societies, such as the Ku Klux Klan, to keep African Americans from the polls through intimidation and violence. Eventually, the Republican effort to claim some of the fruits of victory was lost by the Union leagues, and the machinery of government in the Southern states gradually reverted to traditional white Democratic control by the end of Reconstruction.

AMERICAN EQUAL RIGHTS ASSOCIATION (AERA)

Founded on May 10, 1866, during the Eleventh National Women's Rights Convention, the American Equal Rights Association (AERA) sought to "secure Equal Rights to all American citizens, especially the right of suffrage, irrespective of race, color, or sex." AERA met its first test in 1867. In that year Kansas, a Republican state, voted down two separate referenda granting suffrage to African Americans and women, respectively. During the Kansas campaign, the organization's founders, Elizabeth Cady Stanton and Susan B. Anthony, had accepted the help of a known racist, alienating abolitionist members as well as AERA president Lucretia Mott.

Angry with the wording and passage of the Fifteenth Amendment in 1870 because it ignored women's rights in favour of those of African Americans,

Stanton and Anthony urged the AERA to support a 16th amendment giving women the vote. More cautious leaders refused, and Stanton and Anthony left the AERA in May 1869 to form the exclusively female National Woman Suffrage Association. Unable to reconcile with the radical feminists, Lucy Stone, Julia Ward Howe, and other conservative feminists formed the American Woman Suffrage Association from the ashes of the AERA in November 1869. In 1890 the groups merged as the National American Woman Suffrage Association.

ATLANTA COMPROMISE

Articulated by educator Booker T. Washington, who was seen by most people as the leading African American figure of the late 19th century, the Atlanta Compromise is among the most important statements ever made on race relations in the United States. In a speech at the Cotton States and International Exposition in Atlanta, Ga., on Sept. 18, 1895, Washington asserted that vocational education, which gave black Americans an opportunity for economic security, was more valuable to them than social advantages, higher education, or political office. In one sentence he summarized his concept of race relations appropriate for the times: "In all things that are purely social we can be as separate as the fingers, yet one as the hand in all things essential to mutual progress." In return for African Americans remaining peaceful and socially separate from

Booker T. Washington, 1903. Library of Congress, Washington, D.C. (digital file number cph.3a49671)

whites, the white community needed to accept responsibility for improving the social and economic conditions of all Americans regardless of skin colour, Washington argued. This notion of shared responsibilities is what came to be known as the Atlanta Compromise.

White leaders in both the North and the South greeted Washington's speech with enthusiasm, but it disturbed black intellectuals who feared that Washington's "accommodationist" philosophy would doom African Americans to indefinite subservience to whites. This criticism of the Atlanta Compromise was best articulated by W.E.B. Du Bois in *The Souls of Black Folk* (1903): "Mr. Washington represents in Negro thought the old attitude of adjustment and submission . . . [His] program practically accepts the alleged inferiority of the Negro races." Advocating full civil rights as an alternative to Washington's policy of accommodation, Du Bois organized a faction of black leaders into the Niagara Movement (1905), which led to the founding of the National Association for the Advancement of Colored People (1909).

NATIONAL ASSOCIATION OF COLORED WOMEN (NACW)

Formed at a convention in Washington, D.C., the National Association of Colored Women (NACW) was the product of the merger in 1896 of the National Federation of Afro-American Women and the National League of Colored Women—organizations that had arisen out of the African American women's club movement. Founders of the NACW included Harriet Tubman, Frances E.W. Harper, Ida B. Wells-Barnett, and Mary Church Terrell, who became the organization's first president.

The NACW adopted the motto "Lifting as We Climb," with the intention of demonstrating to "an ignorant and suspicious world that our aims and interests are identical with those of all good aspiring women." Terrell established an ambitious and forward-thinking agenda for the organization, focusing on job training, wage equity, and child care.

The organization raised funds for kindergartens, vocational schools, summer camps, and retirement homes. In addition, the NACW opposed segregated transportation systems and was a strong and visible supporter of the antilynching movement.

In 1912 the organization began a national scholarship fund for college-bound African American women. During that same year it endorsed the suffrage movement, two years before its white counterpart, the General Federation of Women's Clubs. By the middle of the 20th century nearly every state had an

Mary Eliza Church Terrell. Library of Congress, Washington, D.C. (neg. no. LC USZ 62 54724)

NACW chapter. In the latter part of the 20th century the organization continued its traditional community-based service projects, with equal pay and child care remaining as chief issues.

NIAGARA MOVEMENT

Led by W.E.B. Du Bois, the Niagara Movement was an organization of black intellectuals that called for full political, civil, and social rights for African Americans. This stance stood in notable contrast to the accommodation philosophy proposed by Booker T. Washington in the Atlanta Compromise of 1895. In the summer of 1905, 29 prominent blacks, including Du Bois, met secretly at Niagara Falls, Ont., and drew up a manifesto calling for full civil liberties, abolition of racial discrimination, and recognition of human brotherhood. Subsequent annual meetings were held in such symbolic locations as Harpers Ferry, W. Va., and Boston's Faneuil Hall.

Despite the establishment of 30 branches and the achievement of a few scattered civil rights victories at the local level, the group suffered from organizational weakness and lack of funds as well as a permanent headquarters or staff, and it never was able to attract mass support. After the Springfield Race Riot of 1908, however, white liberals joined with the nucleus of Niagara "militants" and founded the National Association for the Advancement of Colored People (NAACP) the following year. The Niagara Movement disbanded in 1910,

with the leadership of Du Bois forming the main continuity between the two organizations.

NATIONAL ASSOCIATION FOR THE ADVANCEMENT OF COLORED PEOPLE (NAACP)

In addition to Du Bois and others who had been associated with the Niagara Movement, the interracial group that created the National Association for the Advancement of Colored People (NAACP) in 1909 included Ida B. Wells-Barnett and Mary White Ovingtons. They worked for the abolition of segregation and discrimination in housing, education, employment, voting, and transportation; opposed racism; and sought to ensure African Americans their constitutional rights.

Many of the NAACP's actions have focused on national issues; for example, the group was instrumental in helping persuade Pres. Woodrow Wilson to denounce lynching in 1918. Other areas of activism have involved political action to secure enactment of civil rights laws, programs of education and public information to win popular support, and direct action to achieve specific goals. In 1939 the NAACP established as an independent legal arm for the civil rights movement the NAACP Legal Defense and Education Fund, which litigated to the Supreme Court *Brown* v. *Board of Education of Topeka*. The organization had also won a significant victory in 1946, with *Morgan* v. *Virginia*, which successfully barred segregation in interstate travel, setting the stage for the Freedom Rides of 1961, and it would play a pivotal role in the civil rights struggles of the 1960s and beyond.

NATIONAL URBAN LEAGUE

The Urban League traces its roots to three organizations—the Committee for the Improvement of Industrial Conditions Among Negroes in New York (founded in 1906), the National League for the Protection of Colored Women (founded 1906), and the Committee on Urban Conditions Among Negroes (founded 1910)—that merged in 1911 to form the National League on Urban Conditions Among Negroes. The new organization sought to help African Americans, especially those moving to New York City from rural locations in the South, to find jobs and housing and generally to adjust to urban life. The model organization established in New York City was imitated in other cities where affiliates were soon established. By 1920 the national organization had assumed the shorter name, National Urban League.

From its founding, the league has been interracial; the organization's very establishment was led by George Edmund Haynes, the first African American to earn a Ph.D. from Columbia University, and Ruth Standish Baldwin, a white New York City philanthropist. The Urban League's primary task of helping migrants gradually evolved over the years into larger concerns. The organization emphasized employment rights for African Americans during the directorship of Eugene Kinkle Jones (1918–41); and his successor, Lester Granger (1941–61), emphasized jobs for African Americans in the defense industry and attempted to breech the colour barrier prevalent in labour unions during World War II.

UNIVERSAL NEGRO IMPROVEMENT ASSOCIATION (UNIA)

Founded by Marcus Garvey, the Universal Negro Improvement Association (UNIA) was dedicated to racial pride, economic self-sufficiency, and the formation of an independent black nation in Africa. Though Garvey had founded the UNIA in his native Jamaica in 1914, its main influence was felt in the principal urban black neighbourhoods of the northern United States after Garvey's arrival in Harlem in 1916.

Garvey had a strong appeal to poor blacks in urban ghettos, but most African American leaders denounced him as an imposter, particularly after he announced, in New York, the founding of the Empire of Africa, with himself as provisional president. In turn, Garvey denounced the NAACP and many African American leaders, asserting that they sought only assimilation into white society. Garvey's leadership was cut short in 1923 when he was indicted and convicted of fraud in his handling of funds raised to establish a black-run

Marcus Garvey chairing a session of the Universal Negro Improvement Association, 1924. Library of Congress, Washington, D.C. (LC-USZ61-1854)

NATIONAL COUNCIL OF NEGRO WOMEN (NCNW)

An umbrella organization founded by Mary McLeod Bethune in New York City on Dec. 5, 1935, the National Council of Negro Women (NCNW) set as its mission "to advance opportunities and the quality of life for African American women, their families and communities."

Disappointed with the lack of unity and cooperation between African American women's groups, Bethune called upon their leaders to create a cohesive body that would express the concerns and beliefs of African American women in regard to national and international affairs. Fourteen organizations sent delegates to the founding meeting of the NCNW, and the organization ultimately grew to represent more than 35 national and 250 community affiliations. Its national headquarters were established in Washington, D.C., in 1942.

steamship line. In 1927, Pres. Calvin Coolidge pardoned Garvey but ordered him deported as an undesirable alien.

The UNIA never revived. Although the organization did not transport a single person to Africa, its influence reached multitudes on both sides of the Atlantic, and it proved to be a forerunner of black nationalism, which emerged in the U.S. after World War II.

SUMMARY

Like several of the other organizations discussed in this section, the NCNW continued to play an important role in the freedom and civil rights movement throughout the 20th and into the 21st century, expanding into a complex organization with activism at the local, national, and international levels. The murder of NAACP field director Medgar

Evers in 1963 gave that group increased national prominence, likely contributing to the passage of the Voting Rights Act in 1965. In the 1980s the NAACP publicized opposition to apartheid policies in South Africa, and at the turn of the 21st century, it sponsored campaigns against youth violence, encouraged economic enterprise among African Americans, and led voter drives to increase participation in the political process. During the presidency of Whitney M. Young, Jr. (1961–71), the Urban League would emerge as one of the strongest forces in the American civil rights struggle. Under his successor, Vernon E. Jordan, Jr. (1971–81), the league went on to broaden its vision by embracing such causes as environmental protection, energy conservation, and the general problems of poverty; by the turn of the 21st century its focus included the concept of achievement as it relates to racial identity, globalization and its economic effects on the African American community, and education.

PRIMARY SOURCES

Following are a number of primary sources related to the discussion of the African American experience in this chapter. Here Frederick Douglass, W.E.B. Du Bois, Booker T. Washington, Ida B. Wells-Barnett, and others speak for themselves of the injustice faced by African Americans, of the fortitude and courage demonstrated by black Americans, and of their plans and hopes for a better future.

JOHN E. BRUCE: AFRICAN AMERICAN PLEA FOR ORGANIZED RESISTANCE TO WHITE MEN

Although African American leaders proposed numerous programs to challenge the reactionary white supremacists who regained power in the South after Reconstruction and imposed a regime of terror and disenfranchisement calculated to override the legal provisions of the Fourteenth and Fifteenth amendments, some African Americans felt helpless. Under these conditions, there was a certain appeal in proposals for direct retaliation such as those in the following speech by African American journalist John Bruce. The manuscript is dated Oct. 5, 1889. *Source: Manuscript in John E. Bruce Collection, Folder No. 7, Schomburg Collection, New York Public Library, 103 West 135th Street, New York, N.Y.*

I fully realize the delicacy of the position I occupy in this discussion and know too well that those who are to follow me will largely benefit by what I shall have to say in respect to the application of force as one of the means to the solution of the problem known as the "Negro problem."

I am not unmindful of the fact that there are those living who have faith in the efficacy of submission, who are still pregnated with the slavish fear which had its origin in oppression and the peculiar environments of the slave period. Those who are thus minded will advise a pacific policy in order as they believe to affect a settlement of this question, with which the statesmanship of a century has grappled without any particularly gratifying results. Agitation is a good thing, organization is a better thing. The million Negro voters of Georgia, and the undiscovered millions in other Southern states — undiscovered so far as our knowledge of their numbers exists — could, with proper organization and intelligent leadership, meet force with force with most beneficial results.

The issue upon us cannot be misunderstood by those who are watching current events. To us it is not a theory (to quote a distinguished Democrat), but a condition that confronts us; a condition big with hope and fear; a condition where cowards quail and brave men stand their ground; a condition demanding the highest courage, the greatest sacrifices, the noblest ambition to overcome, and to set forever at rest the question of the Negro's right to the titles of manhood, self-respect, and honor. The man who will not fight for the protection of his wife and children is a *coward* and deserves to be ill-treated. The man who takes his life in his hand and stands up for what he knows to be right will always command the respect of his enemy.

Submission to the *dicta* of Southern bulldozers is the basest cowardice, and there is no just reason why manly men of any race should allow themselves to be continually outraged and oppressed by their equals before the law ... In all our homogeneous population no race or class has been more loyal, has shown a greater respect for law and order, has been more willing to write its benefits in marble and

its injuries in dust than the Negroes of the United States ...

Under the present condition of affairs the only hope, the only salvation for the Negro is to be found in a resort to force under wise and discreet leaders. He must sooner or later come to this in order to set at rest, for all time to come, the charge that he is a moral coward ... I hate namby-pambyism, or anything that looks like temporizing, when duty calls.

To settle this Southern problem, the Negro must not be rash and indiscreet either in action or in words, but he must be very determined and terribly in earnest, and of one mind to bring order out of chaos and to convince Southern rowdies and cut-throats that more than two can play at the game with which they have amused their fellow conspirators in crime for nearly a quarter of a century.

Under the Mosaic dispensation, it was the custom to require an eye for an eye and a tooth for a tooth. Under a no less barbarous civilization than that which existed at that period of the world's history, let the Negro require at the hands of every white murderer in the South or elsewhere a life for a life. If they burn our houses, burn theirs; if they kill our wives and children, kill theirs; pursue them relentlessly, meet force with force everywhere it is offered. If they demand blood, exchange with them until they are satiated. By a vigorous adherence to this course the shedding of human blood by white men will soon become a thing of the past.

Wherever and whenever the Negro shows himself to be a man, he can always command the respect even of a cutthroat. Organized resistance to organized resistance is the best remedy for the solution of the vexed problem of the century, which to me seems practicable and feasible; and I submit this view of the question, ladies and gentlemen, for your careful consideration.

FREDERICK DOUGLASS: THE COLOR LINE IN AMERICA

After the withdrawal of Union troops from South Carolina, Louisiana, and Florida and the official end of Reconstruction, African Americans were in theory free, but in practice their participation in all phases of American life was qualified by prejudice, and most avenues of social and economic improvement remained closed to them. Frederick Douglass, the best-known and most influential African American spokesman of his time, considered these facts and offered a solution in the following speech of Sept. 24, 1883. *Source: Three Addresses on the Relations Subsisting Between the White and Colored People of the United States, Washington, 1886, pp. 3–23.*

It is our lot to live among a people whose laws, traditions, and prejudices have been against us for centuries, and from these they are not yet free. To assume that they are free from these evils simply because they have changed their laws is to assume what is utterly unreasonable and contrary to facts. Large bodies move slowly. Individuals may be converted on the instant and change their whole course of life. Nations never. Time and events are required for the conversion of nations. Not even the character of a great political organization can be changed by a new platform. It will be the same old snake though in a new skin.

Frederick Douglass. MPI/Hulton Archive/Getty Images

Though we have had war, reconstruction, and abolition as a nation, we still linger in the shadow and blight of an extinct institution. Though the colored man is no longer subject to be bought and sold, he is still surrounded by an adverse sentiment which fetters all his movements. In his downward course he meets with no resistance, but his course upward is resented and resisted at every step of his progress. If he comes in ignorance, rags, and wretchedness, he conforms to the popular belief of his character, and in that character he is welcome. But if he shall come as a gentleman, a scholar, and a statesman, he is hailed as a contradiction to the national faith concerning his race, and his coming is resented as impudence. In the one case he may provoke contempt and derision, but in the other he is an affront to pride and provokes malice. Let him do what he will, there is at present, therefore, no escape for him. The color line meets him everywhere, and in a measure shuts him out from all respectable and profitable trades and callings.

In spite of all your religion and laws, he is a rejected man. He is rejected by trade unions of every trade, and refused work while he lives and burial when he dies; and yet he is asked to forget his color and forget that which everybody else remembers. If he offers himself to a builder as a mechanic, to a client as a lawyer, to a patient as a physician, to a college as a professor, to a firm as a clerk, to a government department as an agent or an officer, he is sternly met on the color line, and his claim to consideration in some way is disputed on the ground of color.

Not even our churches, whose members profess to follow the despised Nazarene, whose home, when on earth, was among the lowly and despised, have yet conquered this feeling of color madness, and what is true of our churches is also true of our courts of law. Neither is free from this all-pervading atmosphere of color hate. The one describes the Deity as impartial, no respecter of persons, and the other the Goddess of Justice as blindfolded, with sword by her side and scales in her hand, held evenly between high and low, rich and poor, white and black; but both are the images of American imagination rather than American practices.

Taking advantage of the general disposition in this country to impute crime to color, white men *color* their faces to commit crime and wash off the hated color to escape punishment. In many places where the commission of crime is alleged against one of our color, the ordinary processes of the law are set aside as too slow for the impetuous justice of the infuriated populace. They take the law into their own bloody hands and proceed to whip, stab, shoot, hang, or burn the alleged culprit, without the intervention of courts, counsel, judges, juries, or witnesses. In such cases it is not the business of the accusers to prove guilt, but it is for the accused to prove his innocence, a thing hard for any man to do, even in a court of law, and utterly impossible for him to do in these infernal lynch courts.

A man accused, surprised, frightened, and captured by a motley crowd, dragged with a rope around his neck in midnight-darkness to the nearest tree, and told in the coarsest terms of profanity to prepare for death, would be more than human if he did not, in his terror-stricken appearance, more confirm suspicion of guilt than the contrary. Worse still, in the presence of such hell-black outrages, the pulpit is usually dumb, and the press in the neighborhood is silent or openly takes sides with the mob. There are occasional cases in which white men are lynched, but one sparrow does not make a summer. Everyone knows that what is called lynch law is peculiarly the law for colored people and for nobody else.

If there were no other grievance than this horrible and barbarous lynch-law custom, we should be justified in assembling, as we have now done, to expose and denounce it. But this is not all. Even now, after twenty years of so-called emancipation, we are subject to lawless raids of midnight riders, who, with blackened faces, invade our homes and perpetrate the foulest of crimes upon us and our families. This condition of things is too flagrant and notorious to require specifications or proof. Thus in all the relations of life and death we are met by the color line. We cannot ignore it if we would, and ought not if we could. It hunts us at midnight, it denies us accommodation in hotels and justice in the courts; excludes our children from schools, refuses our sons the chance to learn trades, and

compels us to pursue only such labor as will bring the least reward.

While we recognize the color line as a hurtful force, a mountain barrier to our progress, wounding our bleeding feet with its flinty rocks at every step, we do not despair. We are a hopeful people. This convention is a proof of our faith in you, in reason, in truth, and justice; our belief that prejudice, with all its malign accompaniments, may yet be removed by peaceful means; that, assisted by time and events and the growing enlightenment of both races, the color line will ultimately become harmless. When this shall come it will then only be used, as it should be, to distinguish one variety of the human family from another. It will cease to have any civil, political, or moral significance, and colored conventions will then be dispensed with as anachronisms, wholly out of place — but not till then.

Do not marvel that we are not discouraged. The faith within us has a rational basis and is confirmed by facts. When we consider how deep-seated this feeling against us is; the long centuries it has been forming; the forces of avarice which have been marshaled to sustain it; how the language and literature of the country have been pervaded with it; how the church, the press, the playhouse, and other influences of the country have been arrayed in its support, the progress toward its extinction must be considered vast and wonderful.

If liberty, with us, is yet but a name, our citizenship is but a sham, and our suffrage thus far only a cruel mockery, we may yet congratulate ourselves upon the fact that the laws and institutions of the country are sound, just, and liberal. There is hope for a people when their laws are righteous, whether for the moment they conform to their requirements or not. But until this nation shall make its practice accord with its Constitution and its righteous laws, it will not do to reproach the colored people of this country with keeping up the color line; for that people would prove themselves scarcely worthy of even theoretical freedom, to say nothing of practical freedom, if they settled down in silent, servile, and cowardly submission to their wrongs from fear of making their color visible.

They are bound by every element of manhood to hold conventions in their own name and on their own behalf, to keep their grievances before the people and make every organized protest against the wrongs inflicted upon them within their power. They should scorn the counsels of cowards and hang their banner on the outer wall. Who would be free, themselves must strike the blow. We do not believe, as we are often told, that the Negro is the ugly child of the national family, and the more he is kept out of sight the better it will be for him. You know that liberty given is never so precious as liberty sought for and fought for. The man outraged is the man to make the outcry. Depend upon it, men will not care much for a people who do not care for themselves.

Our meeting here was opposed by some of our members because it would disturb the peace of the Republican Party. The suggestion came from coward lips and misapprehended the character of that party. If the Republican Party cannot stand a demand for justice and fair play, it ought to go down. We were men before that party was born, and our manhood is more sacred than any party can be. Parties were made for men, not men for parties.

If the 6 million colored people of this country, armed with the Constitution of the United States, with a million votes of their own to lean upon and millions of white men at their back, whose hearts are responsive to the claims of humanity, have not sufficient spirit and wisdom to organize and combine to defend themselves from outrage, discrimination, and oppression, it will be idle for them to expect that the Republican Party or any other political party will organize and combine for them or care what becomes of them. Men may combine to prevent cruelty to animals, for they are dumb and cannot speak for themselves; but we are men and must speak for ourselves, or we shall not be spoken for at all. We have conventions in America for Ireland, but we should have none if Ireland did not speak for herself. It is because she makes a noise and keeps her cause before the people that other people go to her help. It was the sword of Washington and of Lafayette that gave us independence.

In conclusion upon this color objection, we have to say that we meet here in open daylight. There is nothing sinister about us. The eyes of the nation are upon us. Ten thousand newspapers may tell if they choose of whatever is said and done here. They may commend our wisdom or condemn our folly, precisely as we shall be wise or foolish. We put ourselves before them as honest men and ask their judgment upon our work.

W.E.B. Du Bois. Library of Congress, Washington, D.C.

W.E.B. DU BOIS: WHAT AFRICAN AMERICANS WANT

Much has been made about the differences between the two leading African American spokesmen at the turn of the 20th century, Booker T. Washington and W.E.B. Du Bois, and about how they came to represent divergent perspectives on civil rights, but though they disagreed on the means, they often had the same goals. The selection reprinted here comprises parts of two chapters of Du Bois's famous book The Souls of Black Folk (1903). *Source: The Souls of Black Folk, 5th edition, Chicago, 1904, Chs. 1, 3.*

I. THE SPIRITUAL STRIVINGS OF BLACK FOLK

Between me and the other world there is ever an unasked question: unasked by some through feelings of delicacy; by others through the difficulty of rightly framing it. All, nevertheless, flutter round it. They approach me in a half-hesitant sort of way, eye me curiously or compassionately, and then, instead of saying directly, How does it feel to be a problem? they say, I know an excellent colored man in my town; or, I fought at Mechanicsville; or, Do not these Southern outrages make your blood boil? At these I smile, or am interested, or reduce the boiling to a simmer, as the occasion may require. To the real question, How does it feel to be a problem? I answer seldom a word.

And, yet, being a problem is a strange experience — peculiar even for one who has never been anything else, save perhaps in babyhood and in Europe. It is in the early days of rollicking boyhood that the revelation first bursts upon one, all in a day, as it were. I remember well when the shadow swept across me. I was a little thing, away up in the hills of New England, where the dark Housatonic winds between Hoosac and Taghkanic to the sea. In a wee wooden schoolhouse, something put it into the boys' and girls' heads to buy gorgeous visiting cards — ten cents a package — and exchange. The exchange was merry, till one girl, a tall newcomer, refused my card, — refused it peremptorily, with a glance. Then it dawned upon me with a certain suddenness that I was different from the others; or like, mayhap, in heart and life and longing, but shut out from their world by a vast veil.

I had thereafter no desire to tear down that veil, to creep through; I held all beyond it in common contempt and lived above it in a region of blue sky and great wandering shadows. That sky was bluest when I could beat my mates at examination time, or beat them at a foot race, or even beat their stringy heads. Alas, with the years all this fine contempt began to fade; for the worlds I longed for, and all their dazzling opportunities, were theirs, not mine. But they should not keep these prizes, I said; some, all, I would wrest from them. Just

how I would do it I could never decide — by reading law, by healing the sick, by telling the wonderful tales that swam in my head — some way.

With other black boys the strife was not so fiercely sunny: their youth shrunk into tasteless sycophancy or into silent hatred of the pale world about them and mocking distrust of everything white; or wasted itself in a bitter cry — Why did God make me an outcast and a stranger in mine own house? The shades of the prison house closed round about us all: walls strait and stubborn to the whitest, but relentlessly narrow, tall, and unscalable to sons of night who must plod darkly on in resignation, or beat unavailing palms against the stone, or steadily, half-hopelessly, watch the streak of blue above.

After the Egyptian and Indian, the Greek and Roman, the Teuton and Mongolian, the Negro is a sort of seventh son, born with a veil, and gifted with second-sight in this American world — a world which yields him no true self-consciousness, but only lets him see himself through the revelation of the other world. It is a peculiar sensation, this double-consciousness, this sense of always looking at oneself through the eyes of others, of measuring one's soul by the tape of a world that looks on in amused contempt and pity. One ever feels his twoness — an American, a Negro; two souls, two thoughts, two unreconciled strivings; two warring ideals in one dark body, whose dogged strength alone keeps it from being torn asunder.

The history of the American Negro is the history of this strife, this longing to attain self-conscious manhood, to merge his double self into a better and truer self. In this merging he wishes neither of the older selves to be lost. He would not Africanize America, for America has too much to teach the world and Africa. He would not bleach his Negro soul in a flood of white Americanism, for he knows that Negro blood has a message for the world. He simply wishes to make it possible for a man to be both a Negro and an American, without being cursed and spit upon by his fellows, without having the doors of opportunity closed roughly in his face.

This, then, is the end of his striving: to be a co-worker in the kingdom of culture, to escape both death and isolation, to husband and use his best powers and his latent genius. These powers of body and mind have in the past been strangely wasted, dispersed, or forgotten. The shadow of a mighty Negro past flits through the tale of Ethiopia the Shadowy and of Egypt the Sphinx. Throughout history, the powers of single black men flash here and there like falling stars, and die sometimes before the world has rightly gauged their brightness.

Here in America, in the few days since Emancipation, the black man's turning hither and thither in hesitant and doubtful striving has often made his very strength to lose effectiveness, to seem like absence of power, like weakness. And yet it is not weakness — it is the contradiction of double aims. The double-aimed struggle of the black artisan — on the one hand to escape white contempt for a nation of mere hewers of wood and drawers of water, and on the other hand to plow and nail and dig for a poverty-stricken horde — could only result in making him a poor craftsman, for he had but half a heart in either cause.

By the poverty and ignorance of his people, the Negro minister or doctor was tempted toward quackery and demagogy; and, by the criticism of the other world, toward ideals that made him ashamed of his lowly tasks. The would-be black savant was confronted by the paradox that the knowledge his people needed was a twice-told tale to his white neighbors, while the knowledge which would teach the white world was Greek to his own flesh and blood. The innate love of harmony and beauty that set the ruder souls of his people a-dancing and a-singing raised but confusion and doubt in the soul of the black artist; for the beauty revealed to him was the soul-beauty of a race which his larger audience despised, and he could not articulate the message of another people. This waste of double aims, this seeking to satisfy two unreconciled ideals has wrought sad havoc with the courage and faith and deeds of ten thousand thousand people — has sent them often wooing false gods and invoking false means of salvation, and at times has even seemed about to make them ashamed of themselves.

Away back in the days of bondage, they thought to see in one divine event the end of all doubt and disappointment;

few men ever worshiped Freedom with half such unquestioning faith as did the American Negro for two centuries. To him, so far as he thought and dreamed, slavery was indeed the sum of all villainies, the cause of all sorrow, the root of all prejudice; Emancipation was the key to a promised land of sweeter beauty than ever stretched before the eyes of wearied Israelites. In song and exhortation swelled one refrain — Liberty; in his tears and curses the God he implored had Freedom in His right hand. At last it came, — suddenly, fearfully, like a dream. With one wild carnival of blood and passion came the message in his own plaintive cadences:

> *Shout, O children!*
> *Shout, you're free!*
> *For God has bought you liberty!*

Years have passed away since then — ten, twenty, forty; forty years of national life, forty years of renewal and development, and yet the swarthy specter sits in its accustomed seat at the nation's feast. In vain do we cry to this our vastest social problem:

> *Take any shape but that, and*
> *my firm nerves*
> *Shall never tremble!*

The nation has not yet found peace from its sins; the freedman has not yet found in freedom his promised land. Whatever of good may have come in these years of change, the shadow of a deep disappointment rests upon the Negro people, a disappointment all the more bitter because the unattained ideal was unbounded save by the simple ignorance of a lowly people.

The first decade was merely a prolongation of the vain search for freedom, the boon that seemed ever barely to elude their grasp, like a tantalizing will-o'-the-wisp, maddening and misleading the headless host. The holocaust of war, the terrors of the Ku Klux Klan, the lies of carpetbaggers, the disorganization of industry, and the contradictory advice of friends and foes left the bewildered serf with no new watchword beyond the old cry for freedom. As the time flew, however, he began to grasp a new idea. The ideal of liberty demanded for its attainment powerful means, and these the Fifteenth Amendment gave him. The ballot, which before he had looked upon as a visible sign of freedom, he now regarded as the chief means of gaining and perfecting the liberty with which war had partially endowed him. And why not? Had not votes made war and emancipated millions? Had not votes enfranchised the freedmen? Was anything impossible to a power that had done all this? A million black men started with renewed zeal to vote themselves into the kingdom.

So the decade flew away, the revolution of 1876 came, and left the half-free serf weary, wondering, but still inspired. Slowly but steadily, in the following years, a new vision began gradually to replace the dream of political power — a powerful movement, the rise of another ideal to guide the unguided, another pillar of fire by night after a clouded day. It was the ideal of "book learning"; the curiosity, born of compulsory ignorance, to know and test the power of the cabalistic letters of the white man, the longing to know. Here at last seemed to have been discovered the mountain path to Canaan; longer than the highway of Emancipation and law, steep and rugged, but straight, leading to heights high enough to overlook life.

Up the new path the advance guard toiled, slowly, heavily, doggedly; only those who have watched and guided the faltering feet, the misty minds, the dull understandings of the dark pupils of these schools know how faithfully, how piteously this people strove to learn. It was weary work. The cold statistician wrote down the inches of progress here and there, noted also where here and there a foot had slipped or someone had fallen. To the tired climbers, the horizon was ever dark, the mists were often cold, the Canaan was always dim and far away. If, however, the vistas disclosed as yet no goal, no resting place, little but flattery and criticism, the journey at least gave leisure for reflection and self-examination; it changed the child of Emancipation to the youth with dawning self-consciousness, self-realization, self-respect.

In those somber forests of his striving, his own soul rose before him and he saw himself — darkly as through a veil; and yet he saw in himself some faint revelation of his power, of his mission. He began to have a dim feeling that, to attain his place in the world, he must be himself, and not another. For the first time he sought to analyze the burden he bore upon his back, that deadweight of social degradation partially masked behind a half-named Negro problem.

He felt his poverty; without a cent, without a home, without land, tools, or savings, he had entered into competition with rich, landed, skilled neighbors. To be a poor man is hard, but to be a poor race in a land of dollars is the very bottom of hardships. He felt the weight of his ignorance, not simply of letters but of life, of business, of the humanities; the accumulated sloth and shirking and awkwardness of decades and centuries shackled his hands and feet. Nor was his burden all poverty and ignorance. The red stain of bastardy, which two centuries of systematic legal defilement of Negro women had stamped upon his race, meant not only the loss of ancient African chastity but also the hereditary weight of a mass of corruption from white adulterers, threatening almost the obliteration of the Negro home.

A people thus handicapped ought not to be asked to race with the world, but rather allowed to give all its time and thought to its own social problems. But alas! while sociologists gleefully count his bastards and his prostitutes, the very soul of the toiling, sweating black man is darkened by the shadow of a vast despair. Men call the shadow prejudice and learnedly explain it as the natural defense of culture against barbarism, learning against ignorance, purity against crime, the "higher" against the "lower" races. To which the Negro cries Amen! and swears that to so much of this strange prejudice as is founded on just homage to civilization, culture, righteousness, and progress he humbly bows and meekly does obeisance.

But before that nameless prejudice that leaps beyond all this, he stands helpless, dismayed, and well-nigh speechless; before that personal disrespect and mockery, the ridicule and systematic humiliation, the distortion of fact and wanton license of fancy, the cynical ignoring of the better and the boisterous welcoming of the worse, the all-pervading desire to inculcate disdain for everything black, from Toussaint to the devil — before this there rises a sickening despair that would disarm and discourage any nation save that black host to whom "discouragement" is an unwritten word.

But the facing of so vast a prejudice could not but bring the inevitable self-questioning, self-disparagement, and lowering of ideals which ever accompany repression and breed in an atmosphere of contempt and hate. Whisperings and portents came borne upon the four winds: Lo! we are diseased and dying, cried the dark hosts; we cannot write, our voting is vain; what need of education since we must always cook and serve? And the nation echoed and enforced this self-criticism, saying: Be content to be servants, and nothing more; what need of higher culture for half-men? Away with the black man's ballot, by force or fraud

— and behold the suicide of a race! Nevertheless, out of the evil came something of good — the more careful adjustment of education to real life, the clearer perception of the Negroes' social responsibilities, and the sobering realization of the meaning of progress.

So dawned the time of *Sturm und Drang*: storm and stress today rocks our little boat on the mad waters of the world sea; there is within and without the sound of conflict, the burning of body and rending of soul; inspiration strives with doubt, and faith with vain questionings. The bright ideals of the past — physical freedom, political power, the training of brains and the training of hands — all these in turn have waxed and waned, until even the last grows dim and overcast. Are they all wrong — all false? No, not that, but each alone was oversimple and incomplete — the dreams of a credulous race-childhood, or the fond imaginings of the other world which does not know and does not want to know our power. To be really true, all these ideals must be melted and welded into one.

The training of the schools we need today more than ever — the training of deft hands, quick eyes and ears, and, above all, the broader, deeper, higher culture of gifted minds and pure hearts. The power of the ballot we need in sheer self-defense, else what shall save us from a second slavery? Freedom, too, the long-sought, we still seek — the freedom of life and limb, the freedom to work and think, the freedom to love and aspire. Work, culture, liberty, all these we need, not singly but together, not successively but together, each growing and aiding each, and all striving toward that vaster ideal that swims before the Negro people, the ideal of human brotherhood, gained through the unifying ideal of race; the ideal of fostering and developing the traits and talents of the Negro, not in opposition to or contempt for other races but rather in large conformity to the greater ideals of the American republic, in order that some day on American soil two worldraces may give each to each those characteristics both so sadly lack.

We, the darker ones, come even now not altogether empty-handed: there are today no truer exponents of the pure human spirit of the Declaration of Independence than the American Negroes; there is no true American music but the wild sweet melodies of the Negro slave; the American fairy tales and folk-lore are Indian and African; and, all in all, we black men seem the sole oasis of simple faith and reverence in a dusty desert of dollars and smartness. Will America be poorer if she replace her brutal, dyspeptic blundering with lighthearted but determined Negro humility? or her coarse and cruel wit with loving jovial good-humor? or her vulgar music with the soul of the Sorrow Songs?

Merely a concrete test of the underlying principles of the great republic is the Negro Problem, and the spiritual striving of the freedmen's sons is the travail of souls whose burden is almost beyond the measure of their strength, but who bear it in the name of an historic race, in the name of this the land of their fathers' fathers, and in the name of human opportunity.

II. ON MR. BOOKER T. WASHINGTON

Easily the most striking thing in the history of the American Negro since 1876 is the ascendancy of Mr. Booker T. Washington. It began at the time when war memories and ideals were rapidly passing; a day of astonishing commercial development was dawning; a sense of doubt and hesitation overtook the freedmen's sons — then it was that his leading began. Mr. Washington came, with a simple, definite program, at the psychological moment when the nation was a little ashamed of having bestowed so much sentiment on Negroes and was concentrating its energies on dollars.

His program of industrial education, conciliation of the South, and submission and silence as to civil and political rights was not wholly original; the free Negroes from 1830 up to wartime had striven to build industrial schools, and the American Missionary Association had from the first taught various trades; and Price and others had sought a way of honorable alliance with the best of the Southerners. But Mr. Washington first indissolubly linked these things; he put enthusiasm, unlimited energy, and perfect faith into this program, and changed it from a bypath into a veritable way of life. And the tale of the methods by which he did this is a fascinating study of human life.

It startled the nation to hear a Negro advocating such a program after many decades of bitter complaint; it startled and won the applause of the South, it interested and won the admiration of the North; and after a confused murmur of protest, it silenced if it did not convert the Negroes themselves.

To gain the sympathy and cooperation of the various elements comprising the white South was Mr. Washington's first task; and this, at the time Tuskegee was founded, seemed, for a black man, well-nigh impossible. And yet ten years later it was done in the word spoken at Atlanta: "In all things purely social we can be as separate as the five fingers, and yet one as the hand in all things essential to mutual progress." This "Atlanta Compromise" is by all odds the most notable thing in Mr. Washington's career.

The South interpreted it in different ways: the radicals received it as a complete surrender of the demand for civil and political equality; the conservatives, as a generously conceived working basis for mutual understanding. So both approved it, and today its author is certainly the most distinguished Southerner since Jefferson Davis, and the one with the largest personal following.

Next to this achievement comes Mr. Washington's work in gaining place and consideration in the North. Others less shrewd and tactful had formerly essayed to sit on these two stools and had fallen between them; but as Mr. Washington knew the heart of the South from birth and training, so by singular insight he intuitively grasped the spirit of the age which was dominating the North. And so thoroughly did he learn the speech and thought of triumphant commercialism and the ideals of material prosperity that the picture of a lone black boy poring over a French grammar amid the weeds and dirt of a neglected home soon seemed to him the acme of absurdities. One wonders what Socrates and St. Francis of Assisi would say to this.

And yet this very singleness of vision and thorough oneness with his age is a mark of the successful man. It is as though nature must needs make men narrow in order to give them force. So Mr. Washington's cult has gained unquestioning followers, his work has wonderfully prospered, his friends are legion, and his enemies are confounded. Today he stands as the one recognized spokesman of his 10 million fellows, and one of the most notable figures in a nation of 70 million.

One hesitates, therefore, to criticize a life which, beginning with so little, has done so much. And yet the time is come when one may speak in all sincerity and utter courtesy of the mistakes and shortcomings of Mr. Washington's career, as well as of his triumphs, without being thought captious or envious, and without forgetting that it is easier to do ill than well in the world.

The criticism that has hitherto met Mr. Washington has not always been of this broad character. In the South, especially, has he had to walk warily to avoid the harshest judgments, and naturally so, for he is dealing with the one subject of deepest sensitiveness to that section. Twice — once when at the Chicago celebration of the Spanish-American War he alluded to the color prejudice that is "eating away the vitals of the South," and once when he dined with President Roosevelt — has the resulting Southern criticism been violent enough to threaten seriously his popularity. In the North the feeling has several times forced itself into words, that Mr. Washington's counsels of submission overlooked certain elements of true manhood, and that his educational program was unnecessarily narrow.

Usually, however, such criticism has not found open expression, although, too, the spiritual sons of the Abolitionists have not been prepared to acknowledge that the schools founded before Tuskegee, by men of broad ideals and self-sacrificing spirit, were wholly failures or worthy of ridicule. While, then, criticism has not failed to follow Mr. Washington, yet the prevailing public opinion of the land has been but too willing to deliver the solution of a wearisome problem into his hands and say, "If that is all you and your race ask, take it."

Among his own people, however, Mr. Washington has encountered the strongest and most lasting opposition, amounting at times to bitterness, and even today continuing strong and insistent even though largely silenced in outward expression by the public opinion of the nation. Some of this opposition is, of course, mere envy; the disappointment of displaced demagogues and the spite of narrow minds. But aside from this, there is among educated and thoughtful colored men in all parts of the land a feeling of deep regret, sorrow, and apprehension at the wide currency and ascendancy which some of Mr. Washington's theories have gained. These same men admire his sincerity of purpose and are willing to forgive much to honest endeavor which is doing something worth the doing. They cooperate with Mr. Washington as far as they conscientiously can; and, indeed, it is no ordinary tribute to this man's tact and power that, steering as he must between so many diverse interests and opinions, he so largely retains the respect of all.

But the hushing of the criticism of honest opponents is a dangerous thing. It leads some of the best of the critics to unfortunate silence and paralysis of effort and others to burst into speech so passionately and intemperately as to lose listeners. Honest and earnest criticism from those whose interests are most nearly touched — criticism of writers by readers, of government by those governed, of leaders by those led — this is the soul of democracy and the safeguard of modern society. If the best of the American Negroes receive by outer pressure a leader whom they had not recognized before, manifestly there is here a certain palpable gain. Yet there is also irreparable loss — a loss of that peculiarly valuable education which a group receives when by search and criticism it finds and commissions its own leaders.

The way in which this is done is at once the most elementary and the nicest problem of social growth. History is but the record of such group leadership; and yet how infinitely changeful is its type and character! And of all types and kinds, what can be more instructive than the leadership of a group within a group? — that curious double movement where real progress may be negative and actual advance be relative retrogression. All this is the social student's inspiration and despair.

Now, in the past, the American Negro has had instructive experience in the choosing of group leaders, founding thus a peculiar dynasty which in the light of present conditions is worthwhile studying. When sticks and stones and beasts form the sole environment of a people, their attitude is largely one of determined opposition to and conquest of natural forces. But when to earth and brute is added an environment of men and ideas, then the attitude of the imprisoned group may take three main forms: a feeling of revolt and revenge; an attempt to adjust all thought and action to the will of the greater group; or, finally, a determined effort at self-realization and self-development despite environing opinion. The influence of all these attitudes at various times can be traced in the history of the American Negro and in the evolution of his successive leaders.

Before 1750, while the fire of African freedom still burned in the veins of the slaves, there was in all leadership or attempted leadership but the one motive of revolt and revenge, typified in the terrible Maroons, the Danish blacks, and Cato of Stono, and veiling all the Americas in fear of insurrection . . . The slaves in the South . . . made three fierce attempts at insurrection — in 1800 under Gabriel in Virginia, in 1822 under Vesey in Carolina, and in 1831, again in Virginia, under the terrible Nat Turner . . .

After the war and emancipation, the great form of Frederick Douglass, the greatest of American Negro leaders, still led the host. Self-assertion, especially in political lines, was the main program, and behind Douglass came Elliot, Bruce, and Langston, and the Reconstruction politicians, and, less conspicuous but of greater social significance, Alexander Crummell and Bishop Daniel Payne.

Then came the revolution of 1876, the suppression of the Negro votes, the changing and shifting of ideals, and the seeking of new lights in the great night. Douglass, in his old age, still bravely stood for the ideals of his early manhood — ultimate assimilation *through* self-assertion, and on no other terms. For a time, Price arose as a new leader, destined, it seemed, not to give up but to restate the old ideals in a form less repugnant to the white South. But he passed away in his prime.

Then came the new leader. Nearly all the former ones had become leaders by the silent suffrage of their fellows, had sought to lead their own people alone, and were usually, save Douglass, little known outside their race. But Booker T. Washington arose as essentially the leader, not of one race but of two, a compromiser between the South, the North, and the Negro.

Naturally, the Negroes resented, at first bitterly, signs of compromise which surrendered their civil and political rights, even though this was to be exchanged for larger chances of economic development. The rich and dominating North, however, was not only weary of the race problem but was investing largely in Southern enterprises and welcomed any method of peaceful cooperation. Thus, by national opinion, the Negroes began to recognize Mr. Washington's leadership, and the voice of criticism was hushed.

Mr. Washington represents in Negro thought the old attitude of adjustment and submission; but adjustment at such a peculiar time as to make his program unique. This is an age of unusual economic development, and Mr. Washington's program naturally takes an economic cast, becoming a gospel of Work and Money to such an extent as apparently almost completely to overshadow the higher aims of life. Moreover, this is an age when the more advanced races are coming in closer contact with the less developed races, and the race feeling is therefore intensified; and Mr. Washington's program practically accepts the alleged inferiority of the Negro races.

Again, in our own land, the reaction from the sentiment of wartime has given impetus to race prejudice against Negroes, and Mr. Washington withdraws many of the high demands of Negroes as men and American citizens. In other periods of intensified prejudice, all the Negro's tendency to self-assertion has been called forth; at this period, a policy of submission is advocated. In the history of nearly all other races and peoples the doctrine preached at such crises has been that manly self-respect is worth more than lands and houses, and that a people who voluntarily surrender such respect or cease striving for it are not worth civilizing.

In answer to this, it has been claimed that the Negro can survive only through submission. Mr. Washington distinctly asks that black people give up, at least for the present, three things:

First, political power; second, insistence on civil rights; third, higher education of Negro youth; and concentrate all their energies on industrial education, the accumulation of wealth, and the conciliation of the South.

This policy has been courageously and insistently advocated for over fifteen years, and has been triumphant for perhaps ten years. As a result of this tender of the palm branch, what has been the return? In these years there have occurred:

- The disfranchisement of the Negro.
- The legal creation of a distinct status of civil inferiority for the Negro.
- The steady withdrawal of aid from institutions for the higher training of the Negro. These movements are not, to be sure, direct results of Mr.

Washington's teachings; but his propaganda has, without a shadow of doubt, helped their speedier accomplishment.

The question then comes: Is it possible, and probable, that 9 million men can make effective progress in economic lines if they are deprived of political rights, made a servile caste, and allowed only the most meager chance for developing their exceptional men? If history and reason give any distinct answer to these questions, it is an emphatic *No*. And Mr. Washington thus faces the triple paradox of his career:

- He is striving nobly to make Negro artisans businessmen and property owners; but it is utterly impossible, under modern competitive methods, for workingmen and property owners to defend their rights and exist without the right of suffrage.
- He insists on thrift and self-respect, but at the same time counsels a silent submission to civic inferiority such as is bound to sap the manhood of any race in the long run.
- He advocates common-school and industrial training, and depreciates institutions of higher learning; but neither the Negro common schools nor Tuskegee itself could

remain open a day were it not for teachers trained in Negro colleges or trained by their graduates.

HENRY B. BROWN AND JOHN MARSHALL HARLAN: PLESSY V. FERGUSON

By 1896 segregation in railway cars was in effect in all Southern states. In an effort to test the constitutionality of Louisiana's segregation laws, Homer A. Plessy, who was only one-eighth African American and could easily "pass" for white, sat in a white car after having made it known that he was an African American. When he was asked to move to an African American car, Plessy refused. He was arrested and tried, appealing his conviction to the Louisiana Supreme Court. The U.S. Supreme Court heard the case on a writ of error and, in a landmark decision, ruled that "separate but equal accommodations" were constitutional. The judgment sanctioned segregation in the South as well as the North for nearly 60 years. Justice John M. Harlan delivered the sole dissenting opinion; portions of this and of Justice Henry Brown's majority opinion are reprinted here. Source: *United States Reports [Supreme Court], Vol. 163, pp.537ff.*

Mr. Justice Brown:

This case turns upon the constitutionality of an act of the General Assembly of the state of Louisiana, passed in 1890, providing for separate railway carriages for the white and colored races ... The 1st Section of the statute enacts

That all railway companies carry-ing passengers in their coaches in this state shall provide equal but separate accommodations for the white and colored races, by pro-viding two or more passenger coaches for each passenger train, or by dividing the passenger coaches by a partition so as to secure separate accommoda-tions: Provided, that this section shall not be construed to apply to street railroads. No person or per-sons, shall be admitted to occupy seats in coaches, other than, the ones, assigned, to them on account of the race they belong to.

...

By the 2nd Section it was enacted

That the officers of such passen-ger trains shall have power and are hereby required to assign each passenger to the coach or compartment used for the race to which such passenger belongs; any passenger insisting on going into a coach or compartment to which by race he does not belong shall be liable to a fine of $25, or, in lieu thereof, to imprisonment for a period of not more than twenty days in the parish prison; and any officer of any railroad insisting on assigning a passen-ger to a coach or compartment other than the one set aside for the race to which said passenger belongs shall be liable to a fine of $25, or, in lieu thereof, to imprison-ment for a period of not more than twenty days in the parish prison; and should any passenger refuse to occupy the coach or compart-ment to which he or she is assigned by the officer of such railway, said officer shall have power to refuse to carry such passenger on his train, and for such refusal neither he nor the railway company which he represents shall be liable for damages in any of the courts of this state. ...

The constitutionality of this act is attacked upon the ground that it conflicts both with the Thirteenth Amendment of the Constitution, abolishing slavery, and the Fourteenth Amendment, which prohibits certain restrictive legislation on the part of the states.

- That it does not conflict with the Thirteenth Amendment, which abolished slavery and involuntary servitude except as a punishment for crime, is too clear for argument ... A statute which implies merely a legal distinction between the white and colored races — a distinction which is founded in the color of the two races, and which must always exist so long as white men are distinguished from the other race by color — has no tendency to destroy the legal equality of the two races or reestablish a state of involuntary servitude. Indeed, we do not understand that the Thirteenth Amendment is strenuously relied upon by the plaintiff in error in this connection.

· By the Fourteenth Amendment, all persons born or naturalized in the United States and subject to the jurisdiction thereof are made citizens of the United States and of the state wherein they reside; and the states are forbidden from making or enforcing any law which shall abridge the privileges or immunities of citizens of the United States, or shall deprive any person of life, liberty, or property without due process of law, or deny to any person within their jurisdiction the equal protection of the laws.

The proper construction of this amendment was first called to the attention of this court in the *Slaughter-House Cases* . . . which involved, however, not a question of race but one of exclusive privileges. The case did not call for any expression of opinion as to the exact rights it was intended to secure to the colored race, but it was said generally that its main purpose was to establish the citizenship of the Negro; to give definitions of citizenship of the United States and of the states, and to protect from the hostile legislation of the states the privileges and immunities of citizens of the United States as distinguished from those of citizens of the states.

The object of the amendment was undoubtedly to enforce the absolute equality of the two races before the law, but in the nature of things it could not have been intended to abolish distinctions based upon color, or to enforce social as distinguished from political equality, or a commingling of the two races upon terms unsatisfactory to either. Laws permitting, and even requiring, their separation in places where they are liable to be brought into contact do not necessarily imply the inferiority of either race to the other, and have been generally, if not universally, recognized as within the competency of the state legislatures in the exercise of their police power. The most common instance of this is connected with the establishment of separate schools for white and colored children, which has been held to be a valid exercise of the legislative power even by courts of states where the political rights of the colored race have been longest and most earnestly enforced. . .

While we think the enforced separation of the races, as applied to the internal commerce of the state, neither abridges the privileges or immunities of the colored man, deprives him of his property without due process of law, nor denies him the equal protection of the laws, within the meaning of the Fourteenth Amendment, we are not prepared to say that the conductor, in assigning passengers to the coaches according to their race, does not act at his peril, or that the provision of the 2nd Section of the act, that denies to the passenger compensation in damages for a refusal to receive him into the coach in which he properly belongs, is a valid exercise of the legislative power. Indeed, we understand it to be conceded by the state's attorney, that such part of the act as exempts from liability the railway company and its officers is unconstitutional.

The power to assign to a particular coach obviously implies the power to determine to which race the passenger belongs, as well as the power to determine who, under the laws of the particular state, is to be deemed a white and who a colored person. This question, though indicated in the brief of the plaintiff in error, does not properly arise upon the record in this case, since the only issue made is as to the unconstitutionality of the act, so far as it requires the railway to provide separate accommodations and the conductor to assign passengers according to their race.

It is claimed by the plaintiff in error that, in any mixed community, the reputation of belonging to the dominant race, in this instance the white race, is *property*, in the same sense that a right of action, or of inheritance, is property. Conceding this to be so for the purposes of this case, we are unable to see how this statute deprives him of, or in any way affects, his right to such property. If he be a white man and assigned to a colored coach, he may have his action for damages against the company for being deprived of his so-called property. Upon the other hand, if he be a colored man and be so assigned, he has been deprived of no property since he is not lawfully entitled to the reputation of being a white man.

In this connection, it is also suggested by the learned counsel for the plaintiff in error that the same argument that will justify the state legislature in requiring railways to provide separate accommodations for the two races will also authorize them to require separate cars to be provided for people whose hair is of a certain color, or who are aliens, or who belong to certain nationalities, or to enact laws requiring colored people to walk upon one side of the street and white people upon the other, or requiring white men's houses to be painted white and colored men's black, or their vehicles or business signs to be of different colors, upon the theory that one side of the street is as good as the other, or that a house or vehicle of one color is as good as one of another color. The reply to all this is that every exercise of the police power must be reasonable and extend only to such laws as are enacted in good faith for the promotion for the public good and not for the annoyance or oppression of a particular class . . .

So far, then, as a conflict with the Fourteenth Amendment is concerned, the case reduces itself to the question whether the statute of Louisiana is a reasonable regulation, and with respect to this there must necessarily be a large discretion on the part of the legislature. In determining the question of reasonableness, it is at liberty to act with reference to the established usages, customs, and traditions of the people, and with a view to the promotion of their comfort, and the preservation of the public peace and good order. Gauged by this standard, we cannot say that a law which authorizes or even requires the separation of the two races in public conveyances is unreasonable or more obnoxious to the Fourteenth Amendment than the acts of Congress requiring separate schools for colored children in the District of Columbia, the constitutionality of which does not seem to have been questioned, or the corresponding acts of state legislatures.

We consider the underlying fallacy of the plaintiff's argument to consist in the assumption that the enforced separation of the two races stamps the colored race with a badge of inferiority. If this be so, it is not by reason of anything found in the act, but solely because the colored race chooses to put that construction upon it. The argument necessarily assumes that if, as has been more than once the case, and is not unlikely to be so again, the colored race should become the dominant power in the state legislature and should enact a law in precisely similar terms, it would thereby relegate the white race to an inferior position. We imagine that the white race, at least, would not acquiesce in this assumption.

The argument also assumes that social prejudices may be overcome by legislation and that equal rights cannot be secured to the Negro except by an enforced commingling of the two races. We cannot accept this proposition. If the two races are to meet upon terms of social equality, it must be the result of natural affinities, a mutual appreciation of each other's merits, and a voluntary consent of individuals. As was said by the Court of Appeals of New York in *People* v. *Gallagher* . . .

This end can neither be accomplished nor promoted by laws which conflict with the general sentiment of the community upon whom they are designed to operate. When the government, therefore, has secured to each of its citizens equal rights before the law and equal opportunities for improvement and progress, it has accomplished the end for which it was organized and performed all of the functions respecting social advantages with which it is endowed.

Legislation is powerless to eradicate racial instincts or to abolish distinctions based upon physical differences, and the attempt to do so can only result in accentuating the difficulties of the present situation. If the civil and political rights of both races be equal, one cannot be inferior to the other civilly or politically. If one race be inferior to the other socially, the Constitution of the United States cannot put them upon the same plane.

It is true that the question of the proportion of colored blood necessary to constitute a colored person as distinguished from a white person is one upon which there is a difference of opinion in the different states, some holding that any visible admixture of black blood stamps the person as belonging to the colored race (*State* v. *Chavers*, 5 Jones, [N.C.]1, p.11); others that it depends upon the preponderance of blood (*Gray* v. *State*, 4 Ohio, 354; *Monroe* v. *Collins*, 17 Ohio St. 665); and still others that the predominance of white blood must only be in the proportion of three-fourths (*People* v. *Dean*, 14 Michigan, 406; *Jones* v. *Commonwealth*, 80 Virginia, 538). But these are questions to be determined under the laws of each state and are not properly put in issue in this case. Under the allegations of his petition it may undoubtedly become a question of importance whether, under the laws of Louisiana, the petitioner belongs to the white or colored race.

The judgment of the court below is, therefore, *affirmed*.

Mr. Justice Harlan:

In respect of civil rights, common to all citizens, the Constitution of the United States does not, I think, permit any public authority to know the race of those entitled to be protected in the enjoyment of such rights. Every true man has pride of race, and, under appropriate circumstances, when the rights of others, his equals before the law, are not to be affected, it is his privilege to express such pride and to take such action based upon it as to him seems proper. But I deny that any legislative body or judicial tribunal may have regard to the race of citizens when the civil rights of those citizens are involved. Indeed, such legislation as that here in question is inconsistent, not only with that equality of rights which pertains to citizenship, national and state, but with the personal liberty enjoyed by everyone within the United States.

The Thirteenth Amendment does not permit the withholding or the deprivation of any right necessarily inhering in freedom. It not only struck down the institution of slavery as previously existing in the United States but it prevents the imposition of any burdens or disabilities that constitute badges of slavery or servitude. It decreed universal civil freedom in this country. This Court has so adjudged. But that amendment having been found inadequate to the protection of the rights of those who had been in slavery, it was followed by the Fourteenth Amendment, which added greatly to the dignity and glory of American citizenship and to the security of personal liberty by declaring that "all persons born or naturalized in the United States and subject to the jurisdiction thereof are citizens of the United States and of the state wherein they reside," and that "no state shall make or enforce any law which shall abridge the privileges or immunities of citizens of the United States; nor shall any state deprive any person of life, liberty, or property without due process of law, nor deny to any person within its jurisdiction the equal protection of the laws."

These two amendments, if enforced according to their true intent and meaning, will protect all the civil rights that pertain to freedom and citizenship. Finally, and to the end that no citizen should be denied on account of his race the privilege of participating in the political control of his country, it was declared by the Fifteenth Amendment that "the right of citizens of the United States to vote shall not be denied or abridged by the United States or by any state on account of race, color, or previous condition of servitude."

These notable additions to the fundamental law were welcomed by the friends of liberty throughout the world. They removed the race line from our governmental systems. They had, as this Court has said, a common purpose; namely, to secure "to a race recently emancipated, a race that through many generations have been held in slavery, all the civil rights that the superior race enjoy." They declared, in legal effect, this Court has further said, "that the law in the states shall be the same for the black as for the white; that all persons, whether colored or white, shall stand equal before the laws of the states, and, in regard to the colored race, for whose protection the amendment was primarily designed, that no discrimination shall be made against them by law because of their color."

We also said: "The words of the amendment, it is true, are prohibitory, but they contain a necessary implication of a positive immunity, or right, most valuable to the colored race — the right to exemption from unfriendly legislation against them distinctively as colored — exemption from legal discriminations, implying inferiority in civil society, lessening the security of their enjoyment of the rights which others enjoy, and discriminations which are steps toward reducing them to the condition of a subject race." It was, consequently, adjudged that a state law that excluded citizens of the colored race from juries because of their race and however well-qualified in other respects to discharge the duties of jurymen was repugnant to the Fourteenth Amendment . . .

The decisions referred to show the scope of the recent amendments of the Constitution. They also show that it is not within the power of a state to prohibit colored citizens, because of their race, from participating as jurors in the administration of justice.

It was said in argument that the statute of Louisiana does not discriminate against either race, but prescribes a rule applicable alike to white and colored citizens. But this argument does not meet the difficulty. Everyone knows that the statute in question had its origin in the purpose, not so much to exclude white persons from railroad cars occupied by blacks as to exclude colored people from coaches occupied by or assigned to white persons. Railroad corporations of Louisiana did not make discrimination among whites in the matter of accommodation for travelers. The thing to accomplish was, under the guise of giving equal accommodation for whites and blacks, to compel the latter to keep to themselves while traveling in railroad passenger coaches. No one would be so wanting in candor as to assert the contrary.

The fundamental objection, therefore, to the statute is that it interferes with the personal freedom of citizens. "Personal liberty," it has been well said, "consists in the power of locomotion, of changing situation, or removing one's person to whatsoever places one's own inclination may direct, without imprisonment or restraint, unless by due course of law." . . . If a white man and a black man choose to occupy the same public conveyance on a public highway, it is their right to do so, and no government proceeding alone on grounds of race can prevent it without infringing the personal liberty of each.

It is one thing for railroad carriers to furnish, or to be required by law to furnish, equal accommodations for all whom they are under a legal duty to carry. It is quite another thing for government to forbid citizens of the white and black races from traveling in the same public conveyance, and to punish officers of railroad companies for permitting persons of the two races to occupy the same passenger coach. If a state can prescribe, as a rule of civil conduct, that whites and blacks shall not travel as passengers in the same railroad coach, why may it not so regulate the use of the streets of its cities and towns as to compel white citizens to keep on one side of a street and black citizens to keep on the other?

Why may it not, upon like grounds, punish whites and blacks who ride together in street cars or in open vehicles on a public road or street? Why may it not require sheriffs to assign whites to one side of a courtroom and blacks to the other? And why may it not also prohibit the commingling of the two races in the galleries of legislative halls or in public assemblages convened for the consideration of the political questions of the day? Further, if this statute of Louisiana is consistent with the personal liberty of citizens, why may not the state require the separation in railroad coaches of native and naturalized citizens of the United States, or of Protestants and Roman Catholics?

The answer given at the argument to these questions was that regulations of the kind they suggest would be unreasonable and could not, therefore, stand before the law. Is it meant that the determination of questions of legislative power depends upon the inquiry whether the statute whose validity is questioned is, in the judgment of the courts, a reasonable one, taking all the circumstances into consideration? A statute may be unreasonable merely because a sound public policy forbade its enactment. But I do not understand that the courts have anything to do with the policy or expediency of legislation. A statute may be valid, and yet, upon grounds of public policy, may well be characterized as unreasonable. Mr. Sedgwick correctly states the rule when he says that the legislative intention being clearly ascertained, "the courts have no other duty to perform than to execute the legislative will, without any regard to their views as to the wisdom or justice of the particular enactment." ...

There is a dangerous tendency in these latter days to enlarge the functions of the courts by means of judicial interference with the will of the people as expressed by the legislature. Our institutions have the distinguishing characteristic that the three departments of government are coordinate and separate. Each must keep within the limits defined by the Constitution, and the courts best discharge their duty by executing the will of the lawmaking power, constitutionally expressed, leaving the results of legislation to be dealt with by the people through their representatives.

Statutes must always have a reasonable construction. Sometimes they are to be construed strictly; sometimes, liberally, in order to carry out the legislative will. But however construed, the intent of the legislature is to be respected if the particular statute in question is valid, although the courts, looking at the public interests, may conceive the statute to be both unreasonable and impolitic. If the power exists to enact a statute, that ends the matter so far as the courts are concerned. The adjudged cases in which statutes have been held to be void because unreasonable are those in which the means employed by the legislature were not at all germane to the end to which the legislature was competent.

The white race deems itself to be the dominant race in this country. And so it is, in prestige, in achievements, in education, in wealth, and in power. So, I doubt not, it will continue to be for all time if it remains true to its great heritage and holds fast to the principles of constitutional liberty. But in view of the Constitution, in the eye of the law, there is in this country no superior, dominant, ruling class of citizens. There is no caste here. Our Constitution is color-blind and neither knows nor tolerates classes among citizens.

In respect of civil rights, all citizens are equal before the law. The humblest is the peer of the most powerful. The law regards man as man and takes no account of his surroundings or of his color when his civil rights as guaranteed by the supreme law of the land are involved. It is therefore to be regretted that this high tribunal, the final expositor of the fundamental law of the land, has reached the conclusion that it is competent for a state to regulate the enjoyment by citizens of their civil rights solely upon the basis of race.

In my opinion, the judgment this day rendered will, in time, prove to be quite as pernicious as the decision made by this tribunal in the *Dred Scott Case*. It was adjudged in that case that the descendants of Africans who were imported into this country and sold as slaves were not included nor intended to be included under the word "citizens" in the Constitution and could not claim any of the rights and privileges which that instrument provided for and secured to citizens of the United States; that at the time of the adoption of the Constitution they were "considered as a subordinate and inferior class of beings who had been subjugated by the dominant race, and, whether emancipated or not, yet remained subject to their authority, and had no rights or privileges but such as those who held the power and the government might choose to grant them." ...

The recent amendments of the Constitution, it was supposed, had eradicated these principles from our institutions. But it seems that we have yet, in some of the states, a dominant race — a superior class of citizens, which assumes to regulate the enjoyment of civil rights, common to all citizens, upon the basis of race. The present decision, it may well be apprehended, will not only stimulate aggressions, more or less brutal and irritating, upon the admitted rights of colored citizens, but will encourage the belief that it is possible, by means of state enactments, to defeat the beneficent purposes which the people of the United States had in view when they adopted the recent amendments of the Constitution, by one of which the blacks of this country were made citizens of the United States and of the states in which they respectively reside, and whose privileges and immunities as citizens the states are forbidden to abridge.

Sixty millions of whites are in no danger from the presence here of 8 million blacks. The destinies of the two races in this country are indissolubly linked together, and the interests of both require that the common government of all shall not permit the seeds of race hate to be planted under the sanction of law. What can more certainly arouse race hate, what more certainly create and perpetuate a feeling of distrust between these races than state enactments, which, in fact, proceed on the ground that colored citizens are so inferior and degraded that they cannot be allowed to sit in public coaches occupied by white citizens? That, as all will admit, is the real meaning of such legislation as was enacted in Louisiana.

The sure guarantee of the peace and security of each race is the clear, distinct, unconditional recognition by our governments, national and state, of every right that inheres in civil freedom and of the equality before the law of all citizens of the United States without regard to race. State enactments regulating the enjoyment of civil rights upon the basis of race, and cunningly devised to defeat legitimate results of the war under the pretense of recognizing equality of rights, can have no other result than to render permanent peace impossible and to keep alive a conflict of races, the continuance of which must do harm to all concerned.

This question is not met by the suggestion that social equality cannot exist between the white and black races in this country. That argument, if it can be properly regarded as one, is scarcely worthy of consideration; for social equality no more exists between two races when traveling in a passenger coach or a public highway than when members of the same races sit by each other in a streetcar or in the jury box, or stand or sit with each other in a political assembly, or when they use in common the streets of a city or town, or when they are in the same room for the purpose of having their names placed on the registry of voters, or when they approach the ballot box in order to exercise the high privilege of voting.

There is a race so different from our own that we do not permit those belonging to it to become citizens of the United States. Persons belonging to it are, with few exceptions, absolutely excluded from our country. I allude to the Chinese race. But by the statute in question, a Chinaman can ride in the same passenger coach with white citizens of the United States, while citizens of the black race in Louisiana, many of whom, perhaps, risked their lives for the preservation of the Union, who are entitled, by law, to participate in the political control of the state and nation, who are not excluded, by law or by reason of their race, from public stations of any kind, and who have all the legal rights that belong to white citizens, are yet declared to be criminals, liable to imprisonment, if they ride in a public coach occupied by citizens of the white race.

It is scarcely just to say that a colored citizen should not object to occupying a public coach assigned to his own race. He does not object, nor, perhaps, would he object to separate coaches for his race, if his rights under the law were recognized. But he objects, and ought never to cease objecting to the proposition that citizens of the white and black races can be adjudged criminals because they sit, or claim the right to sit, in the same public coach on a public highway.

The arbitrary separation of citizens, on the basis of race, while they are on a public highway, is a badge of servitude wholly inconsistent with the civil freedom and the equality before the law established by the Constitution. It cannot be justified upon any legal grounds.

If evils will result from the commingling of the two races upon public highways established for the benefit of all, they will be infinitely less than those that will surely come from state legislation regulating the enjoyment of civil rights upon the basis of race. We boast of the freedom enjoyed by our people above all other peoples. But it is difficult to reconcile that boast with a state of law which, practically, puts the brand of servitude and degradation upon a large class of our fellow citizens, our equals before the law. The thin disguise of "equal" accommodations for passengers in railroad coaches will not mislead anyone, nor atone for the wrong this day done.

The result of the whole matter is that while this Court has frequently adjudged, and at the present term has recognized the doctrine, that a state cannot, consistently with the Constitution of the United States, prevent white and black citizens, having the required qualifications for jury service, from sitting in the same jury box, it is now solemnly held that a state may prohibit white and black citizens from sitting in the same passenger coach on a public highway, or may require that they be separated by a "partition," when in the same passenger coach . . .

I am of opinion that the statute of Louisiana is inconsistent with the personal liberty of citizens, white and black, in that state, and hostile to both the spirit and letter of the Constitution of the United States. If laws of like character should be enacted in the several states of the Union, the effect would be in the highest degree mischievous. Slavery, as an institution tolerated by law, would, it is true, have disappeared from our country, but there would remain a power in the states, by sinister legislation, to interfere with the full enjoyment of the blessings of freedom; to regulate civil rights, common to all citizens, upon the basis of race; and to place in a condition of legal inferiority a large body of American citizens now constituting a part of the political community called the People of the United States, for whom, and by whom through representatives, our government is administered. Such a system is inconsistent with the guarantee given by the Constitution to each state of a republican form of government and may be stricken down by Congressional action or by the courts in the discharge of their solemn duty to maintain the supreme law of the land, anything in the constitution or laws of any state to the contrary notwithstanding.

For the reasons stated, I am constrained to withhold my assent from the opinion and judgment of the majority.

Booker T. Washington, first principal and chief developer of Tuskegee Institute in Alabama. Library of Congress, Washington, D.C.

BOOKER T. WASHINGTON: THE ROAD TO AFRICAN AMERICAN PROGRESS

When he introduced speaker Booker T. Washington to the crowd at the Cotton States and International Exposition in Atlanta, on Sept. 18, 1895, Georgia governor Rufus Bullock called him a "representative of Negro enterprise and Negro civilization." By emphasizing his belief that African Americans wanted responsibilities rather than rights, Washington allayed any fears his white audience might have had about the ambitions of Southern African Americans. That speech, printed here, lay the groundwork for the Atlanta Compromise. *Source: The Story of My Life and Work, Revised edition, Naperville, Ill. and Atlanta, Ga., 1900, pp. 165–171.*

Mr. President and Gentlemen of the Board of Directors and Citizens:

One-third of the population of the South is of the Negro race. No enterprise seeking the material, civil, or moral welfare of this section can disregard this element of our population and reach the highest success. I but convey to you, Mr. President and Directors, the sentiment of the masses of my race when I say that in no way have the value and manhood of the American Negro been more fittingly and generously recognized than by the managers of this magnificent exposition at every stage of its progress. It is a recognition that will do more to cement the friendship of the two races than any occurrence since the dawn of our freedom.

Not only this, but the opportunity here afforded will awaken among us a new era of industrial progress. Ignorant and inexperienced, it is not strange that in the first years of our new life we began at the top instead of at the bottom; that a seat in Congress or the state legislature was more sought than real estate or industrial skill; that the political convention or stump speaking had more attractions than starting a dairy farm or truck garden.

A ship lost at sea for many days suddenly sighted a friendly vessel. From the mast of the unfortunate vessel was seen a signal: "Water, water; we die of thirst." The answer from the friendly vessel at once came back: "Cast down your bucket where you are." A second time the signal, "Water, water, send us water!" ran up from the distressed vessel, and was answered: "Cast down your bucket where you are." And a third and fourth signal for water was answered: "Cast down your bucket where you are." The captain of the distressed vessel, at last heeding the injunction, cast down his bucket, and it came up full of fresh, sparkling water from the mouth of the Amazon River.

To those of my race who depend on bettering their condition in a foreign land or who underestimate the importance of cultivating friendly relations with the Southern white man, who is their next-door neighbor, I would say: Cast down your bucket where you are; cast it down in making friends, in every manly way, of the people of all races by whom we are surrounded. Cast it down in agriculture, mechanics, in commerce, in domestic service, and in the professions. And in this connection it is well to bear in mind that whatever other sins the South may be called to bear, when it comes to business, pure and simple, it is in the South that the Negro is given a man's chance in the commercial world, and in nothing is this exposition more eloquent than in emphasizing this chance.

Our greatest danger is that, in the great leap from slavery to freedom, we may overlook the fact that the masses of us are to live by the productions of our hands and fail to keep in mind that we shall prosper in proportion as we learn to dignify and glorify common labor, and put brains and skill into the common occupations of life; shall prosper in proportion as we learn to draw the line between the superficial and the substantial, the ornamental gewgaws of life and the useful. No race can prosper till it learns that there is as much dignity in tilling a field as in writing a poem. It is at the bottom of life we must begin, and not at the top. Nor should we permit our grievances to overshadow our opportunities.

To those of the white race who look to the incoming of those of foreign birth and strange tongue and habits for the prosperity of the South, were I permitted I would repeat what I say to my own race, "Cast down your bucket where you are." Cast it down among the 8 million Negroes whose habits you know, whose fidelity and love you have tested in days when to have proved treacherous meant the ruin of your firesides. Cast down your bucket among these people who have, without strikes and labor wars, tilled your fields, cleared your forests, builded your railroads and cities, and brought forth treasures from the bowels of the earth and helped make possible this magnificent representation of the progress of the South. Casting down your bucket among my people, helping and encouraging them as you are doing on these grounds, and, with education of head, hand, and heart, you will find that they will buy your surplus land, make blossom the waste places in your fields, and run your factories.

While doing this, you can be sure in the future, as in the past, that you and your families will be surrounded by the most patient, faithful, law-abiding, and unresentful people that the world has seen. As we have proved our loyalty to you in the past, in nursing your children, watching by the sickbed of your mothers and fathers, and often following them with tear-dimmed eyes to their graves, so in the future, in our humble way, we shall stand by you with a devotion that no foreigner can approach, ready to lay down our lives, if need be, in defense of yours; interlacing our industrial, commercial, civil, and religious life with yours in a way that shall make the interests of both races one. In all things that are purely social we can be as separate as the fingers, yet one as the hand in all things essential to mutual progress.

There is no defense or security for any of us except in the highest intelligence and development of all. If anywhere there are efforts tending to curtail the fullest growth of the Negro, let these efforts be turned into stimulating, encouraging, and making him the most useful and intelligent citizen. Effort or means so invested will pay a thousand percent interest. These efforts will be twice blessed — "blessing him that gives and him that takes."

There is no escape, through law of man or God, from the inevitable:

The laws of changeless justice
bind Oppressor with oppressed;
And close as sin and suffering
joined We march to fate abreast.

Nearly 16 million hands will aid you in pulling the load upward, or they will pull against you the load downward. We shall constitute one-third and more of the ignorance and crime of the South, or one-third its intelligence and progress; we shall contribute one-third to the business and industrial prosperity of the South, or we shall prove a veritable body of death, stagnating, depressing, retarding every effort to advance the body politic.

Gentlemen of the exposition, as we present to you our humble effort at an exhibition of our progress, you must not expect overmuch. Starting thirty years ago with ownership here and there in a few quilts and pumpkins and chickens (gathered from miscellaneous sources), remember: the path that has led from these to the invention and production of agricultural implements, buggies, steam engines, newspapers, books, statuary, carving, paintings, the management of drugstores and banks, has not been trodden without contact with thorns and thistles. While we take pride in what we exhibit as a result of our independent efforts, we do not for a moment forget that our part in this exhibition would fall far short of your expectations but for the constant help that has come to our educational life, not only from the Southern states but especially from Northern philanthropists who have made their gifts a constant stream of blessing and encouragement.

The wisest among my race understand that the agitation of questions of social equality is the extremest folly, and that progress in the enjoyment of all the privileges that will come to us must be the result of severe and constant struggle rather than of artificial forcing. No race that has anything to contribute to the markets of the world is long in any degree ostracized. It is important and right that all privileges of the law be ours, but it is vastly more important that we be prepared for the exercise of those privileges. The opportunity to earn a dollar in a factory just now is worth infinitely more than the opportunity to spend a dollar in an opera house.

In conclusion, may I repeat that nothing in thirty years has given us more hope and encouragement and drawn us so near to you of the white race as this opportunity offered by the exposition; and here bending, as it were, over the altar that represents the results of the struggles of your race and mine, both starting practically empty-handed three decades ago, I pledge that, in your effort to work out the great and intricate problem which God has laid at the doors of the South, you shall have at all times the patient, sympathetic help of my race; only let this be constantly in mind that, while from representations in these buildings of the product of field, of forest, of mine, of factory, letters, and art, much good will come — yet far above and beyond material benefits will be that higher good, that let us pray God will come, in a blotting out of sectional differences and racial animosities and suspicions, in a determination to administer absolute justice, in a willing obedience among all classes to the mandates of law. This, coupled with our material prosperity, will bring into our beloved South a new heaven and a new earth.

IDA B. WELLS-BARNETT: LYNCHING AND THE EXCUSE FOR IT

In the 20 years after 1885, there were more lynchings in the United States than legal executions. The great majority of victims were Southern African Americans. Lynching and discrimination, however, were national rather than particularly Southern problems. Neither state nor federal governments took any effective action to combat lynchings. But the issue was brought before the public by African American spokesmen, foremost of whom was journalist Ida B. Wells-Barnett, head of the antilynching crusade, who lectured throughout the United States and Europe on the subject for several years. In the following article published in 1901, Wells-Barnett attacks the premise that lynching was merely an extralegal means of securing justice. *Source: The Independent, May 16, 1901.*

It was eminently befitting that the *Independent*'s first number in the new century should contain a strong protest against lynching. The deepest dyed infamy of the 19th century was that which, in its supreme contempt for law, defied all constitutional guarantees of citizenship, and during the last fifteen years of the century put to death 2,000 men, women, and children by shooting, hanging, and burning alive. Well would it have been if every preacher in every pulpit in the land had made so earnest a plea as that which came from Miss Addams' forceful pen.

Appreciating the helpful influences of such a dispassionate and logical argument as that made by the writer referred to, I earnestly desire to say nothing to lessen the force of the appeal. At the same time, an unfortunate presumption used as a basis for her argument works so serious, though doubtless unintentional, an injury to the memory of thousands of victims of mob law that it is only fair to call attention to this phase of the writer's plea. It is unspeakably infamous to put thousands of people to death without a trial by jury; it adds to that infamy to charge that these victims were moral monsters, when, in fact, four-fifths of them were not so accused even by the fiends who murdered them.

Almost at the beginning of her discussion, the distinguished writer says: "Let us assume that the Southern citizens who take part in and abet the lynching of Negroes honestly believe that that is the only successful method of dealing with a certain class of crimes."

It is this assumption, this absolutely unwarrantable assumption, that vitiates every suggestion which it inspires Miss Addams to make. It is the same baseless assumption which influences ninety-nine out of every one hundred persons who discuss this question. Among many thousand editorial clippings I have received in the past five years, 99 percent discuss the question upon the presumption that lynchings are the desperate effort of the Southern people to protect their women from black monsters, and, while the large majority condemn lynching, the condemnation is tempered with a plea for the lyncher — that human nature gives way under such awful provocation and that the mob, insane for the moment, must be pitied as well as condemned. It is strange that an intelligent, law-abiding, and fair-minded people should so persistently shut their eyes to the facts in the discussion of what the civilized world now concedes to be America's national crime.

This almost universal tendency to accept as true the slander which the lynchers offer to civilization as an excuse for their crime might be explained if the true facts were difficult to obtain; but not the slightest difficulty intervenes. The Associated Press dispatches, the press clipping bureau, frequent book publications, and the annual summary of a number of influential journals give the lynching record every year. This record, easily within the reach of everyone who wants it, makes inexcusable the statement and cruelly unwarranted the assumption that Negroes are lynched only because of their assaults upon womanhood.

For an example in point: For fifteen years past, on the first day of each year, the *Chicago Tribune* has given to the public a carefully compiled record of all the lynchings of the previous year. Space will not permit a résumé of these fifteen years, but as fairly representing the entire time, I desire to briefly tabulate here the record of the five years last past. The statistics of the ten years preceding do not vary; they simply emphasize the record here presented.

The record gives the name and nationality of the man or woman lynched, the alleged crime, the time and place of the lynching. With this is given a résumé of the offenses charged, with the number of persons lynched for the offenses named. That enables the reader to see at a glance the causes assigned for the lynchings, and leaves nothing to be assumed. The lynchers, at the time and place of the lynching, are the best authority for the causes which actuate them. Every presumption is in favor of this record, especially as it remains absolutely unimpeached. This record gives the following statement of the colored persons lynched and the causes of the lynchings for the years named.

With this record in view, there should be no difficulty in ascertaining the alleged offenses given as justification for lynchings during the last five years. If the Southern citizens lynch Negroes because "that is the only successful method of dealing with a certain class of crimes," then that class of crimes should be shown unmistakably by this record. Now consider the record.

It would be supposed that the record would show that all, or nearly all, lynchings were caused by outrageous assaults upon women; certainly that this particular offense would outnumber all other causes for putting human beings to death without a trial by jury and the other safeguards of our Constitution and laws.

But the record makes no such disclosure. Instead, it shows that five women have been lynched, put to death with unspeakable savagery, during the past five years. They certainly were not under the ban of the outlawing crime. It shows that men, not a few but hundreds, have been lynched for misdemeanors, while others have suffered death for no offense known to the law, the causes assigned being "mistaken identity," "insult," "bad reputation," "unpopularity," "violating contract," "running quarantine," "giving evidence," "frightening child by shooting at rabbits," etc. Then, strangest of all, the record shows that the sum total of lynchings for these offenses — not crimes — and for the alleged offenses which are only misdemeanors greatly exceeds the lynchings for the very crime universally declared to be the cause of lynching.

A careful classification of the offenses which have caused lynchings during the past five years shows that contempt for law and race prejudice constitute the real cause of all lynching. During the past five years, 147 white persons were lynched. It may be argued that fear of the "law's delays" was the cause of their being lynched. But this is not true. Not a single white victim of the mob was wealthy or had friends or influence to cause a miscarriage of justice. There was no such possibility; it was contempt for law which incited the mob to put so many white men to death without a complaint under oath, much less a trial.

In the case of the Negroes lynched, the mobs' incentive was race prejudice. Few white men were lynched for any such trivial offenses as are detailed in the causes for lynching colored men. Negroes are lynched for "violating contracts," "unpopularity," "testifying in court," and "shooting at rabbits." As only Negroes are lynched for "no offense," "unknown offenses," offenses not criminal, misdemeanors, and crimes not capital, it must be admitted that the real cause of lynching in all such cases is race prejudice, and should be so classified.

Grouping these lynchings under that classification and excluding rape, which in some states is made a capital offense, the record for the five years, so far as the Negro is concerned, reads as follows:

This table tells its own story and shows how false is the excuse which lynchers offer to justify their fiendishness. Instead of being the sole cause of lynching, the crime upon which lynchers build their defense furnishes the least victims for the mob. In 1896 less than 39 percent of the Negroes lynched were charged with this crime; in 1897, less than 18 percent; in 1898, less than 16 percent; in 1899, less than 14 percent; and in 1900, less than 15 percent were so charged.

No good result can come from any investigation which refuses to consider the facts. A conclusion that is based upon a presumption instead of the best evidence is unworthy of a moment's consideration. The lynching record, as it is compiled from day to day by unbiased, reliable, and responsible public journals, should be the basis of every investigation which seeks to discover the cause and suggest the remedy for lynching. The excuses of lynchers and the specious pleas of their apologists should be considered in the light of the record, which they invariably misrepresent or ignore.

The Christian and moral forces of the nation should insist that misrepresentation should have no place in the discussion of this all important question, that the figures of the lynching record should be allowed to plead, trumpet-tongued, in defense of the slandered dead, that the silence of concession be broken, and that truth, swift-winged and courageous, summon this nation to do its duty to exalt justice and preserve inviolate the sacredness of human life.

CHAPTER 7

RELIGION

In his seminal history of black America, *Before the Mayflower*, Lerone Bennett, Jr., calls the black church the dominant institutional force in African American life. Its dominance has been evident from its role as a cornerstone of the abolitionist movement through the Jim Crow era and the civil rights struggle in the 1960s. Presented in roughly chronological order of their founding, what follows is an examination of the churches (and other religious organizations) that established the longstanding tradition of self-management, activism, spirituality, idealism, community, and courage that sustained African Americans in the struggle for equality.

AFRICAN METHODIST EPISCOPAL CHURCH

The African Methodist Episcopal Church developed from a congregation formed by a group of African Americans who withdrew in 1787 from St. George's Methodist Episcopal Church in Philadelphia because of restrictions in seating; black people had been confined to the gallery of the church. Those who withdrew formed the Free African Society, the forerunner of the African Methodist Episcopal Church, and built Bethel African Methodist Church in Philadelphia. In 1799 Richard Allen was ordained its minister by Bishop Francis Asbury of the Methodist Episcopal Church. In 1816 Asbury consecrated Allen bishop of the newly organized

African Methodist Episcopal Church, which accepted Methodist doctrine and discipline. The church speaks of Allen, William Paul Quinn, David A. Payne, and Henry M. Turner as the "Four Horsemen" of its establishment.

AFRICAN METHODIST EPISCOPAL ZION CHURCH

Organized in 1821, the African Methodist Episcopal Zion Church adopted its present name in 1848. It developed from a congregation formed by a group of black Americans who in 1796 left the John Street Methodist Church in New York City because of discrimination. They built their first church (Zion) in 1800 and were served for many years by white ministers of the Methodist Episcopal Church. In 1821 a conference attended by representatives of six black churches and presided over by a white Methodist minister elected an African American bishop, James Varick.

After the Civil War the church, which is Methodist in doctrine and government, grew rapidly in the North and the South. Foreign-mission programs were established in South America, Africa, and the West Indies.

AMERICAN MISSIONARY ASSOCIATION (AMA)

The nondenominational American Missionary Association (AMA) worked to develop educational opportunities for African Americans and other minorities in the United States. The society originally grew out of a committee organized in 1839 to defend the group of African slaves who had mutinied on *Amistad*. The AMA itself was incorporated in 1846 by the merger of three missionary antislavery societies whose goal was to establish missions for freed slaves overseas. After 1850 the AMA turned primarily to abolitionist activities. When the Union armies began freeing slaves during the Civil War, the AMA opened schools and churches for them, founding more than 500 schools for freed slaves in the South in the decades following the Civil War. These schools were actually open to all students and often operated as integrated institutions during the Reconstruction period.

As the South recovered from the effects of the war and developed public school systems, the AMA turned over its elementary and secondary schools to the public systems and instead concentrated on improving and expanding colleges for African Americans in the South. The AMA founded nine predominantly African American colleges: Atlanta University, Dillard University, Fisk University, Hampton Institute (now Hampton University), Howard University, Huston-Tillotson College, LeMoyne College (now LeMoyne-Owen College), Talladega College, and Tougaloo College; it was also instrumental in founding the racially integrated Berea College. The AMA ceased operations as an independent body in the mid-20th century, and its papers and other collections became part of the Amistad Research Center at Tulane University.

CHRISTIAN METHODIST EPISCOPAL CHURCH

Organized in 1870 as the Colored Methodist Episcopal Church, the Christian Methodist Episcopal Church did not officially adopt its present name until 1956. The church originated from a movement begun in 1866 within the Methodist Episcopal Church, South, to organize African American members into an independent church. At the founding convention in 1870, two bishops from the Methodist Episcopal Church, South, consecrated two African American elders as the first bishops of the new church.

NATIONAL BAPTIST CONVENTION, U.S.A., INC.

The National Baptist Convention, U.S.A., Inc., is an association of black Baptist churches formed in 1895 in Atlanta, from the merger of the Foreign Mission Baptist Convention (established 1880), the American National Baptist Convention (1886), and the Baptist National Education Convention (1893). A schism in 1915 resulted in the formation of the National Baptist Convention of America. In 1961 a dispute within the National Baptist Convention, U.S.A., Inc., would result in the establishment of a third

organization, the Progressive National Baptist Convention, Inc.

CHURCH OF GOD AND SAINTS OF CHRIST

Prophet William S. Crowdy founded the Church of God and Saints of Christ in 1896. He passed his mantle of leadership to Bishop William Plummer, who announced himself as "Grand Father Abraham." This group believes that all Jews were originally black and that modern-day blacks are descendants of the "lost tribes of Israel." These beliefs are centred on the "Seven Keys," the "Stone of Truth," and the Ten Commandments.

NATIONAL PRIMITIVE BAPTIST CONVENTION, INC.

The National Primitive Baptist Convention, Inc., is an association of independent black Baptist churches in the United States that were joined in a national convention in 1907. The convention developed from African American congregations formed after the Civil War by emancipated slaves who had previously attended Primitive Baptist churches with whites.

MOORISH SCIENCE TEMPLE OF AMERICA

The Moorish Science Temple of America was founded in Newark, N.J., in 1913 by Timothy Drew (1886–1929), known to followers as Noble Drew Ali and also as the Prophet. Drew Ali taught that all blacks were of Moorish origins but had their Muslim identity taken away from them through slavery and segregation. He advocated that they should "return" to the Islam of their Moorish forefathers, redeeming themselves from racial oppression by reclaiming their historical spiritual heritage. He also encouraged use of the term "Moor" rather than "black" in self-identification. Many of the group's formal practices were derived from Muslim observances. Rigorous obedience to the Prophet's regulations was required, and certain foods were forbidden. The group's sacred text was the Holy Koran, which was distinct from the Qur'ān of orthodox Islam and which members considered to have been divinely revealed by Allah to Drew Ali. The work begins with a long narrative spanning from the Fall of Man to the Resurrection of Jesus; it includes moral instructions by Drew Ali and closes with a prophecy of the imminent "uplift of fallen humanity."

Drew Ali moved his organization several times and ultimately settled in the mid-1920s in Chicago, where he found success. He died under mysterious circumstances during a period of internal strife, and the Moorish Science Temple of America split into several factions. The Nation of Islam grew out of the contested succession to Drew Ali and became a separate organization in Detroit in 1932. Several men claimed to carry on the spiritual lineage of Noble Drew Ali and founded similar organizations.

NATIONAL BAPTIST CONVENTION OF THE UNITED STATES OF AMERICA, INC.

The National Baptist Convention of the United States of America, Inc., is the larger of two associations of black Baptist churches that formed after a schism in 1915 in the National Baptist Convention.

The National Baptist Convention had its origins in the period after the Civil War, when many independent African American Baptist congregations were established. Eventually they joined in various national organizations, and the merger of the Foreign Mission Baptist Convention (1880), the American National Baptist Convention (1886), and the Baptist National Educational Convention (1893) in Atlanta in 1895 produced the National Baptist Convention. Disagreements over the organization's publishing house and adoption of a charter resulted in a schism in 1915, when one group adopted the charter and took the name National Baptist Convention of the United States of America, Inc., and the other group rejected the charter and continued as the National Baptist Convention of America. In 1961 a dispute within the National Baptist Convention, U.S.A., Inc., would result in the establishment of a third organization, the Progressive National Baptist Convention, Inc. By the late 20th century, the National Baptist Convention of the

United States of America, Inc., was the largest African American church in the United States

APOSTOLIC OVERCOMING HOLY CHURCH OF GOD

The Apostolic Overcoming Holy Church of God was founded in 1919 as the Ethiopian Overcoming Holy Church of God by Bishop W.T. Phillips in Mobile, Ala. The Pentecostal church adopted its present name in 1927. The founder left the Methodist Episcopal Church, which he served as a minister, after becoming concerned about the doctrine of holiness and the process of sanctification.

PEACE MISSION

The Peace Mission was founded and led by Father Divine (1878/80–1965), who was regarded, or worshiped, by his predominantly African American followers as God, Dean of the Universe, and Harnesser of Atomic Energy. According to most accounts, Father Divine was born George Baker and reared in Savannah, Ga., during the post-Reconstruction period, when black messiahs flourished in an atmosphere of misery and degradation. He received indelible impressions from his immersion in primitive mysticism and the Holiness and Pentecostal movements.

The transition from George Baker to Major J. Devine to Father Divine essentially was completed when he set up his first "heaven" in Sayville, Long Island, N.Y., in 1919. Legal entanglements forced him to relocate in Harlem and Philadelphia, but the Peace Mission continued to grow and spread through many cities of the Northern and Western United States.

Heaven, according to Father Divine, was symbolized by separation of sexes and union of all races in a communion composed of a multicourse feast. He also preached total racial integration, that all things and persons are to be forsaken for the Father, and that heaven is on earth. Although he owned almost nothing directly, his 500,000 to 2,000,000 followers provided him free access to a fortune worth at least $1,500,000.

The Peace Mission supported African Americans in businesses that became successful and fulfilled basic needs. The key to Father Divine's success was the devotion of competent disciples. By the late 20th century this cohesion would diminish and the movement would dwindle.

SUMMARY

The centrality of the black church, not just to the spiritual and social lives of African Americans but also to the freedom movement, becomes even clearer when the events of the 1950s and '60s are considered. So too, the biographies of African American political leaders show that so many have been formed in the church or drawn from the clergy.

CHAPTER 8

EDUCATION

Arguably the most lasting accomplishment of Reconstruction was the creation and proliferation of the public school system in the South. In tandem with this spread of primary and secondary education, which all too soon would become separate and distinctly unequal, was the founding and growth of colleges and universities that were dedicated to educating African Americans. From these institutions would come many of the leaders who shaped the future not just for African Americans and Americans but for all people. W.E.B. Du Bois, for example, was a graduate of Fisk University, which was also attended by Ida B. Wells-Barnett; Martin Luther King, Jr., graduated from Morehouse College. This chapter considers the broad spectrum of institutions now usually referred to as historically black colleges and universities as well as other institutions that have played a role in African American history.

ALABAMA AGRICULTURAL AND MECHANICAL UNIVERSITY

Alabama Agricultural and Mechanical University (better known simply as Alabama A&M University) was founded in 1875 in Huntsville as the Huntsville Normal School. In 1891 the school moved to its Normal campus, was designated a land-grant school for African Americans, and was renamed State Agricultural and Mechanical College for Negroes. The college was re-formed as a junior college in 1919 and became a four-year college in 1939. Its name was changed to Alabama Agricultural and Mechanical College in 1948, and it was granted university status in 1969.

Today the university comprises the schools of Agricultural and Environmental Sciences, Graduate Studies and Extended Education, Arts and Sciences, Business, Education, and Engineering and Technology. It offers a range of bachelor's, master's, and doctoral degree programs. University College provides services for new students. Research facilities include the Center of Excellence in Nonlinear Optics and Nonlinear Optical Materials, Howard J. Foster Center for Irradiation of Materials, and the Center for Forestry and Ecology. The university is the home of the State Black Archives, Research Center and Museum, which collects materials on African American history and culture. Total enrollment is more than 5,000.

ALABAMA STATE UNIVERSITY

Alabama State University began in 1867 as the Lincoln Normal School, a private school for African Americans in Marion. In 1874 the school was reorganized as a state-supported college. It moved to Montgomery in 1887. After years of steady growth and a series of name changes, Alabama State achieved university status in 1969. Among its graduates was civil rights leader Ralph Abernathy, cofounder of the Southern Christian Leadership Conference.

Alabama State now offers bachelor's and master's degree programs in the schools of Music and Graduate Studies and colleges of Business Administration, Education, and Arts and Sciences. An educational specialist degree is available. University College provides academic services and a basic program of study to prepare new students for degree programs. Total enrollment is more than 5,600.

ALCORN STATE UNIVERSITY

The history of Alcorn State University, located near Lorman, Miss., began in 1830 with the establishment of Oakland College, a Presbyterian college for white male students. The college, closed during the Civil War, was unable to reopen after the war's conclusion, and it was sold to the state as an institution for the instruction of African American students, founded in 1871 as Alcorn University. Hiram R. Revels, the first African American to serve in the U.S. Senate, was the university's first president. In 1878 the university was made a land-grant institution, and the name was changed to Alcorn Agricultural and Mechanical College. Women first attended in 1895, and it became coeducational in 1903. The school acquired its present name in 1974. Civil rights activist Medgar Evers was a graduate of Alcorn.

The present-day university consists of schools of Arts and Sciences, Business,

Education and Psychology, Nursing, and Agriculture and Applied Sciences. The university's School of Nursing is located in Natchez. In addition to undergraduate studies, Alcorn State offers several master's degree programs and a specialist degree in elementary education. Total enrollment exceeds 3,000.

CHICAGO STATE UNIVERSITY

Chicago State University was established in 1867 as an experimental teacher-training school. Its student body was predominantly white until the late 20th century, when the changing demographics of the surrounding area contributed to shift to a predominantly African American enrollment. Today Chicago State is often listed among historically black colleges and universities. It offers bachelor's degree programs in health sciences, business, education, and arts and sciences. Master's degree programs are also available in education and in arts and sciences. Notable facilities on campus include an electron microscopy laboratory and an art gallery. Its University Without Walls program allows students to combine academic training with practical experience in a profession and in the community. Total enrollment is about 7,000.

DELAWARE STATE UNIVERSITY

Delaware State University, located in Dover, was founded in 1891 as a land-grant institution for African American students, and the student body continues to be predominantly black. In 1947 the college became Delaware State College. It was granted university status in 1993.

The university consists of a College of Arts and Sciences and schools of Management; Education and Professional Studies, including aviation, education, and nursing; and Agriculture, Natural Resources, Family and Consumer Services. In addition to undergraduate studies, the university offers master's degree programs in business, social work, education, biology, chemistry, and physics. Facilities at the university include an observatory, an herbarium, and the William W.W. Baker Center of Agriculture and Natural Resources. Total enrollment is approximately 3,400.

UNIVERSITY OF THE DISTRICT OF COLUMBIA

The University of the District of Columbia had its beginnings in Miner Normal (teacher-training) School, founded as a "school for colored girls" in 1851, and in Washington Normal School, founded for white female students in 1873. Both schools became four-year teachers colleges in 1929. In 1955 the colleges merged into District of Columbia Teachers College. Federal City College and Washington Technical Institute, which had been founded in 1966 and had received land-grant status in 1968, merged with the teachers college in 1977 to form the University of the District of Columbia. The District of Columbia Water Resources Research Center and the district's Agricultural Experiment Station are operated by the university, which also conducts research on social and economic urban problems at the Center for Applied Research and Urban Policy.

There are three campuses—the Georgia/Harvard Street campus, the Mount Vernon Square campus, and the Van Ness campus. The university consists of the University College, which all students attend until they declare their majors, and the colleges of Business and Public Management; Education and Human Ecology; Liberal and Fine Arts; Life Sciences; and Physical Science, Engineering, and Technology. The Graduate Studies Division offers master's degree programs in business administration, urban policy, and other areas. Total enrollment is approximately 14,000.

FISK UNIVERSITY

One of the most notable historically black institutions of higher education, Fisk University is affiliated with the United Church of Christ. It opened in Nashville, Tenn., in 1866 as Fisk School, named for Gen. Clinton B. Fisk of the Tennessee Freedmen's Bureau, who gave the school its original facilities in a former Union army barracks. It became a university the next year. In severe debt by 1871, the school emptied its treasury to finance a fundraising concert tour by a student group, the Fisk Jubilee Singers. As well as successfully raising funds, the Singers' concerts in the United States and Europe helped establish spirituals as an art form.

Fisk University offers undergraduate degree programs in business administration; humanities and fine arts, including religion and philosophy; natural science and mathematics, including computer science; and social sciences, including psychology and public administration. Master's degree programs in biology, chemistry, physics, general or clinical psychology, sociology, and social gerontology are also available, and a master's in business administration can be earned through a joint program with Vanderbilt University. The Center for Photonic Materials and Devices, funded by the National Aeronautics and Space Administration, and the Molecular Spectroscopy Research Laboratory are research units of the university. Enrollment is approximately 800 students.

Much of the important modern art collection of photographer Alfred Stieglitz was donated to the university by his wife, Georgia O'Keeffe, including paintings by O'Keeffe, Pablo Picasso, and Paul Cézanne. Among the collections at the university library are the papers of John Mercer Langston, George Gershwin, W. C. Handy, and alumnus W.E.B. Du Bois.

FLORIDA AGRICULTURAL AND MECHANICAL UNIVERSITY

Florida Agricultural and Mechanical University (better known as Florida A&M University) was founded in Tallahassee in 1887 as the State Normal College for Colored Students. In 1891 it was designated Florida's land-grant institution for African Americans, and its name was changed to the State Normal and Industrial College for Colored Students. It became Florida Agricultural and Mechanical College for Negroes in 1909 and awarded its first bachelor's degree the following year. Florida A&M was granted university status in 1953, and it became a full member of the state university system in 1971.

With an enrollment that remains predominantly African American, the present-day university includes colleges of Arts and Sciences, Education, Pharmacy and Pharmaceutical Sciences, and Engineering Sciences, Technology, and Agriculture. The university cooperates in a college of engineering with nearby Florida State University. It also includes the Environmental Sciences Institute and schools of Allied Health Sciences; Architecture; Business and Industry; Journalism, Media, and Graphic Arts; Nursing; General Studies; and Graduate Studies and Research. Graduate degree programs are available in many fields of study, and a professional degree in pharmacy is also offered. The College of Pharmacy and Pharmaceutical Sciences has extension campuses in Tampa and Miami. The campus is home to the Black Archives Research Center and Museum. Total enrollment is approximately 11,000.

GRAMBLING STATE UNIVERSITY

Grambling State University, located in Grambling, La., was founded in 1901 as The Colored Industrial and Agricultural School by the North Louisiana Colored Agricultural Relief Association in 1901. The name was changed in 1905 to the North Louisiana Agricultural and Industrial School. The school came under the control of the Lincoln Parish School Board in 1919, and its mission was expanded to include teacher training. In 1928 it became the Louisiana Negro Normal and Industrial Institute, a junior college under state control. In 1944 the institute began awarding bachelor's degrees, and in 1946 it was renamed Grambling College. It was elevated to university standing in 1974. Grambling's Eddie Robinson was among the most successful college gridiron-football coaches, being the first to win more than 400 games during his career.

The university comprises colleges of Basic Studies, Business, Education, Liberal Arts, and Science and Technology and the Earl Lester Cole Honors College. The university also includes schools of Nursing and Social Work. In addition to undergraduate studies, Grambling offers a variety of master's degree programs and a doctoral program in education. Total enrollment is approximately 6,000.

HAMPTON UNIVERSITY

Hampton University is a private institution located in Hampton, Va. Samuel Chapman Armstrong, a Union general during the Civil War and an agent for the Freedmen's Bureau after the war, recognized the need to educate the recently freed slaves. Armstrong raised funds for land and for construction of a school that would train African Americans as teachers, who would in turn educate the larger black population. The Hampton Normal and Agricultural Institute opened in 1868. From 1872 to 1920 the school received U.S. land-grant funds. The institute began awarding bachelor's degrees in 1922 and was accredited as a college in 1933; the school was raised to university status in 1984. The Peabody Collection at the university's main library contains a wealth of material on African American culture and history. Educator Booker T.

Washington is among the school's notable alumni.

The Undergraduate College consists of schools of Business, Liberal Arts and Education, Engineering and Technology, Nursing, Pharmacy, and Science. The Graduate College offers master's degree programs in business, nursing, education, and science, and doctoral

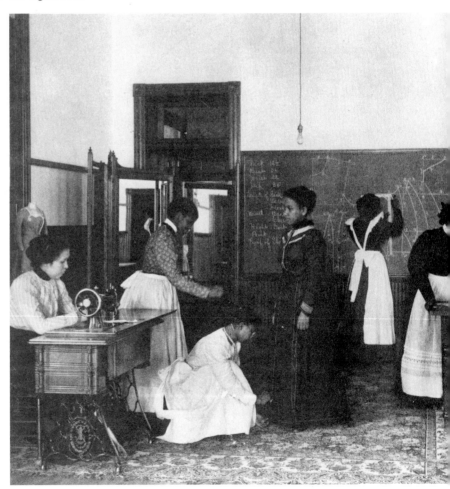

Students learning dressmaking at Hampton University, c. 1900. Library of Congress, Washington, D.C.

programs in physics, pharmacy, and physical therapy. Total enrollment is approximately 5,700.

HOWARD UNIVERSITY

Howard University was founded in 1867 in Washington, D.C., and named for General Oliver Otis Howard, head of the post-Civil War Freedmen's Bureau, who influenced Congress to appropriate funds for the school. The university is financially supported in large part by the U.S. government but is privately controlled.

Although Howard University has always been open to students of any ethnicity or creed, it was founded with a special obligation to provide advanced studies for African Americans. Its library is the leading research library on African American history. Academic divisions include the colleges or schools of Arts and Sciences; Business; Communications; Dentistry; Divinity; Education; Engineering, Architecture, and Computer Sciences; Law; Medicine; Pharmacy, Nursing, and Allied Health Sciences; and Social Work. There is also a graduate school. Although the student body at one time was virtually all black, students of other races began attending after World War II, especially in the graduate schools.

Many of Howard's graduates have advanced to leadership positions in education, social reform, and government. Among the most prominent have been U.S. Sen. Edward William Brooke of Massachusetts; sociologist E. Franklin Frazier; playwright Amiri Baraka (LeRoi Jones); statesman Ralph Bunche, a longtime member of the United Nations and recipient of the 1950 Nobel Prize for Peace, who established

Pharmacy students at Howard University, c. 1900. Library of Congress, Washington, D.C.

the school's political science department; soprano Jessye Norman; and Nobel Prize-winning author Toni Morrison.

KENTUCKY STATE UNIVERSITY

Kentucky State University was founded in Frankfort, Ky., in 1886 as the State Normal School for Colored Persons. The normal school opened in 1887 to prepare teachers for African American schools. In 1890 it was designated a land-grant college, and it graduated its first class that year. The name was changed to Kentucky Normal and Industrial Institute for Colored Persons in 1902 and to Kentucky State College for Negroes in 1938, shortened to Kentucky State College in 1952. Kentucky State was granted university standing in 1972.

The university consists of colleges of Arts and Sciences, Professional Studies, Schools of Business and Public Administration, and Whitney M. Young, Jr., College of Leadership Studies. The School of Public Administration offers bachelor's and master's degree programs in public policy and administration. The Whitney M. Young, Jr., College, which honours the university's most-noted alumnus, offers a great-books curriculum to undergraduate students. Historically an African American institution, Kentucky State University now has a racially balanced student body. Total enrollment is approximately 2,300. The campus also includes a 203-acre (82-hectare) agricultural research farm and aquaculture research program.

LANGSTON UNIVERSITY

Langston University was established by Oklahoma's territorial legislature in 1897 in Langston as the Colored Agricultural and Normal University. It was coeducational from the outset. African American settlers raised money to buy land for the school, which opened in a Presbyterian church in 1898. It was renamed Langston University (for African American educator and public official John Mercer Langston) in 1941. The E (Kika) de la Garza Institute for Goat Research is located there, and the university also conducts extension and research programs on topics such as grasslands resources.

It includes schools of Arts and Sciences, Business, Education and Behavioral Sciences, Agricultural and Applied Sciences, and Nursing and Health Professions. Graduate programs lead to a Master of Education degree or a Master of Science in rehabilitation counseling. The Airway Science program trains aviation personnel, including pilots, in cooperation with the Federal Aviation Administration and Oklahoma State University. The university maintains its Urban Centers in Tulsa and Oklahoma City. Total enrollment is approximately 4,000.

LINCOLN UNIVERSITY

Lincoln University, located in Jefferson City, Mo., had its origins in Lincoln Institute, conceived by Missouri soldiers of the 62nd U.S. Colored Infantry who were stationed near Galveston, Texas, during the Civil War. The 65th Colored Infantry also contributed to the school's founding. Classes for African American students were inaugurated in 1866. In 1870 the state began funding Lincoln's teacher-training program. College work was added to the curriculum in 1877, and two years later the school became a state institution. Under the provisions of the second Morrill Act, in 1890, Lincoln Institute became a land-grant institution. It achieved university status in 1921.

The university offers associate's, bachelor's, and master's degrees through colleges of Agriculture, Applied Sciences and Technology, Arts and Sciences, and business. Greenberry Farm and several other farms owned by the university are important to its agricultural education programs. Total enrollment is about 3,500 students.

MOREHOUSE COLLEGE

The origins of Morehouse College, a private liberal arts college for men, stem from the Augusta Institute, which was founded in 1867 in Augusta, Ga., and moved to Atlanta in 1879, becoming Atlanta Baptist Seminary. When it became Atlanta Baptist College in 1897, much of its curriculum resembled that of a high school. After the noted educator John Hope became president in 1906, the curriculum expanded, and the school became Morehouse College. In 1929 Atlanta University and Morehouse and Spelman colleges agreed to share resources. The agreement led to the

formation of the Atlanta University Center, in which six institutions of higher learning exchange faculty, students, facilities, and curricula. The Morehouse School of Medicine was founded as part of the college in 1978 and became independent three years later. Notable alumni include Martin Luther King, Jr., civil rights leader Julian Bond, and filmmaker Spike Lee.

The university offers bachelor's degree programs in business, education, humanities, and physical and natural sciences. Interdisciplinary majors are also available, as are study abroad programs in Africa, Central America, and Europe; joint engineering programs in cooperation with Georgia Institute of Technology, Boston and Auburn universities, and several other institutions; and a joint architecture program with the University of Michigan. The American Institute for Managing Diversity is affiliated with the college, and the Andrew Young Center for International Affairs and the Morehouse Research Institute are Morehouse College facilities. Total enrollment is approximately 3,000 students.

MORGAN STATE UNIVERSITY

Morgan State University dates to 1867, when the Methodist Episcopal Church established it in Baltimore as the Centenary Biblical Institute. In 1890 the school was given the name Morgan College, in honour of donor Lyttleton F. Morgan. The Methodists continued to operate the school until it was purchased by the state of Maryland in 1939. The School of Graduate Studies was authorized in 1963. Morgan State was elevated to university status in 1975.

Today the university is a coeducational institution with an emphasis on liberal arts and sciences, particularly urban studies. University-sponsored research and public service programs also focus on issues of urban life. The College of Arts and Sciences is the largest academic division. The university also includes the Institute of Architecture and Planning and Schools of Business and Management, Education and Urban Studies, Engineering, and Graduate Studies. Morgan State offers both bachelor's degree and master's degree programs; doctorates are awarded in urban educational leadership, history, mathematics education, and science education. Campus facilities include a supercomputer, the Entrepreneur Center, and the Soper Library, which houses collections of African and African American books and materials. There are approximately 5,000 full-time students enrolled at the university.

OBERLIN COLLEGE

Although not a historically black institution, Oberlin College, a private coeducational college located in Oberlin, Ohio, has a place in African American history because it admitted blacks on an equal footing with whites, and it, along with the town, became a station on the Underground Railroad. It was founded by Presbyterian minister John J. Shipherd and Philo P. Stewart in 1833 as the Oberlin Collegiate Institute to educate ministers and schoolteachers for the West. It was named for the Alsatian pastor Johann Friedrich Oberlin and was designated a college in 1850. The institution was coeducational from its beginning. Charles Grandison Finney, the college's president from 1851 to 1866, was a well-known evangelist. Charles Martin Hall, an alumnus who had in 1886 developed an inexpensive method of making aluminum commercially, bequeathed to the college a large endowment and the funds to construct Hall Auditorium. Oberlin now consists of a college of Arts and Sciences and the Oberlin Conservatory of Music (1865), which is one of the oldest professional music schools in the United States.

SOUTH CAROLINA STATE UNIVERSITY

South Carolina State University traces its origins to 1872 with the creation of the South Carolina Agricultural and Mechanical Institute within Claflin College, an African American institution of higher education in Orangeburg, S.C. The institute was separated from Claflin in 1896 and established as the Colored Normal, Industrial, Agricultural and Mechanical College of South Carolina, the state's land-grant college for African American students. The college was renamed South Carolina State College in 1954 and was granted university status in 1992.

The public coeducational university offers numerous bachelor's degree programs through schools of Applied Professional Sciences, Arts and Humanities, Business, Education, and Engineering Technology and Sciences. Master's degree programs are offered in agribusiness, education, and human services. There is also a doctorate program in education. Total enrollment is about 4,500.

SOUTHERN UNIVERSITY

Based on a state constitutional convention mandate of 1879, Southern University was chartered and incorporated in 1880 "for the education of persons of color." It opened in Baton Rouge in 1881. In 1890 an agricultural and mechanical department was added. Two years later it became a land-grant institution under the aegis of the Federal Act of 1890, known as the Second Morrill Act. In 1914 it closed and was relocated to Scotlandville, a suburb adjoining Baton Rouge. The Law Center, established in 1946, opened the following year, while the Graduate School began operations in 1957. The campus at New Orleans was founded in 1956 and opened in 1959. The campus was integrated after a white woman sued the institution in 1964. That same year the Shreveport campus was established; it opened in 1967. Notable among the school's courses of study is a unique associate degree program in jazz, with an emphasis on Louisiana music.

The main unit of this state-supported university system, Southern University and Agricultural and Mechanical College, in Baton Rouge, offers about 65 undergraduate degree programs and some 30 graduate programs. John B. Cade Library contains a Black Heritage Collection. University centres conduct research in such fields as energy and the environment, sickle-cell disease, agriculture, business, and social issues. Southern conducts various programs in conjunction with Louisiana State University, which is also based in Baton Rouge. The New Orleans campus comprises colleges of Arts and Social Sciences, Education, Business, and Science, as well as a School of Social Work. The Shreveport campus is a two-year college that grants three associate degrees. Total enrollment on all three campuses exceeds 15,000 students.

SPELMAN COLLEGE

A private liberal arts institution for women in Atlanta, Spelman College traces its history to 1881, when two Boston women, Sophia Packard and Harriet Giles, began teaching a small group of African American women, mostly ex-slaves, in an Atlanta church basement. Two years later the school moved to the site of Fort McPherson, which had been a Union training site during the Civil War. Donations from industrialist and philanthropist John D. Rockefeller, beginning in 1884, assured the school's security and growth in its early decades. The school was named Spelman Seminary for Rockefeller's wife's mother. It began awarding college degrees in 1901 and became Spelman College in 1924. In 1929 an agreement between Spelman College, Morehouse College, and Atlanta University formed what would become the Atlanta University Center, which consists of Spelman and five other African American institutions in Atlanta sharing students, faculty, facilities, and curricula. Notable alumnae include lawyer and civil rights activist Marian Wright Edelman, musician and historian Bernice Johnson Reagon, and writer Alice Walker.

Spelman offers bachelor's degrees in more than 20 fields, including arts, sciences, psychology, computer science, economics, languages, philosophy, political science, religion, and sociology. It also offers an independent-major option, premedical and prelaw programs, and dual-degree engineering programs with a dozen other institutions. Total enrollment is about 2,000.

TENNESSEE STATE UNIVERSITY

The institution that became Tennessee State University was created by a 1909 act of the Tennessee state legislature and opened in Nashville in 1912 as the Agricultural and Industrial State Normal School. It became a four-year teachers college in 1922 and awarded its first bachelor's degree in 1924; university standing was granted in 1951. The university absorbed the University of Tennessee at Nashville in 1979. A historically black university, it still has a largely African American enrollment. Notable graduates

include talk-show host Oprah Winfrey and Olympic athletes Ralph Boston, Wilma Rudolph, and Wyomia Tyus.

Part of the State University and Community College System of Tennessee and a land-grant school, the university consists of colleges of Arts and Sciences, Business, Education, and Engineering and Technology and schools of Agriculture and Home Economics, Nursing, and Graduate Studies and Research; the School of Allied Health Professions is administered jointly with Meharry Medical College, also in Nashville. The university offers a range of undergraduate and graduate degree programs. There are also doctoral programs in education, psychology, biological science, and public administration. Total enrollment exceeds 8,000.

TUSKEGEE UNIVERSITY

Tuskegee University's establishment in Tuskegee, Ala., as a school for training African American teachers was approved by the Alabama state legislature in 1880. Founder Booker T. Washington opened the school in 1881 in a one-room shanty, serving as Tuskegee's principal until his death in 1915. The Tuskegee Normal and Industrial Institute (the school's fourth name; 1891–1937) inculcated Washington's principles of providing practical training for African Americans and helping them develop economic self-reliance through the mastery of manual trades and agricultural skills. In the 1920s Tuskegee shifted from

ANONYMOUS: ON EDUCATING AFRICAN AMERICAN WOMEN

Freedom's Journal, the first African American newspaper, served not only as a forum for the abolitionist sentiments of educated African Americans but also as an official sounding board for the average African American whose views heretofore had seldom been published. The Aug. 10, 1827, issue of the paper carried the following letter, in which an anonymous author, "Matilda," made a humble plea for female education. It is noteworthy not only as one of the earliest entreaties for women's rights made by an African American but also because it was written when Emma Hart Willard and Catharine Beecher were just beginning their crusades for the educational rights of women. Source: Freedom's Journal, Aug. 10, 1827.

Messrs. Editors,

Will you allow a female to offer a few remarks upon a subject that you must allow to be all-important? I don't know that in any of your papers you have said sufficient upon the education of females. I hope you are not to be classed with those who think that our mathematical knowledge should be limited to "fathoming the dish-kettle," and that we have acquired enough of history if we know that our grandfather's father lived and died. It is true the time has been when to darn a stocking and cook a pudding well was considered the end and aim of a woman's being. But those were days when ignorance blinded men's eyes. The diffusion of knowledge has destroyed those degrading opinions, and men of the present age allow that we have minds that are capable and deserving of culture.

There are difficulties, and great difficulties, in the way of our advancement; but that should only stir us to greater efforts. We possess not the advantages with those of our sex whose skins are not colored like our own, but we can improve what little we have and make our one talent produce twofold. The influence that we have over the male sex demands that our minds should be instructed and improved with the principles of education and religion, in order that this influence should be properly directed. Ignorant ourselves, how can we be expected to form the minds of our youth and conduct them in the paths of knowledge? How can we "teach the young idea how to shoot" if we have none ourselves? There is a great responsibility resting somewhere, and it is time for us to be up and doing.

I would address myself to all mothers, and say to them that while it is necessary to possess a knowledge of cookery and the various mysteries of pudding making, something more is requisite. It is their bounden duty to store their daughters' minds with useful learning. They should be made to devote their leisure time to reading books, whence they would derive valuable information which could never be taken from them.

I will not longer trespass on your time and patience. I merely throw out these hints in order that some more able pen will take up the subject.

Matilda

vocational education to academic higher education and became an accredited, degree-granting institute. It was renamed Tuskegee Institute in 1937 and began offering graduate-level instruction in 1943; the institute was elevated to university status in 1985. The renowned agricultural chemist George Washington Carver, who headed the school's agriculture department, conducted most of his research at Tuskegee from 1896 until his death in 1943. The school's third president, Frederick Douglass Patterson (served 1935–53), was the founder of the United Negro College Fund (1944).

The private coeducational university, which still serves a predominantly African American student body, offers a wide variety of bachelor's, master's, and doctorate degrees and is renowned for its science and engineering programs. The George Washington Carver Museum on campus includes the laboratory used by Carver for his work on the peanut (groundnut) and sweet potato. The university's library contains a notable collection of books pertaining to African Americans. The Booker T. Washington

Monument shows the institute's founder lifting a "veil of ignorance" from the head of a former slave. Washington's home, The Oaks, is also preserved on campus. A section of the campus was declared a national historic site in 1974. The National Center for Bioethics in Research and Health Care was established at the university in 1998 as a response to the infamous Tuskegee syphilis study (1932–72) conducted through the auspices of the school. The university's enrollment is more than 3,000 students.

Booker T. Washington (front row, centre left), *with Andrew Carnegie and other sponsors of Tuskegee Institute, Alabama, 1903.* Library of Congress, Washington, D.C.

VIRGINIA STATE UNIVERSITY

In 1882, Alfred W. Harris, an African American state legislator, sponsored the bill that founded Virginia Normal and Collegiate Institute, forerunner of Virginia State University. An antagonistic lawsuit delayed the school's opening in Petersburg, Va., until October 1883, and insufficient support from the state hindered its progress in its early years. In 1902 the legislature reduced the school's collegiate programs and changed its name to Virginia Normal and Industrial Institute. It became Virginia's African American land-grant school in 1920, and three years later its collegiate programs were reinstated. It was renamed Virginia State College for Negroes in 1930 and Virginia State College in 1946; it was raised to university status in 1979. Norfolk State University, Virginia State's Norfolk branch, was founded in 1944 and became independent in 1969.

The public coeducational institution consists of schools of Agriculture, Business, Liberal Arts and Education, Science and Technology, and Graduate Studies and Continuing Education. It awards a variety of bachelor's degrees, and more than half of its departments offer graduate programs. Total enrollment is approximately 4,000 students.

WILBERFORCE UNIVERSITY

The oldest historically black private college in the United States, Wilberforce University was founded in Wilberforce, Ohio, in 1856 by members of the Methodist Episcopal Church. Hardships resulting from the Civil War caused the university to close in 1862, but the next year it was bought by the African Methodist Episcopal Church and reopened. The state of Ohio established a normal and industrial department at the university in 1887. Prominent alumni have included educator Hallie Quinn Brown and composer William Grant Still.

The liberal arts university offers undergraduate programs in business, engineering, sciences, humanities, and other areas. All students must participate in the cooperative education program, which complements traditional campus study with work experience.

SUMMARY

The dramatic desegregation in the 1960s of American colleges and universities—such as the University of Georgia by Charlayne Hunter and Hamilton Holmes in 1961 and the University of Mississippi by James Meredith in 1962—helped to open higher education more widely to African Americans. Nevertheless, the historically black colleges and universities described in this chapter remain an essential part of the academy, albeit, in many cases, with their own increasingly diverse student bodies.

CHAPTER 9

LITERATURE AND THE ARTS

AFRICAN AMERICAN LITERATURE TO THE 1940S

Since the pre-Revolutionary War period, African American writers have engaged in a creative if often contentious dialogue with American letters. The result is a literature rich in expressive subtlety and social insight, offering illuminating assessments of American identities and history. This literature has been recognized nationally as well as internationally since its inception in the late 18th century.

SLAVE NARRATIVES

In the wake of the bloody Nat Turner rebellion in Southampton county, Virginia, in 1831, an increasingly fervent antislavery movement in the United States sponsored firsthand autobiographical accounts of slavery by fugitives from the South in order to make abolitionists of a largely indifferent white Northern readership. From 1830 to the end of the slavery era, the fugitive slave narrative dominated the literary landscape of antebellum black America. The *Narrative of the Life of Frederick Douglass, an American Slave, Written by Himself* (1845) gained the most attention, establishing Frederick Douglass as the leading African American man of letters of his time. By predicating his struggle for freedom on his

solitary pursuit of literacy, education, and independence, Douglass portrayed himself as a self-made man, which appealed strongly to middle-class white Americans. In his second, revised autobiography, *My Bondage and My Freedom* (1855), Douglass depicted himself as a product of a slave community in Maryland's Eastern Shore and explained how his struggles for independence and liberty did not end when he reached the so-called "free states" of the North. Harriet Jacobs's *Incidents in the Life of a Slave Girl* (1861), the first autobiography by a formerly enslaved African American woman, candidly describes her experience of the sexual exploitation that made slavery especially oppressive for black women. Chronicling what she called "the war" of her life, which ultimately won both her own freedom and that of her two children, Jacobs proved the inadequacy of the image of victim that had been applied pervasively to female slaves. Her work and the antislavery and feminist oratory of the New York ex-slave who renamed herself Sojourner Truth (from Isabella Van Wagener) enriched early African American literature with unprecedented models of female eloquence and heroism.

PROSE, DRAMA, AND POETRY

Through the slave narrative, African Americans entered the world of prose and dramatic literature. In 1853 William Wells Brown, an internationally known fugitive slave narrator, authored the first black American novel, *Clotel; or, The President's Daughter*. It tells the tragic story of the beautiful light-skinned African American daughter of Thomas Jefferson and his slave mistress; Clotel dies trying to save her own daughter from slavery. Five years later Brown also published the first African American play, *The Escape; or, A Leap for Freedom*, based on scenes and themes familiar to readers of fugitive slave narratives. In the late 1850s Martin R. Delany, a black journalist and physician who would later serve as a major in the Union army during the Civil War, wrote *Blake; or, The Huts of America* (serially published in 1859), a novel whose hero plots a slave revolt in the South. In 1859 the first African American women's fiction appeared: "The Two Offers," a short story by Frances Ellen Watkins Harper dealing with middle-class women whose race is not specified, and Harriet E. Wilson's *Our Nig; or, Sketches from the Life of a Free Black*, an autobiographical novel about the life of a working-class black woman in the North. *The Bondwoman's Narrative* (2002), an apparently fictionalized slave narrative discovered in manuscript in the early 21st century, also may be among the earliest contributions to African American women's fiction, but the identity of its author, Hannah Crafts, has yet to be confirmed. Harper, by contrast, was renowned in mid-19th-century black America as the poetic voice of her people, a writer whose verse was direct, impassioned, and poignant. She and James M. Whitfield, author of a volume of spirited protest poetry entitled *America and Other Poems* (1853), helped ensure that the 1850s would become the first African American literary renaissance.

ORAL TRADITION

Behind the achievements of individual African American writers during the antislavery era lies the communal consciousness of millions of slaves, whose oral tradition in song and story has given form and substance to much subsequent literature by black Americans. Douglass recalled that the plantation spiritual *Run to Jesus* had first suggested to him the thought of making his escape from slavery. When slaves sang "I thank God I'm free at last," only they knew whether they were referring to freedom from sin or from slavery. A second great fund of Southern black folklore, the beast fables that originated in Africa testified to the slaves' commonsense understanding of human psychology and everyday justice. The slaves selected for special celebration trickster figures.

TRICKSTER TALE

In oral traditions worldwide, trickster tales feature a protagonist (often an anthropomorphized animal) who has magical powers and is characterized as a compendium of opposites. Simultaneously an omniscient creator and an innocent fool, a malicious destroyer and a childlike prankster, the trickster-hero serves as a sort of folkloric scapegoat onto which are projected the fears, failures, and unattained ideals of the source culture.

Trickster stories may be told for amusement as well as on serious or sacred occasions. Depending on the context, either a single tale or a series of interrelated stories might be told. The typical tale recounts a picaresque adventure: the trickster is "going along," encounters a situation to which he responds with knavery, stupidity, gluttony, or guile (or, most often, some combination of these), and meets a violent or ludicrous end. Often the trickster serves as a transformer and culture hero who creates order out of chaos. He may teach humans the skills of survival, usually through negative examples that end with his utter failure to accomplish these tasks. Frequently he is accompanied by a companion who either serves as a stooge or ultimately tricks the trickster.

As with other forms of culture, trickster tales are apt to develop and evolve when differing societies interact. One such case occurred during the colonial period in North America, as Hare (or Rabbit) was a common trickster in Africa as well as in the New World. Over time, as Native Americans and enslaved Africans met and exchanged elements of culture, their separate Hare traditions produced a new trickster, Brer, or Brother, Rabbit, who was popularized in the United States in the stories of Joel Chandler Harris (1848–1908). The Brer Rabbit tales share many features of traditional African trickster stories: the trickster is an underdog,

MINSTREL SHOW

One of the most curious and revealing American art forms of the 19th and early 20th centuries was the minstrel show (also called minstrelsy), a theatrical form that reached its zenith between 1850 and 1870 and that was founded on the comic enactment of stereotypes of African Americans. The earliest minstrel shows were staged by white male minstrels (traveling musicians) who, with their faces painted black, caricatured the singing and dancing of slaves. Scholars usually distinguish this form of the tradition as blackface minstrelsy. The father of the blackface show was Thomas Dartmouth Rice, popularly known as "Jim Crow," an early African American impersonator whose performances created a vogue for the genre. The pioneer company, the Virginia Minstrels, a quartet headed by Daniel Decatur Emmett, first performed in 1843. Other noteworthy companies were Bryant's, Campbell's, and Haverly's, but the most important of the early companies was the Christy Minstrels, who played on Broadway for nearly 10 years; Stephen Foster wrote songs for this company.

The format of the minstrel show, usually in two parts, was established by the Christy company and changed little thereafter. In part one the performers were arranged in a semicircle, with the interlocutor in the centre and the end men—Mr. Tambo, who played the tambourine, and Mr. Bones, who rattled the bones (a pair of clappers, named after the original material from which they were made)—at the ends. The interlocutor, in whiteface, usually wore formal attire; the others, in blackface, wore gaudy swallow-tailed coats and striped trousers. The program opened with a chorus, often as a grand entrance, and at the conclusion of the song the interlocutor gave the command, "Gentlemen, be seated." Then followed a series of jokes between the interlocutor and end men, interspersed with ballads, comic songs, and instrumental numbers, chiefly on the banjo and violin. The second part, or olio (mixture or medley), consisted of a series of individual acts that concluded with a hoedown or walk-around in which every member did a specialty number while the others sang and clapped. Occasionally there was a third part consisting of a farce, burlesque, or comic opera.

Minstrel troupes composed of African American performers were formed after the Civil War, and a number of these, including the Hicks and Sawyer Minstrels, had black owners and managers. Some, such as Callendar's Consolidated Spectacular Colored Minstrels, were popular in both the United States and Britain in the late 19th and early 20th centuries. The larger African American minstrel shows included bands of multitalented instrumentalists to play marches for the troupe's parades in the daytime and perform string accompaniments for the evening shows. In addition to some music by Foster, their repertoire featured music by black composers such as James Bland, a popular singer-banjoist who wrote some 700 songs, including Carry Me Back to Old Virginny. In general, these minstrel shows were the only theatrical medium in which gifted African performers of the period could support themselves.

A few of the larger companies employed both black and white performers. By the 20th century, women also began appearing in minstrel shows; the great blues singers Ma Rainey and Bessie Smith were both minstrel performers early in their careers. Minstrel shows had effectively disappeared by the mid-20th century. However, vestiges of their racial stereotyping and performance aesthetics would persist for decades in various performance mediums.

smaller in stature and strength than his opponents (thus gaining the audience's sympathy) but much cleverer and always well in control of the situation. However, African trickster tales usually centre upon a particular victim, such as Hyena, Lion, or Elephant, while Brer Rabbit tales, like their Native American counterparts, tend to repeatedly revisit the same cast of characters—Brer Fox, Brer Wolf, and Brer Bear. In African tales the trickster's prey is usually earnest, hardworking, and slow-witted and soon yields to the smooth arguments and attractive promises of his opponent; in contrast, it is usually Brer Rabbit's opponents who instigate conflict, forcing him to rely upon his charm, speed, diminutive size, and guile—characteristics that save him from trouble in some cases only to ensnare him in difficulty in others.

THE CIVIL WAR AND RECONSTRUCTION

With the outbreak of the Civil War, many African Americans deployed their pens and voices to convince President Abraham Lincoln that the nation was engaged in nothing less than a war to end slavery, which black men, initially barred from enlisting, should be allowed to fight. This agitation led eventually to a decisive force of 180,000 black soldiers joining the Union army. Charlotte Forten, daughter of a wealthy Philadelphia civil rights activist and author of the most important African American diary of the 19th century (a recent edition of which is

The Journals of Charlotte Forten Grimké [1988]), spoke for most black Americans when she wrote of Lincoln's Emancipation Proclamation: "Ah, what a grand, glorious day this has been. The dawn of freedom which it heralds may not break upon us at once; but it will surely come." When the Civil War effectively ended with Robert E. Lee's surrender on April 9, 1865, African Americans hoped finally to witness a new era of freedom and opportunity.

The short-lived era of Reconstruction in the United States (1865–77) elicited an unprecedented optimism from African

A portrait of Elizabeth Keckley, by an unknown artist, from the frontispiece to her autobiography, Behind the Scenes; or, Thirty Years a Slave and Four Years in the White House *(1868).*

American writers. Elizabeth Keckley, who rose from slavery in St. Louis to become the modiste (dressmaker) and confidante of first lady Mary Todd Lincoln, articulated in her autobiography, *Behind the Scenes; or, Thirty Years a Slave and Four Years in the White House* (1868), a spirit of sectional reconciliation espoused by many other leading African Americans of the Reconstruction era. Autobiographies such as Brown's *My Southern Home* (1880) and Douglass's *Life and Times of Frederick Douglass* (1881) joined Keckley's in anticipating progress for the newly freed men and women of the South under the benevolent eye of reformed government in the South. In *Sketches of Southern Life* (1872), a volume of poems based on her own travels among the freed people of the South, Harper created an effective counter to the popular white stereotype of the passive and incompetent ex-slave in the person of Aunt Chloe Fleet, whose wit and wisdom expressed in Southern folk vernacular evinced the literary potential of African American dialect writing.

THE LATE 19TH AND EARLY 20TH CENTURIES

As educational opportunity expanded among African Americans after the war, a self-conscious black middle class with serious literary ambitions emerged in the later 19th century. Their challenge lay in reconciling the genteel style and sentimental tone of much popular American literature, which middle-class black writers often imitated, to a real-world sociopolitical agenda that, after the abandonment of Reconstruction in the South, obliged African American writers to argue the case for racial justice to an increasingly indifferent white audience. In the mid-1880s Oberlin College graduate Anna Julia Cooper, a distinguished teacher and the author of *A Voice from the South* (1892), began a speaking and writing career that highlighted the centrality of educated black women in the broad-gauged reform movements in black communities of the post-Reconstruction era.

African American poetry developed along two paths after 1880. The traditionalists were led by Albery Allson Whitman, who made his fame among black readers with two book-length epic poems, *Not a Man, and Yet a Man* (1877) and *The Rape of Florida* (1884), the latter written in Spenserian stanzas.

PAUL LAURENCE DUNBAR

On Aug. 25, 1893, Whitman shared the platform for African American literature at the Chicago World's Fair with a 21-year-old Ohioan named Paul Laurence Dunbar, who had just that year published his first volume of poetry, *Oak and Ivy*. Though not the first black American to write poetry in so-called Negro dialect, Dunbar was by far the most successful, both critically and financially. Deeply ambivalent about his white readers' preference for what he called "a jingle in a broken tongue," Dunbar wrote a great deal of verse in standard diction and form, including a handful of lyrics, such as *We Wear the Mask,Sympathy,* and *The Haunted Oak,* that testify candidly and movingly to his frustrated aspirations as a black poet in a white supremacist era. The first professional African American writer, Dunbar also authored a large body of fiction, including four novels, the most important of which—*The Sport of the Gods* (1901)—offered a bleak view of African American prospects in urban America that anticipated the work of Richard Wright.

THE NOVEL AS SOCIAL ANALYSIS

While most of Dunbar's fiction was designed primarily to entertain his white readers, in the hands of Harper, Sutton E. Griggs, and Charles W. Chesnutt, the novel became an instrument of social analysis and direct confrontation with the prejudices, stereotypes, and racial mythologies that allowed whites to ignore worsening social conditions for blacks in the last decades of the 19th century. Harper's *Iola Leroy; or, Shadows Uplifted* (1892) attempted to counter specious notions of slavery popularized by white writers who idealized plantation life, while offering models of socially committed

middle-class African Americans who exemplified the ideals of uplift that motivated much of Harper's writing. Griggs, a Baptist minister who wrote five novels and founded a publishing company, excoriated racism in his fiction, stressing the need for his educated middle-class heroes

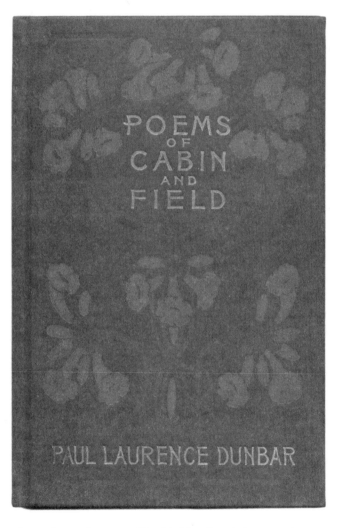

The embossed cover of Dodd, Mead and Company's 1899 illustrated edition of Paul Laurence Dunbar's Poems of Cabin and Field. Between the Covers Rare Books, Merchantville, N.J.

and heroines to turn away from whiteness as a standard of value and rely instead on self-determination and racial solidarity. Unlike Harper and Griggs, whose fiction won few readers outside black communities, Chesnutt attracted the backing of prestigious publishing houses in Boston and New York. Between 1899 and 1905 he published two books of short stories and three novels of purpose that addressed the causes and consequences of racial problems in the postwar South. Based on the Wilmington, N.C., racial massacre of 1898, Chesnutt's *The Marrow of Tradition* (1901) was reviewed extensively throughout the United States as a timely study of troubling contemporary issues, but its commercial success was limited, probably because of its unsparing assessment of white supremacy.

BOOKER T. WASHINGTON AND W.E.B. DU BOIS

As segregation regimes took hold in the South in the 1890s with the tacit approval of the rest of the country, many African Americans found a champion in Booker T. Washington and adopted his self-help autobiography, *Up from Slavery* (1901), as their guidebook to improved fortunes. Washington portrayed his own life in such a way as to suggest that even the most disadvantaged of black people could attain dignity and prosperity in the South by proving themselves valuable, productive members of society deserving

of fair and equal treatment before the law. A classic American success story, *Up from Slavery* solidified Washington's reputation as the most eminent African American of the new century. Yet Washington's primacy was soon challenged. In his landmark collection of essays, *The Souls of Black Folk* (1903), William Edward Burghardt Du Bois, a professor of sociology at Atlanta University, disputed the main principle of Washington's political program, the idea that voting and civil rights were less important to black progress than acquiring property and achieving economic self-sufficiency. Unlike Washington, who foresaw the steady obliteration of racial prejudice and discrimination, Du Bois prophesied in the opening lines of *The Souls of Black Folk*: "The problem of the Twentieth Century is the problem of the color-line." An uncompromising advocate of civil and voting rights, Du Bois asserted in *The Souls of Black Folk* that through "work, culture, and liberty" the dual heritage of African Americans—what he called "double-consciousness"—could be melded into a force for positive social and cultural change in the United States. Du Bois's striving to dramatize in his narrator a synthesis of racial and national consciousness dedicated to "the ideal of human brotherhood" made *The Souls of Black Folk* one of the most provocative and influential works of African American literature in the 20th century.

THE CRISIS

Founded in 1910 and, for its first 24 years, edited by W.E.B. Du Bois, the monthly magazine The Crisis (its full name was The Crisis: A Record of the Darker Races) was published by the National Association for the Advancement of Colored People (NAACP). By the end of its first decade it had achieved a monthly circulation of 100,000 copies. In its pages, Du Bois displayed the evolution of his thought from his early, hopeful insistence on racial justice to his resigned call for black separatism.

The Crisis was an important medium for the young black writers of the Harlem Renaissance, especially from 1919 to 1926, when Jessie Redmon Fauset was its literary editor. The writers she discovered or encouraged included the poets Arna Bontemps, Langston Hughes, and Countee Cullen and the novelist-poet Jean Toomer. Under Fauset's literary guidance The Crisis, along with the magazine Opportunity, was the leading publisher of young black authors. After Fauset's departure The Crisis was unable to sustain its high literary standards.

THE RISE OF THE NEW NEGRO

During the first two decades of the 20th century, rampant racial injustices, led by weekly reports of grisly lynchings, gave strong impetus to protest writing. From the editor's desk of the *Colored American Magazine*, Pauline E. Hopkins wrote novels, short stories, editorials, and social commentary in the early 1900s that attempted to revive the fervour of the antislavery era. The founding of the National Association for the Advancement of Colored People (NAACP) in 1909 in New York City put Du Bois in charge of its organ, *The Crisis*, which, as its editor from 1910 to 1934, he fashioned into the most widely read African American magazine of its time. In 1912 future NAACP leader James Weldon Johnson, poet, diplomat, and journalist, published anonymously *The Autobiography of an Ex-Colored Man*, a psychological novel that employed the theme of passing for white to explore the double consciousness of its protagonist with a dispassionate objectivity unattempted in African American fiction up to that point. By the time the United States entered World War I in 1917, Harlem was well on its way to becoming what Johnson called "the greatest Negro city in the world," attracting key intellectual leaders and artists such as Du Bois and Johnson, not to mention thousands of migrants from the South and Midwest whose talents and aspirations would fuel in the 1920s the second great renaissance of African American culture.

THE HARLEM RENAISSANCE

The phenomenon known as the Harlem Renaissance represented the flowering in literature and art of the New Negro movement of the 1920s, epitomized in *The New Negro* (1925), an anthology edited by Alain Locke that featured the early work of some of the most gifted Harlem Renaissance writers, including the poets Countee Cullen, Langston Hughes, and Claude McKay and the novelists Rudolph Fisher, Zora Neale Hurston, and Jean Toomer. The "New Negro," Locke announced, differed from the "Old Negro" in assertiveness and self-confidence, leading New Negro writers to question traditional "white" aesthetic standards, to eschew parochialism and propaganda, and to cultivate personal self-expression, racial pride, and literary experimentation. Spurred by an unprecedented receptivity to black writing on the part of major American magazines, book publishers, and white patrons, the literary vanguard of the Harlem Renaissance enjoyed critical favour and financial rewards that lasted, at least for a few, until well into the Great Depression of the 1930s.

CLAUDE McKAY, LANGSTON HUGHES, AND COUNTEE CULLEN

McKay is generally regarded as the first major poet of the Harlem Renaissance. His best poetry, including sonnets ranging from the militant *If We Must Die* (1919) to the brooding self-portrait *Outcast*, was collected in *Harlem Shadows* (1922), which some critics have called the first great literary achievement of the Harlem Renaissance. Admiring McKay as well as Dunbar, Hughes exchanged McKay's formalism for the free verse of Walt Whitman and Carl Sandburg. Hughes also found ways to write in an African American street vernacular that registers a much wider and deeper spectrum of mood than Dunbar was able to represent in his poetry. Hughes earned his greatest praise for his experimental jazz and blues poetry in *The Weary Blues* (1926) and *Fine Clothes to the Jew* (1927). While McKay and Hughes embraced the rank and file of black America and proudly identified themselves as black poets, Cullen sought success through writing in traditional forms and employing a lyricism informed by the work of John Keats. His lingering ambivalence about racial identification as a man or a poet is movingly evoked in his most famous poem, *Heritage* (1925). In contrast, James Weldon Johnson embraced the African American oral tradition in *God's Trombones* (1927), his verse tribute to the folk sermon tradition of Southern blacks.

NOVELISTS

McKay and Hughes made names for themselves in prose as well. McKay's novel *Home to Harlem* (1928) garnered a substantial readership, especially among those curious about the more lurid side of Harlem's nightlife. A lasting achievement in autobiography was Hughes's *The Big*

Sea (1940), arguably the most insightful and unsentimental first-person account of the Harlem Renaissance ever published. Yet the most notable narratives produced by the Harlem Renaissance came from Toomer (himself an accomplished poet), Fisher, Wallace Thurman, Hurston, and Nella Larsen. Toomer's *Cane* (1923), an avant-garde collection of sketches, fiction, poetry, and drama, set a standard for experimentalism that few practitioners of any one of these genres could match for the rest of the decade. Like T. S. Eliot's modernist classic *The Waste Land* (1922), *Cane*, although deliberately fragmented, was designed to achieve a unified effect through its impressionistic use of language and its recurrent attention to questions of African American identity. Fisher's *The Walls of Jericho* (1928) won critical applause because of the novel's balanced satire of class and colour prejudice among black New Yorkers. In 1932 Fisher brought out *The Conjure Man Dies*, often referred to as the first African American detective novel. Thurman's *The Blacker the Berry* (1929) exposes colour prejudice among African Americans and is among the first African American novels to broach the topic of homosexuality. The struggles and frustrations Larsen revealed in the black female protagonists of her novels *Quicksand* (1928) and *Passing* (1929) likely register the problems their creator faced as a sophisticated New Negro woman trying to find her own way in the supposedly liberated racial and sexual atmosphere of the 1920s. Like

Toomer, Larsen fell silent after the Harlem Renaissance. Of the major fiction writers of the Harlem Renaissance, only Florida native Hurston, whose early short stories appeared in the late 1920s but who did not publish a novel until after the Harlem Renaissance had ended, published a masterwork that guaranteed her permanent reputation among African American novelists. In *Their Eyes Were Watching God* (1937), Hurston embodied the sustaining ethos of a vibrant working-class Southern black community in a woman whose sassy tongue and heroic reclamation of herself make Janie Crawford what many would consider the greatest single literary character created by the New Negro generation.

PLAYWRIGHTS AND EDITORS

Although the most memorable literary achievement of the Harlem Renaissance was in narrative prose and poetry, the movement also inspired dramatists such as Willis Richardson, whose *The Chip Woman's Fortune* (produced 1923) was the first nonmusical play by an African American to be produced on Broadway. African American editors such as Charles S. Johnson, whose monthly *Opportunity* was launched in 1923 under the auspices of the National Urban League, and the respected Caribbean-born short-story writer Eric Walrond, who published young black writers in *Negro World*, the organ of Marcus Garvey's Universal Negro Improvement Association, provided significant visibility for New

Negro writers. Anthologies, particularly of poetry, abounded during the Harlem Renaissance, enhancing the literary reputations of both the writers represented in them and their editors. The editors included James Weldon Johnson (*The Book of American Negro Poetry* [1922] and *The Book of American Negro Spirituals* [1925, 1926]), Charles S. Johnson (*Ebony and Topaz* [1927]), and Cullen (*Caroling Dusk* [1927]), to mention only a handful of the most noteworthy.

THE ADVENT OF URBAN REALISM

Despite the enormous outpouring of creativity during the 1920s, the vogue of black writing, black art, and black culture waned markedly in the early 1930s as the Great Depression took hold in the United States. African American pundits in the 1930s and '40s tended to depreciate the achievements of the New Negroes, calling instead for a more politically engaged, socially critical realism in literature.

THE 1940S

During the 1930s and '40s Hughes and Sterling A. Brown kept the folk spirit alive in African American poetry. An admirer of Hughes, Margaret Walker dedicated *For My People* (1942), the title poem of which remains one of the most popular texts for recitation and performance in African American literature, to the same black American rank and file whom Hughes and Brown celebrated. By

the early 1940s three figures, Melvin B. Tolson, Robert Hayden, and Chicagoan Gwendolyn Brooks, were showing how the vernacular tradition could be adapted to modernist experimentation. The variety of expressiveness and formal innovation in African American poetry of the 1940s is reflected in Tolson's densely allusive *Rendezvous with America* (1942), Hayden's meditative history poems such as *Middle Passage* (1945) and *Frederick Douglass* (1947), and Brooks's tribute to the vitality and rigours of black urban life in *A Street in Bronzeville* (1945) and her Pulitzer Prize-winning volume, *Annie Allen* (1949). The 1940s was also a decade of creative experimentation in autobiography, led by Du Bois's *Dusk of Dawn* (1940), a self-styled "essay toward an autobiography of a race concept"; Hurston's *Dust Tracks on a Road* (1942), an early venture in "autoethnography," the writing of self via the characterization of a culture (in this case, the rural Southern black culture of Hurston's roots); J. Saunders Redding's *No Day of Triumph* (1942), the story of an alienated Northern professional's quest for redemptive immersion in Southern black working-class communities; and Wright's *Black Boy*.

RALPH ELLISON

In 1949 the young New York essayist James Baldwin, a protégé of Wright, published *Everybody's Protest Novel*, a criticism of protest fiction from Harriet Beecher Stowe's *Uncle Tom's Cabin* to

OPPORTUNITY

Published from 1923 to 1949 and associated with the Harlem Renaissance, the magazine Opportunity (full name: Opportunity: Journal of Negro Life) was editor Charles S. Johnson's effort to give voice to black culture, hitherto neglected by mainstream American publishing. To encourage young writers to submit their work, Johnson sponsored three literary contests. In 1925 the winners included Zora Neale Hurston, Langston Hughes, and Countee Cullen. Ebony and Topaz, A Collectanea (1927) was an anthology of the best works published in the magazine.

Native Son. Baldwin's charge that the protest novel was prone to categorize humanity rather than reflect its full "beauty, dread, and power" heralded a shift in the 1950s away from Wright's brand of realism. The most enduring African American novel of the 1950s, *Invisible Man* (1952), by another Wright protégé, Ralph Ellison, answered Baldwin's call for "a new act of creation," a new kind of black hero, and a new way of picturing that hero's participation in post-Depression, post–World War II American reality. The protagonist of Ellison's novel is an unnamed black everyman who makes the traditional journey in African American literature from the South to the North, where he goes in search of conventional success and ends up, through a series of ironic revelations, discovering himself. The Invisible Man has been called a modern Odysseus and a 20th-century Candide, in tribute to Ellison's ability to invest in his central character a universality that bespeaks its author's wide reading in Western myth and European, British, and American literature. But foremost the Invisible Man is a black American engaged, willy-nilly, in an often painful process of education. Part Douglass, part Washington, and part Du Bois, he struggles with the dominant "isms," from Freudianism to Marxism, of the first half of the 20th century to decide what black intellectual leadership can and should be in the second half of the century. Encountering a volatile American reality that defies every political or philosophical attempt to define and control it, the Invisible Man comes to realize that his African American folk and cultural heritage, embodied in a series of black antagonists and enigmatic mentors, represents some of the most valuable wisdom he needs in order to discover his role and responsibilities in modern America. *Invisible Man* won the National Book Award in 1953, reflecting the enormously positive critical reception the novel enjoyed. Ellison never published another novel during his lifetime, but his essays, reviews, and interviews, published as *Shadow and Act* (1964) and *Going to the Territory* (1986), acknowledged his unwavering commitment to a pluralistic ideal of art that knows no allegiance to any school or program.

RICHARD WRIGHT

The chief proponent of this position was Richard Wright, whose fiction, autobiography, and social commentary dominated African American literature from the late 1930s to the early 1950s. A migrant from Mississippi with barely a ninth-grade education, Wright set the tone for the post–New Negro era with *Uncle Tom's Children* (1938), a collection of novellas set in the Jim Crow South that evidenced Wright's strong affinity with Marxism and the influence of American Naturalist writers such as Theodore Dreiser. In 1940 Wright's monumental novel *Native Son* appeared, winning thunderous critical acclaim as well as unprecedented financial success. Charting the violent life and death of a Chicago ghetto youth, *Native Son* revived the protest tradition of 19th-century African American literature while eschewing its moralizing, sentimentality, and political conservatism. Wright's autobiography *Black Boy* (1945) also revisited a 19th-century tradition, the slave narrative, to chronicle his quest, as much intellectual as physical, from an oppressive South to anticipated freedom in Chicago. After the critical and popular success of *Black Boy* in the mid-1940s, Wright moved to Paris, where he continued to publish fiction and travel books, though none matched the achievement of

his work in the 1940s. Nevertheless, the stamp Wright placed on African American prose remained evident in the work of novelists such as William Attaway, Chester Himes, and Ann Petry, which has often been interpreted as belonging to "the Wright school" of social realism. Petry's *The Street* (1946) adopted Wright's pitiless assessment of the power of environment in the lives of black urban dwellers, but, unlike Wright, whose female characters generally exemplify demoralization and passivity, Petry created a female protagonist who fights back.

CHICAGO WRITERS

The *Chicago Defender*, one of the premier African American newspapers of the 20th century, portrayed the Windy City as a cultural and economic mecca for black migrants fleeing the South during the Great Depression. Wright, who moved from Memphis, Tenn., to Chicago in 1927, found in the South Side of Chicago a lively community of young African American writers, among them poet Margaret Walker, playwright Theodore Ward, poet and journalist Frank Marshall Davis, and novelist and children's book author Arna Bontemps. Chicago-based *Abbott's Monthly* (1930–33), established by the *Defender*'s editor, Robert Abbott, published the work of Wright and Himes for the first time, while *New Challenge* (1937), coedited by novelist Dorothy West and Wright, helped the fledgling Chicago black literary renaissance expound its purpose. In the 1940s

CHICAGO DEFENDER

Founded in 1905 by Robert S. Abbott, the Chicago Defender *originally was a four-page weekly newspaper. Like the white-owned Hearst and Pulitzer newspapers, the* Defender, *under Abbott, used sensationalism to boost circulation. Editorials attacking white oppression and the lynching of African Americans helped increase the paper's circulation in Southern states. During World War I the* Defender *urged equal treatment of black soldiers. It published dispatches contrasting opportunities for African Americans in the urban North with the privations of the rural South, contributing actively to the northward migration of millions of black Southerners between World War I and the Great Depression. By 1929 the* Defender *was selling more than 250,000 copies each week.*

Along with other African American newspapers, the Defender *protested the treatment of African American servicemen fighting in World War II and urged the integration of the armed forces. As a result of their protests, the U.S. government threatened to indict African American publishers for sedition; however, the* Defender's *publisher, John H. Sengstacke, negotiated a compromise with the Justice Department that protected the First Amendment rights of the African American press.*

The Defender *would become a daily newspaper in 1956. It was noted for the quality of its writers, among them novelist Willard Motley, poet Gwendolyn Brooks, and Langston Hughes, whose "Simple" stories first appeared in 1942 in the* Defender *column he wrote for more than 20 years. After Sengstacke's death in 1997, however, the* Defender's *national influence diminished.*

Negro Digest and *Negro Story*, also literary products of Chicago's South Side, provided outlets for fiction writers, poets, and essayists. Encouraged by the Chicago and New York units of the Federal Theater Project, African American drama advanced during the Depression, led by Abram Hill, founder of the American Negro Theater in Harlem; Hughes, whose play *Mulatto* (produced 1935) reached Broadway with a searching examination of miscegenation; and Ward, whose *Big White Fog* (produced 1938) was the most widely viewed African American drama of the period.

THE HARLEM RENAISSANCE UP CLOSE

The Harlem Renaissance, which lasted from about 1918 until about 1937, was a blossoming of African American culture, particularly in the creative arts, and the most influential movement in African American literary history. Embracing literary, musical, theatrical, and visual arts, participants sought to reconceptualize "the Negro" apart from the white stereotypes that had influenced black people's relationship to their heritage and to each other. They also sought to break free of Victorian moral values and bourgeois shame about aspects of their lives that might, as seen by whites, reinforce racist beliefs. Never dominated by a particular school of thought but rather characterized by intense debate, the movement laid the groundwork for all later African American literature and had an enormous impact on subsequent black literature and consciousness worldwide. While the renaissance was not confined to the Harlem district of New York City, Harlem attracted a remarkable concentration of intellect and talent and served as the symbolic capital of this cultural awakening.

THE BACKGROUND

The Harlem Renaissance was a phase of a larger New Negro movement that had emerged in the early 20th century and in some ways ushered in the civil rights movement of the late 1940s and early 1950s. The social foundations of this movement included the Great Migration of African Americans from rural to urban spaces and from South to North; dramatically rising levels of literacy; the creation of national organizations dedicated to pressing African American civil rights, "uplifting" the race, and opening socioeconomic opportunities; and developing race pride, including pan-African sensibilities and programs. Black exiles and expatriates from the Caribbean and Africa crossed paths in metropoles such as New York City and Paris after World War I and had an invigorating influence on each other that gave the broader

"Negro renaissance" (as it was then known) a profoundly important international cast.

The Harlem Renaissance is unusual among literary and artistic movements for its close relationship to civil rights and reform organizations. Crucial to the movement were magazines such as *The Crisis*, published by the National Association for the Advancement of Colored People (NAACP); *Opportunity*, published by the National Urban League; and *The Messenger*, a socialist journal eventually connected with the Brotherhood of Sleeping Car Porters, a black labour union. *Negro World*, the newspaper of Marcus Garvey's Universal Negro Improvement Association, also played a role, but few of the major authors or artists identified with Garvey's "Back to Africa" movement, even if they contributed to the paper.

The renaissance had many sources in black culture, primarily of the United States and the Caribbean, and manifested itself well beyond Harlem. As its symbolic capital, Harlem was a catalyst for artistic experimentation and a highly popular nightlife destination. Its location in the communications capital of North America helped give the New Negroes visibility and opportunities for publication not evident elsewhere. Located just north of Central Park, Harlem was a formerly white residential district that by the early 1920s was becoming virtually a black city within the borough of Manhattan. Other boroughs of New York City were also home to people now identified with the renaissance, but they often crossed paths in Harlem or went to special events at the 135th Street Branch of the New York Public Library. Black intellectuals from Washington, Baltimore, Philadelphia, Los Angeles, and other cities (where they had their own intellectual circles, theatres, and reading groups) also met in Harlem or settled there. New York City had an extraordinarily diverse and decentred black social world in which no one group could monopolize cultural authority. As a result, it was a particularly fertile place for cultural experimentation.

While the renaissance built on earlier traditions of African American culture, it was profoundly affected by trends—such as primitivism—in European and white American artistic circles. Modernist primitivism was inspired partly by Freudian psychology, but it tended to extol "primitive" peoples as enjoying a more direct relationship to the natural world and to elemental human desires than "overcivilized" whites. The keys to artistic revolution and authentic expression, some intellectuals felt, would be found in the cultures of "primitive races," and preeminent among these, in the stereotypical thinking of the day, were the cultures of sub-Saharan Africans and their descendants. Early in the 20th century, European avant-garde artists had drawn inspiration from African masks as they broke from realistic representational styles toward abstraction in painting and sculpture. The prestige of such experiments caused African American intellectuals to look on their African heritage with new eyes and in many cases with a desire to reconnect with a heritage long despised or misunderstood by both whites and blacks.

BLACK HERITAGE AND AMERICAN CULTURE

This interest in black heritage coincided with efforts to define an American culture distinct from that of Europe, one that would be characterized by ethnic pluralism as well as a democratic ethos. The concept of cultural pluralism (a term coined by the philosopher Horace Kallen in 1915) inspired notions of the United States as a new kind of nation in which diverse cultures should develop side by side in harmony rather than be "melted" together or ranked on a scale of evolving "civilization." W.E.B. Du Bois had advocated something like this position in his *The Souls of Black Folk* (1903), a defining text of the New Negro movement because of its profound effect on an entire generation that formed the core of the Harlem Renaissance. As various forms of cultural-pluralist thought took hold, a fertile environment for the blossoming of African American arts developed. Moreover, the effort on the part of some American intellectuals to distinguish American literature and culture from European cultural forms dovetailed with African American intellectuals' beliefs about their relationship to American national identity.

Du Bois and his NAACP colleague James Weldon Johnson asserted that the only uniquely "American" expressive traditions in the United States had been developed by African Americans. They, more than any other group, had been forced to remake themselves in the New World, Du Bois and Johnson argued, while whites continued to look to Europe or sacrificed artistic values to commercial ones. (Native American cultures, on the other hand, seemed to be "dying out," they claimed.) African Americans' centuries-long struggle for freedom had made them the prophets of democracy and the artistic vanguard of American culture.

This judgment began unexpectedly to spread as African American music, especially the blues and jazz, became a worldwide sensation. Black music provided the pulse of the Harlem Renaissance and of the Jazz Age more generally. The rise of the "race records" industry, beginning with OKeh's recording of Mamie Smith's *Crazy Blues* in 1920, spread the blues to audiences previously unfamiliar with the form. Smith, Alberta Hunter, Clara Smith, Bessie Smith, and Ma Rainey—who had been performing for years in circuses, clubs, and tent shows—found themselves famous. Frequently ironic and often bawdy, the music expressed the longings and philosophical perspectives of the black working class. Black writers such as Langston Hughes, Sterling Brown, and Jean Toomer valued the blues as an indigenous art form of the country's most oppressed people, a secular equivalent of the spirituals, and an antidote to bourgeois black assimilationism.

Out of the blues came jazz, migrating to Northern urban centres such as Chicago and New York City during and after World War I. In the 1920s jazz orchestras grew in size and incorporated new instruments as well as methods of performance. Louis Armstrong became the first great jazz soloist when he moved from King Oliver's Creole Jazz Band in Chicago to Fletcher Henderson's band in New York City in 1924. Henderson's band soon had competitors in "big bands" led by the likes of Cab Calloway, Duke Ellington, Chick Webb, and Jimmie Lunceford—not to mention such "white" bands as Paul Whiteman's. Once associated with brothels and traveling circuses, jazz gained respectability as a form of high art. Moreover, dance forms associated with jazz, most famously the Charleston (also a product of the 1920s) and tap dance, became international fads as a result of hugely popular all-black musical revues.

The popularity of jazz among whites helped spark a "Negro Vogue" in cities such as New York and Paris in the mid- to late 1920s. Simultaneously, European dramatists extolled the body language of African American dance and stage humour (descended from the blackface minstrel show, the most popular and original form of American theatrical comedy). The best-known white man to bring attention to the Harlem Renaissance was undoubtedly Carl Van Vechten, whose music criticism trumpeted the significance of jazz and blues and whose provocatively titled novel *Nigger Heaven* (1926) helped spread the Negro Vogue. It served virtually as a tourist guide to Harlem, capitalizing on the supposed "exotic" aspects of black urban life even while focusing, primarily, on the frustrations of black urban professionals and aspiring writers. Although vilified by some, Van Vechten became a key contact for several black artists and authors because of his interracial parties and publishing connections. Nowhere was the Negro Vogue more evident than in nightclubs such as the Cotton Club and Connie's Inn, which became especially popular with whites in the late 1920s. Both of these nightclubs excluded blacks from the audience; others, called "black and tans," catered to "mixed" audiences, while still others excluded whites so as to avoid the police raids to which black and tans were often subjected.

THE QUESTION OF "NEGRO ART"

The international appeal of jazz and its connection to common black life, accompanied by the sheer virtuosity of its musicians, encouraged black intellectuals in other fields to turn increasingly to specifically "Negro" aesthetic forms as a basis for innovation and self-expression. The tendency appeared in concert music, choral programs, and Broadway musicals as well as literature. Eubie Blake and Noble Sissle's musical revue *Shuffle Along* opened on Broadway in 1921 and established a model that would shape

black musicals for 60 years. Florence Mills, a spritely dancer and phenomenal singer, achieved enormous fame across racial lines in the United States and Europe before suddenly succumbing to appendicitis in 1927. Josephine Baker, who began as a chorus girl in a popular revue, became an international star when *La Revue nègre* opened in 1925 in Paris, where she ultimately settled as a celebrity and played a variety of "exotic" roles exploiting the glamour of the "primitive." Popular revues and vaudeville acts drew all-black audiences throughout the United States in cities on the Theatre Owners Booking Association circuit. In the 1920s black-produced shows came to Broadway again and again, and many white-produced shows featured black casts. The success of such shows helped fuel the optimism of the Harlem Renaissance. Amid worsening socioeconomic conditions in Harlem itself and political setbacks in what was a very conservative and racist era—it was during the 1920s that the Ku Klux Klan reached its peak in membership and political influence in the South and the Midwest—some black leaders hoped that achievement in the arts would help revolutionize race relations while enhancing blacks' understanding of themselves as a people.

Important new publishing houses opened their doors to black authors. These publishers—particularly Alfred A. Knopf, Harcourt Brace, and Boni & Liveright—were breaking away from an earlier emphasis on British literary

JOSEPHINE BAKER

American-born French dancer and singer Josephine Baker symbolized the beauty and vitality of black American culture, taking Paris by storm in the 1920s. Baker (born Freda Josephine McDonald on June 3, 1906) grew up fatherless and in poverty. Between the ages of 8 and 10 she was out of school, helping to support her family. As a child Baker developed a taste for the flamboyant that was later to make her famous. As an adolescent she became a dancer, touring at 16 with a dance troupe from Philadelphia. In 1923 she joined the chorus in a road company performing the musical comedy Shuffle Along and then moved to New York City, where she advanced steadily through the show Chocolate Dandies on Broadway and the floor show of the Plantation Club.

In 1925 she went to Paris to dance at the Théâtre des Champs-Élysées in La Revue nègre and introduced her danse sauvage to France. She went on to become one of the most popular music-hall entertainers in France and achieved star billing at the Folies-Bergère, where she cre-

A 1920s photograph of Josephine Baker in Paris. AFP/Getty Images

ated a sensation by dancing seminude in a G-string ornamented with bananas. She sang professionally for the first time in 1930, made her screen debut as a singer four years later, and appeared in several more films before World War II curtailed her career.

During the German occupation of France, Baker, who had become a French citizen in 1937, worked with the Red Cross and the Résistance. As a member of the Free French forces she entertained troops in Africa and the Middle East. Baker was later awarded the Croix de Guerre and the Legion of Honour with the rosette of the Résistance. After the war much of her energy was devoted to Les Milandes, her estate in southwestern France, from which she began in 1950 to adopt babies of all nationalities in the cause of what she defined as "an experiment in brotherhood" and her "rainbow tribe." She retired from the stage in 1956, but to maintain Les Milandes she was later obliged to return, starring in Paris in 1959. Baker traveled several times to the United States to participate in civil rights demonstrations. In 1968 her estate was sold to satisfy accumulated debt. She continued to perform occasionally until her death in 1975, during the celebration of the 50th anniversary of her Paris debut.

tradition. They were publishing translated Modernist works from a variety of nationalities previously unread in the United States except by immigrants in their native languages. Interested too in the notions of American cultural pluralism—in some cases influenced by left-wing thought, in others involved in the drive for black civil rights—and aware of the vogue of primitivism, they saw a market for black-authored books on "Negro" topics. Their interest was accelerated by the efforts of African American magazine editors who organized literary prize contests and other events showcasing black literary talent. The most often cited event of this sort was a banquet at the liberal Civic Club in downtown New York organized by Charles S. Johnson, editor of *Opportunity*, in 1924. The event had the effect of announcing what had come to resemble a "movement"—a cohort of talented African American writers ready to be noticed. In 1925 appeared the ultimate result: *The New Negro: An Interpretation*, edited by Alain Locke, which sold well and garnered positive critical attention in addition to inspiring black readers and would-be authors.

Locke attempted to direct the "movement" he announced in *The New Negro*, stressing a turn away from social protest or propaganda toward self-expression built on what he termed "folk values"—a movement, in other words, akin to the Irish literary renaissance that had slightly preceded it. Yet the writers of the Harlem Renaissance were not unified in artistic aims or methods. Disagreement helps account for the renaissance's importance. Locke believed that black authors and artists should develop distinct aesthetic tendencies inspired by African American folk sources and African traditions. The satirist George Schuyler lampooned the very idea of "Negro art" in America as "hokum" artificially stimulated by white decadents.

POETRY

Countee Cullen, an early protégé of Locke's, came to resist any suggestion that his racial background should determine his notion of poetic inheritance. Devoted to the examples of John Keats and Edna St. Vincent Millay, Cullen considered the Anglo-American poetic heritage to belong as much to him as to any white American of his age. In contrast, Hughes famously announced in his manifesto *The Negro Artist and the Racial Mountain* (1926) that black poets should create a distinctive "Negro" art, combating the "urge within the race toward whiteness."

Hughes's position reveals how, in addition to primitivism, the tendency to press for "authentic" American art forms—and to find them in black America—led black writers to "the folk." Their focus on the folk also came at a time when American anthropologists influenced by Franz Boas were revolutionizing their discipline with arguments against the racist paradigms of the past. The folk—people of the rural South particularly, but also the new migrants to

Northern cities—were presumed to carry the seeds of black artistic development with relative autonomy from "white" traditions. Thus, James Weldon Johnson, beginning with his poem *The Creation* (1920) and then in the book *God's Trombones* (1927), set traditional African American sermons in free-verse poetic forms modeled on the techniques of black preachers.

Inspired by Southern folk songs and jazz, Toomer experimented with lyrical modifications of prose form in his dense and multigeneric book *Cane* (1923), which to many seemed a radical new departure in writing about black life. *Cane* refrained from moralizing or explicit protest while the symbols, phrases, tones, and rhythms of black folk music and jazz infused its structure. Weaving together poems, sketches, short stories, and dramatic narratives, the book seamlessly melded high Modernist literary techniques with African American style and subject matter that alternated between the rural South and the urban North. Though it exposed the brutal effects of white supremacy, it did so without seeming to preach or moralize, and it dealt with sexuality more overtly than any preceding black-authored text in American literary history. For many young black writers, *Cane* therefore marked the literary future. Ironically, however, even as Toomer completed *Cane*, he thought of himself not as a Negro but as the first member of a "new race" resulting from a uniquely American mixture of Old World peoples. Denying identification with the "Negro renaissance," he regarded the label Negro as inappropriate and limiting for his work.

By exploring black vernacular speech and lyrical forms, Hughes, on the other hand, built his artistic project on identification with the Negro masses. Influenced by such contemporary white poets as Carl Sandburg and Vachel Lindsay but inspired also by the example of Paul Laurence Dunbar, Hughes in his first book, *The Weary Blues* (1926), wrote of working-class life and black popular culture as well as his own vagabond experiences in the Caribbean, Africa, and Europe. In his next book, *Fine Clothes to the Jew* (1927), he turned to the blues for a poetic form derived from and answering to the desires, needs, and aesthetic sensibilities of the black working class. In these poems Hughes also took on working-class personae. Sterling Brown followed Hughes in a similar spirit with ballads and other poetic forms that attempted to catch the spirit of the folk heritage without merely imitating "folk" performance.

Other black poets continued to write primarily in traditional English literary forms, at times turning these forms to new uses. Claude McKay was a Jamaican immigrant and radical socialist who had begun his poetic career with two volumes of verse primarily in Jamaican dialect. But after moving to the United States, he wrote poems exclusively in a standard English dialect and used traditional stanzaic forms, most notably the sonnet. He turned these forms to new uses, with poems of political invective being his most famous (*If We Must Die*), although he wrote many lyrics of nostalgia for his homeland as well as about love or exile (*The Tropics in New York, Harlem Dancer*). The work of McKay, who was an admirer of English Romantics such as Percy Bysshe Shelley, blends a romantic sensibility with a race-conscious and at times revolutionary one.

Cullen also adhered to traditional English poetics, but his work was less politically radical. In poems of love, praise, or racial self-questioning as well as protest, Cullen appealed to the sensibilities of the black middle class. Believing great poetry must transcend racial identity, Cullen was not averse to writing on racial subjects—as he did in his most memorable poems, such as *Heritage, Incident,* and *From the Dark Tower*—but he felt the tradition of poetry in English was a more important resource for the poet than any supposed "racial" heritage.

While the most celebrated poets of the Harlem Renaissance were men— Hughes, McKay, Cullen—black women's poetry was far from incidental to the movement. Poems by Alice Dunbar Nelson, Helene Johnson, Georgia Douglas Johnson, Angelina Weld Grimké, Gwendolyn Bennett, and Anne Spencer appeared frequently in periodicals, although only Georgia Douglas Johnson published full volumes of poetry (including *The Heart of a Woman, and Other Poems* [1918] and *Bronze* [1922]).

Women poets negotiated a number of difficulties concerning gender and tradition as they sought to extricate themselves from stereotypes of hypersexuality and primitive abandon. Attempting to claim femininity on terms denied them by the dominant society, they worked variously within and against inherited constraints concerning the treatment of love and nature as well as racial experience in poetry.

A significant proportion of poets, as well as other participants in the Harlem Renaissance, were gay or bisexual, including McKay, Cullen, Locke, Dunbar Nelson, Richard Bruce Nugent, and perhaps Hughes. References to lesbian sexuality were also well-known in blues songs by Ma Rainey and Bessie Smith. The renaissance participated in what one scholar termed "the invention of homosexuality" in American culture during the early 20th century, when sexual identities came to be defined and policed in new ways. Drag balls were reported in black newspapers, sometimes disparagingly. In part because of lax policing, Harlem was known as a destination for whites seeking illicit sexual thrills, but it also allowed for discreet liaisons through which long-term same-sex relationships developed both within and between the races. According to some critics, the renaissance was as gay as it was Negro. However, with the exception of Nugent, gay sexuality among the well-known writers and artists was discreet and mostly closeted.

FIRE!!

The idea for the experimental, apolitical African American literary journal Fire!! was conceived in Washington, D.C., by Langston Hughes and writer and graphic artist Richard Nugent. The two, along with an editorial board comprising Zora Neale Hurston, Gwendolyn Bennett, John Davis, and Aaron Douglas, selected the brilliant young critic and novelist Wallace Henry Thurman to edit the publication. Thurman solicited art, poetry, fiction, drama, and essays from his editorial advisers, as well as from such leading figures of the New Negro movement as Countee Cullen and Arna Bontemps.

Responses to the magazine (published from 1926 until the early 1930s) ranged from minimal notice in the white press to heated contention among African American critics. Among the latter, the senior rank of intellectuals, such as W.E.B. Du Bois, tended to dismiss it as self-indulgent, while younger figures reacted with enthusiasm. Financial viability quickly proved unattainable, and several hundred undistributed copies met with an ironic fate when the building they were stored in burned to the ground.

FICTION

Fiction of the Harlem Renaissance is notable for its concentration on contemporary life and its cultural instability—in other words, for its modernity. Anticipated by earlier novelists such as James Weldon Johnson in *The Autobiography of an Ex-Colored Man* (published anonymously in 1912; republished under his name in 1927) and Du Bois in *The Quest of the Silver Fleece* (1911), the novelists of the renaissance explored the diversity of black experience across boundaries of class, colour, and gender while implicitly or explicitly protesting antiblack racism. In *There Is Confusion* (1924) Jessie Redmon Fauset considered the transformation of mainstream culture effected by the new black middle class and by the black creative arts. Using the conventions of the novel of manners, Fauset advanced themes of racial uplift, patriotism, optimism for the future, and black solidarity. Walter White's *The Fire in the Flint* (1924) focused on the career and then the lynching of a black physician and veteran of World War I. Protesting racial oppression and exposing its most barbaric expressions, White's novel also brought attention to a distinguished black professional class whose progress was being blocked by prejudice.

After the publication of Toomer's, Fauset's, and White's books, which proved that black authors could place their work with prestigious publishing firms, black writers and critics debated the directions black fiction might take away from the propaganda of racial uplift and toward more nuanced and psychologically complex treatments of black experience. The question also arose as to whether new styles and literary forms might be needed to convey black experience and sensibilities in fiction. On the other hand, were there elements of black experience that, considering the continuing power of damaging white stereotypes, would be better left untouched? Du Bois worried that white editors and readers would draw black authors into an empty aestheticism or salacious modes of primitivism. The immense sales of Van Vechten's *Nigger Heaven* seemed to confirm his fears, especially after some younger black authors came to that novel's defense and, about the same time, Harlem became a popular nightlife destination for slumming whites. Interracial parties, hosted by blacks as well as whites, also developed supportive networks and patronage for the movement. The extent to which such patronage led the movement astray and ultimately destroyed it has been a point of contention ever since.

Nella Larsen and Rudolph Fisher were two significant novelists (and friends) whose work explores issues of racial psychology, class, and sexuality in the modern city. Larsen explored the psychology of urban sophisticates in her novels *Quicksand* (1928) and *Passing* (1929), analyzing the psychological intricacies of race consciousness and exposing the massive pressures to subordinate women's sexuality to the rules of race and class. The daughter of a white immigrant from Denmark and a black West Indian cook, Larsen knew intimately the price colour-line culture exacted of those who transgressed its most fundamental rules, and her fiction remains unequaled for the originality and incisiveness with which it exposes the contradictions of identities founded on the assertion of absolute difference between "black" and "white." Hers was a unique achievement at a time when de facto and de jure segregation were becoming ever more entrenched features of American society.

Overall, Fisher's work presented a nuanced interpretation of the urban geography—and modernity—of Harlem. He expertly explored the ethnic and class diversity of the black metropolis as rural Southern and Caribbean migrants adjusted to and transformed it. In his short stories his use of black music as well as its contexts of performance to complement or advance narrative tensions and thematic concerns was groundbreaking. His novels *The Walls of Jericho* (1928) and *The Conjure-Man Dies* (1932)—the latter among the earliest black detective novels—also display a keen concern with black male psychology that in some respects prefigures the work of much later authors in the canon of African American fiction, particularly Richard Wright, James Baldwin, and John Edgar Wideman.

Two prolific and central figures of the renaissance produced significant, politically radical novels that envision black political identity in a global framework: Du Bois in *Dark Princess* (1928) and McKay in *Banjo* (1929). Both novels show the strong influence of Marxism and the anti-imperialist movements of the early 20th century, and both place their hopes in the revolutionary potential of transnational solidarity to end what they consider to be the corrupt and decadent rule of Western culture. However, in many respects the books could hardly be more different, both formally and thematically: Du Bois's takes the form of the quest romance, McKay's that of the picaresque tale. The similarities and contrasts between the novels both reveal the importance of Marxist and anti-imperialist thought to the Harlem Renaissance and suggest enduring tensions in the black radical tradition.

The decade of the 1920s was an age of satire and "debunking"—urbane, sophisticated, sometimes cynical and decadent. H.L. Mencken, a white magazine editor and satirist at the height of his career in the 1920s, was greatly admired by a number of major Harlem Renaissance authors, especially White, George Schuyler, and Wallace Thurman. Schuyler's *Black No More* (1931) explores the possibilities of satirical fiction more thoroughly than any other novel of the era by centring on American racial mores. Thurman's novels *The Blacker the Berry...* (1929) and *Infants of the Spring* (1932) also direct fundamentally satirical barbs at the contradictions in American racial culture and at the "Negro renaissance" itself. *Black No More* and *Infants of the Spring* are often read as comments on the failure of the Harlem Renaissance, but they were much in tune with the spirit of the age of burlesque and debunking. Satire of the Negro Vogue was an important aspect of the renaissance.

The Harlem Renaissance also coincided with a rising interest in "folk

fiction," particularly that about the black South. White authors such as Paul Green and Julia Peterkin enjoyed tremendous success in the mid-1920s, indicating the existence of an audience for work that took a more realistic, if still limited and sentimental, approach to the black Southern "folk." Black authors and critics felt the time had come for black writers to reveal the truth of black Southern experience as no white authors could, and no one was more successful in doing this than Zora Neale Hurston. A native of the rural South who was intimate with black folklore as well as modernist ethnography, Hurston departed from the scholarly ethnographic practice of the time as her literary ambition grew. A dialectical relationship can be noted between her ethnographic and "purely" fictional texts. The novel *Their Eyes Were Watching God* (1937) treats the maturation of Janie Crawford through a series of relationships and dramatic experiences while using a free indirect discourse (a mode of representing a character's consciousness from a third-person point of view but in an informal, colloquial style seemingly identical to the character's) that melds vernacular language and folk motifs with a more standard "literary" voice. It is widely regarded as one of the signal achievements of the Harlem Renaissance.

DRAMA

Drama of the Harlem Renaissance sought to overcome the decades-long hold on the popular imagination exerted by blackface minstrelsy, which had created a powerful range of damaging stereotypes that constrained theatrical presentation of black life. Critics, playwrights, and actors debated the function of drama, as well as its subject matter and the style of presentation of "Negro experience." A number of white-authored plays about black life gained great critical and box-office success from the late 1910s through the mid-1930s, giving valuable experience to black performers and inspiring black dramatists. Most notable were Ridgely Torrence's *Plays for a Negro Theater* (1917), Eugene O'Neill's *The Emperor Jones* (1921), Green's *In Abraham's Bosom* (1927), and Marc Connelly's *The Green Pastures* (1929). These plays also moved some black playwrights to present more authentic examples of what were called "Negro plays." New all-black theatre groups arose in several cities.

Alain Locke, partly influenced by the Abbey Theatre of Ireland, believed that black drama should develop from the "folk play" and reveal the soul of a people rather than focusing on protest or promoting a political agenda. Du Bois, on the other hand, emphasized that "all art is propaganda." The tension between these two positions defined much of black-authored drama between 1917 and 1937. Playwrights included Dunbar Nelson, Grimké, Hurston, Thurman, Hughes, Mary P. Burrill, Marita Bonner, Georgia Douglas Johnson, Willis Richardson, Eulalie Spence, Frank Wilson, and Randolph Edmonds. Richardson was the

most prolific. Much influenced by Locke's ideas, he focused his early plays on folk experience in the South, but over time his plays came to have more of an educational or encouraging message. *The Chip Woman's Fortune* was picked up by the Ethiopian Art Theater of Chicago (a "black" company organized by white director Raymond O'Neil), and, when the troupe played a season in New York City in 1923, it became the first black-authored nonmusical drama on Broadway. Other significant plays by Richardson include *Compromise: A Folk Play* (1925) and *Broken Banjo* (1925).

A friend and admirer of Locke, Georgia Douglas Johnson also authored a number of plays in the 1920s and '30s. Her plays tended to focus on folk experience, often centring on women, but they also protested racial oppression and especially lynching—a common theme in Harlem Renaissance drama by women. Hurston held a position similar to that of Locke about the importance of folk plays, but she went further, suggesting that such drama should grow from the styles and modes of performance found in rural Southern "juke joints" (small-town nightclubs) and storefront porches and in urban all-black cabarets. In her view, mimicry, ostentatiousness, angular movement, and playfulness characterized black folk expression, whereas Locke (more influenced by the folk theatre of Europe and Romantic aesthetic theory) emphasized simplicity, poise, and formal symmetry. Hurston's plays drew on her vast firsthand knowledge of rural

BILL ROBINSON

Bill "Bojangles" Robinson, who is best remembered for his roles with Shirley Temple in films of the 1930s, began dancing for pennies at the age of eight, when he had also begun to work as a stableboy. He eventually made a swing of a vaudeville circuit and in 1908 entered a business association with Marty Forkins, actors' agent, who helped him to fame.

Robinson went on to become a star of black musical comedies, later a top vaudeville star, and finally a star of motion pictures, appearing in 14 films, notably *The Little Colonel* (1935), *In Old Kentucky* (1935), *The Littlest Rebel* (1935), *Rebecca of Sunnybrook Farm* (1938), and *Just Around the Corner* (1938). He also appeared in the wartime all-black musical film *Stormy Weather* (1943).

His soft-shoe and tap routines were widely copied by other dancers, but Robinson was probably unmatched for ingenuity in creating new steps, especially his famous "stair dance." He also was famed for a unique ability to run backward—almost as fast as other men could run forward; he once ran 75 yards (68 meters) backward in 8.2 seconds.

Entertainer Bill "Bojangles" Robinson, as photographed by Carl Van Vechten, Apr. 18, 1941. Library of Congress Prints and Photographs Division

Despite his earnings, which reached $6,600 a week for at least one year, he died in relative poverty, chiefly because of his spendthrift generosity and habits of gambling. On his death, he received tributes from royalty, the White House, and members of the U.S. president's cabinet.

Southern folklore and freely used humour and exaggeration in depicting everyday black life, risking charges even today that they reinforce stereotypes. Some of her short plays made Broadway after being incorporated into the musicals *Fast and Furious* (first performed 1931) and *The Great Day* (first performed 1932).

Thurman cowrote with William Jourdan Rapp the successful and somewhat controversial play *Harlem*, a fast-paced slice of the "lower" end of Harlem life, notable for its vernacular and slang-ridden dialogue. It landed on Broadway for 93 performances, and, while it drew much praise in the white press, had a mixed reception among blacks, some of whom resented its concern with only the "lowest" aspects of a population too often identified in the mainstream imagination with vice, crime, and moral lassitude.

Most successful of all the black-written plays of the Harlem Renaissance was Hughes's *Mulatto* (written 1931, first performed 1935), adapted from his short story *Father and Son*. Set on a plantation in Georgia in contemporary times, it concerns the tragic consequences of a white man's inability to acknowledge his only children because they are mulatto, born to the black house servant with whom he lives in a common-law marriage of sorts. The play explores the Oedipal struggle between the plantation owner and his eldest son, who is much like him and demands acknowledgment, and it ends with the patriarch's death at the son's hands and the subsequent lynching of both the eldest son and his younger, less rebellious brother, their mother cursing the corpse of the white man she once loved.

Overall, black drama of the Harlem Renaissance shows a steady development of dramatic form, with folk drama becoming a successful vehicle of reflection on the nature and significance of the black American experience that often included an indictment of white institutions. At the same time, black actors gained unprecedented opportunities (though still limited by racism) to perform before all-white, mixed, and all-black audiences. By the mid-1930s a Negro Actors Guild had formed, and black actors had achieved a significant foothold in American theatre.

VISUAL ART

Visual artists of the Harlem Renaissance, like the dramatists, attempted to win control over representation of their people from white caricature and denigration while developing a new repertoire of images. Prior to World War I, black painters and sculptors had rarely concerned themselves with African American subject matter. By the end of the 1920s, however, black artists had begun developing styles related to black aesthetic traditions of Africa or to folk art. Meta Warrick Fuller anticipated this development with her sculpture *Ethiopia Awakening* (1914). Appearing from a distance like a piece of Egyptian funerary sculpture, it depicts a black woman

Dust jacket by the African American artist Aaron Douglas for James Weldon Johnson's God's Trombones *(1927), a collection of black dialect sermons.* Between the Covers Rare Books, Merchantville, N.J.

The signature artist of the renaissance was Aaron Douglas, who turned away from traditional landscape painting after moving to New York City from Kansas and studying under the German immigrant Winold Reiss. Influenced by Art Deco, the flat profile designs of ancient Egyptian art, and what he called the abstract qualities of spirituals, Douglas created his own style of geometrical figural representation in dealing with "Negro" subject matter. His stylized, silhouette-like rendering of recognizably black characters, imbued with qualities of spiritual yearning and racial pride, became closely identified with the Harlem Renaissance generally. In his illustrations for James Weldon Johnson's book *God's Trombones*, Douglas transformed white Christian iconography by putting black subjects in central roles and evoking the identification of black Americans with the suffering of Jesus. In the 1930s he turned more specifically to the collective historical experience of African Americans, his work subtly inflected with a new Marxist orientation, as in his well-known mural series *Aspects of Negro Life* (1934).

wrapped like a mummy from the waist down. But her upper torso aspires upward, suggesting rebirth from a long sleep. In the 1920s, as African art became better known in Western art circles, West African cultural models gained importance for black American artists.

Despite Douglas's importance, most black artists of the 1920s spent little time in Harlem. Paris was the mecca of black painters and sculptors in that decade. Yet traveling exhibits and contests in the United States encouraged black artists in the late 1920s and early '30s. Notable figures include the painter Palmer C. Hayden, who interpreted black folklore and working-class life; Archibald J. Motley, best known for his paintings of urban black social life and his realistic portraits of refined "New Negro" types; Augusta Savage and Richmond Barthé, both sculptors; and other visual artists such as Sargent Johnson, William H. Johnson, Hale Woodruff, Lois Mailou Jones, and James VanDerZee. Many of these artists produced their best work in the 1930s and helped cultivate the next generation. The Great Depression forced many artists to return "home" from Europe and brought them together in a critical mass previously unknown. In that decade New York City became a centre of art education with new galleries, schools, and museums, including the Museum of Modern Art, which had been founded in 1929. Most important for aspiring black artists were the School of Arts and Crafts, founded by Savage, and the Harlem Community Art Center, of which Savage served as the first director after its creation in 1937 with Works Progress Administration (WPA) aid. In the middle and late 1930s, federal arts projects under the New Deal provided an unprecedented level of encouragement to the development of black artists and helped start the careers of a new generation of artists that included Romare Bearden, Jacob Lawrence, and Norman Lewis.

THE LEGACY

In the late 1930s, African American writers, influenced by the Great Depression and the strains of Marxist thought that had been a less-prominent aspect of the 1920s, attempted to differentiate their work from that of what was known then as the "Harlem movement" or the "Negro renaissance" of the previous decade. They castigated its bourgeois propensities and supposed sponsorship by white decadents, which had allegedly encouraged "weak-kneed" black writers and artists to go begging to white America for acceptance.

Yet a number of writers continued to produce texts that clearly developed from their work in the 1920s, most notably Hughes, Hurston, and Brown, as well as Arna Bontemps, who wrote for the magazines *Opportunity* and *The Crisis* in the 1920s and whose first novel, *God Sends Sunday* (1931), is often considered the final work of the Harlem Renaissance. Moreover, the movement of the 1920s had opened the doors of publishing houses and theatres to a significant extent. Even in the midst of the Depression, African American writing continued to appear from prestigious houses; likewise, black actors such as Ethel Waters starred on Broadway, and black visual arts blossomed. While

Richard Wright castigated the writers of the 1920s for playing decorous cultural ambassadors rather than making common cause with the aspirations of the black working class, his own use of Southern black folklore and language in his early fiction owed much to the experiments of such writers of the previous generation as Hurston, McKay, and Hughes. The satirical approaches of Schuyler, Thurman, and Hughes would be revived in the 1960s and afterward by such authors as William Demby, Charles R. Johnson, and Ishmael Reed. Hurston's use of folklore and her focus on women's experiences and voices would inspire subsequent black women writers beginning with Alice Walker. Later yet, Larsen's fiction inspired African American authors of interracial parentage and attracted expanding appreciation from scholars interested in the psychology of race and in black women's sexuality.

Moreover, the Harlem Renaissance had a strong international impact. White's *The Fire in the Flint* was translated into French, as was McKay's *Banjo*. Nancy Cunard's anthology *Negro* (1934) helped advance the reputation of black writers among the European left. Francophone black intellectuals based in Paris, including the leaders of the anti colonial and antiassimilationist movement that came to be known as Negritude (such as Aimé Césaire and Léopold Senghor), were inspired by the work of Harlem Renaissance authors, particularly McKay and Hughes. While the renaissance did not achieve the socio political transformation for which some had hoped, today it is clear that this movement marked a turning point in black cultural history: it helped to establish the authority of black writers and artists over the representation of black culture and experience, and it created for those writers and artists a continually expanding space within Western high culture.

PRIMARY SOURCES

The following documents, by Langston Hughes and W.E.B. Du Bois, provide evaluations of the state of African American literature during one of its most vibrant periods, the 1920s, by two of the most prominent writers of the era.

LANGSTON HUGHES: THE NEGRO ARTIST AND THE RACIAL MOUNTAIN (1926)

A novelist, short-story writer, and poet, Langston Hughes was one of the most prolific writers of the Harlem Renaissance. The ideas that he popularized were influential in shaping the attitudes of African American writers toward their art, especially in the matter of black pride. In this article he castigates the African American artist who shies away from racial identity. *Source: Nation, June 23, 1926.*

One of the most promising of the young Negro poets said to me once, "I want to be a poet—not a Negro poet," meaning, I believe, "I want to write like a white poet"; meaning subconsciously, "I would like to be a white poet"; meaning behind that, "I would like to be white." And I was sorry the young man said that, for no great poet has ever been afraid of being himself. And I doubted then that, with his desire to run away spiritually from his race, this boy would ever be a great poet. But this is the mountain standing in the way of any true Negro art in America—this urge within the race toward whiteness, the desire to pour racial individuality into the mold of American standardization, and to be as little Negro and as much American as possible.

But let us look at the immediate background of this young poet. His family is of what I suppose one would call the Negro middle class: people who are by no means rich yet never uncomfortable nor hungry—smug, contented, respectable folk, members of the Baptist Church. The father goes to work every morning. He is a chief steward at a large white club. The mother sometimes does fancy sewing or supervises parties for the rich families of the town. The children go to a mixed school. In the home they read white papers and magazines. And the mother often says "Don't be like niggers" when the children are bad. A frequent phrase from the father is, "Look how well a white man does things." And so the word white comes to be unconsciously a symbol of all the virtues. It holds for the children beauty, morality, and money. The whisper of "I want to be white" runs silently through their minds. This young poet's home is, I believe, a fairly typical home of the colored middle class. One sees immediately how difficult it would be for an artist born in such a home to interest himself in interpreting the beauty of his own people. He is never taught to see that beauty. He is taught rather not to see it, or if he does, to be ashamed of it when it is not according to Caucasian patterns.

For racial culture the home of a self-styled "high-class" Negro has nothing better to offer. Instead there will perhaps be more aping of things white than in a less cultured or less wealthy home. The father is perhaps a doctor, lawyer, landowner, or politician. The mother may be a social worker, or a teacher, or she may do nothing and have a maid. Father is often dark but he has usually married the lightest woman he could find. The family attend a fashionable church where few really colored faces are to be found. And they themselves draw a color line. In the North they go to white theaters and white movies. And in the South they have at least two cars and a house "like white folks." Nordic manners, Nordic faces, Nordic hair, Nordic art (if any), and an Episcopal heaven. A very high mountain indeed for the would-be racial artist to climb in order to discover himself and his people.

But then there are the low-down folks, the so-called common element, and they are the majority—may the Lord be praised! The people who have their nip of gin on Saturday nights and are not too important to themselves or the community, or too well fed, or too learned to watch the lazy world go round. They live on Seventh Street in Washington or State Street in Chicago and they do not particularly care whether they are like white folks or anybody else. Their joy runs, bang! into ecstasy. Their religion soars to a shout. Work maybe a little today, rest a little tomorrow. Play awhile. Sing awhile. O, let's dance! These common people are not afraid of spirituals, as for a long time their more intellectual brethren were, and jazz is their child. They furnish a wealth of colorful, distinctive material for any artist because they still hold their own individuality in the face of American standardizations. And perhaps these common people will give to the world its truly great Negro artist, the one who is not afraid to be himself. Whereas the better-class Negro would tell the artist what to do, the people at least let him alone when he does appear. And they are not ashamed of him—if they know he exists at all. And they accept what beauty is their own without question.

Certainly there is, for the American Negro artist who can escape the restrictions the more advanced among his own group would put upon him, a great field of unused material ready for his art. Without going outside his race, and even among the better classes with their "white" culture and conscious American manners, but still Negro enough to be different, there is sufficient matter to furnish a black artist with a lifetime of creative work. And when he chooses to touch on the relations between Negroes and whites in this country with their innumerable overtones and undertones, surely, and especially for literature and the drama, there is an inexhaustible supply of themes at hand. To these the Negro artist can give his racial individuality, his heritage of rhythm and warmth, and his incongruous humor that so often, as in the blues, becomes ironic laughter mixed with tears. But let us look again at the mountain.

A prominent Negro clubwoman in Philadelphia paid $11 to hear Raquel Meller sing Andalusian popular songs. But she told me a few weeks before she would not think of going to hear "that woman," Clara Smith, a great black artist, sing Negro folk songs. And many an upper-class Negro church, even now, would not dream of employing a spiritual in its services. The drab melodies in white folks' hymnbooks are much to be preferred. "We want to worship the Lord correctly and quietly. We don't believe in 'shouting.' Let's be dull like the Nordics," they say, in effect.

The road for the serious black artist, then, who would produce a racial art is most certainly rocky and the mountain is high. Until recently he received almost no encouragement for his work from either white or colored people. The fine novels of Chestnutt go out of print with neither race noticing their passing. The quaint charm and humor of Dunbar's dialect verse brought to him, in his day, largely the same kind of encouragement one would give a sideshow freak (A colored man writing poetry! How odd!) or a clown (How amusing!).

To present vogue in things Negro, although it may do as much harm as good for the budding colored artist, has at least done this: it has brought him forcibly to the attention of his own people among whom for so long, unless the other race had noticed him beforehand, he was a prophet with little honor. I understand that Charles Gilpin acted for years in Negro theaters without any special acclaim from his own, but when Broadway gave him eight curtain calls, Negroes, too, began to beat a tin pan in his honor. I know a young colored writer, a manual worker by day, who had been writing well for the colored magazines for some years, but it was not until he recently broke into the white publications and his first book was accepted by a prominent New York publisher that the "best" Negroes in his city took the trouble to discover that he lived there. Then almost immediately they decided to give a grand dinner for him. But the society ladies were careful to whisper to his mother that perhaps she'd better not come. They were not sure she would have an evening gown.

The Negro artist works against an undertow of sharp criticism and misunderstanding from his own group and unintentional bribes from the whites. "O, be respectable, write about nice people, show how good we are," say the Negroes. "Be stereotyped, don't go too far, don't shatter our illusions about you, don't amuse us too seriously. We will pay you," say the whites. Both would have told Jean Toomer not to write *Cane*. The colored people did not praise it. The white people did not buy it. Most of the colored people who did read *Cane* hate it. They are afraid of it. Although the critics gave it good reviews the public remained indifferent. Yet (excepting the work of Du Bois), *Cane* contains the finest prose written by a Negro in America. And like the singing of Robeson, it is truly racial.

But in spite of the Nordicized Negro intelligentsia and the desires of some white editors we have an honest American Negro literature already with us. Now I await the rise of the Negro theater. Our folk music, having achieved worldwide fame, offers itself to the genius of the great individual American Negro composer who is to come. And within the next decade I expect to see the work of a growing school of colored artists who paint and model the beauty of dark faces and create with new technique the expressions of their own soul world. And the Negro dancers who will dance like flame and the singers who will continue to carry our songs to all who listen—they will be with us in even greater numbers tomorrow.

Most of my own poems are racial in theme and treatment, derived from the life I know. In many of them I try to grasp and hold some of the meanings and rhythms of jazz. I am sincere as I know how to be in these poems and yet after every reading I answer questions like these from my own people: Do you think Negroes should always write about Negroes? I wish you wouldn't read some of your poems to white folks. How do you find anything interesting in a place like a cabaret? Why do you write about black people? You aren't black. What makes you do so many jazz poems?

But jazz to me is one of the inherent expressions of Negro life in America: the eternal tom-tom beating in the Negro soul—the tom-tom of revolt against weariness in a white world, a world of subway trains, and work, work, work; the tom-tom of joy and laughter, and pain swallowed in a smile. Yet the Philadelphia clubwoman is ashamed to say that her race created it and she does not like me to write about it. The old subconscious "white is best" runs through her mind. Years of study under white teachers, a lifetime of white books, pictures, and papers, and white manners, morals, and Puritan standards made her dislike the spirituals. And now she turns up her nose at jazz and all its manifestations—likewise almost everything else distinctly racial. She doesn't care for the Winold Reiss portraits of Negroes because they are "too Negro." She does not want a true picture of herself from anybody. She wants the artist to flatter her, to make the white world believe that all Negroes are as smug and near white in soul as she wants to be. But, to my mind, it is the duty of the younger Negro artist, if he accepts any duties at all from outsiders, to change through the force of his art that old whispering "I want to be white," hidden in the aspirations of his people, to "Why should I want to be white? I am a Negro—and beautiful."

So I am ashamed for the black poet who says "I want to be a poet, not a Negro poet," as though his own racial world were not as interesting as any other world. I am ashamed, too, for the colored artist who runs from the painting of Negro faces to the painting of sunsets after the manner of the academicians because he fears the strange unwhiteness of his own features. An artist must be free to choose what he does, certainly, but he must also never be afraid to do what he might choose.

Let the blare of Negro jazz bands and the bellowing voice of Bessie Smith singing blues penetrate the closed ears of the colored near intellectuals until they listen and perhaps understand. Let Paul Robeson singing "Water Boy," and Rudolph Fisher writing about the streets of Harlem, and Jean Toomer holding the heart of Georgia in his hands, and Aaron Douglas drawing strange black fantasies cause the smug Negro middle class to turn from their white, respectable, ordinary books and papers to catch a glimmer of their own beauty. We younger Negro artists who create now intend to express our individual dark-skinned selves without fear or shame. If white people are pleased we are glad. If they are not, it doesn't matter. We know we are beautiful. And ugly too. The tom-tom cries and the tom-tom laughs. If colored people are pleased we are glad. If they are not, their displeasure doesn't matter either. We build our temples for tomorrow, strong as we know how, and we stand on top of the mountain, free within ourselves.

W.E.B. DU BOIS: NEGRO LITERATURE

What follows is a brief summary of the unique contribution of African Americans to American literature, written for the 13th edition (1926) of Encyclopædia Britannica by W.E.B. Du Bois. The essay was written when the Harlem Renaissance was in full swing. One can sense both the troubled spirit of the author and his full awareness of the significance of the moment in which he wrote.

The plight of the Africans brought to America during the slave trade and of their descendants is one of the most dramatic in human history. That there should arise a literature written by black Americans touching their own situation depended on many things—their education, their economic condition, their growth in group consciousness. Before 1910, the books written by American Negroes were with some exceptions either a part of the general American literature or individual voices of Americans of Negro descent.

There began, however, about 1910 something that can be called a renaissance. It came because of oppression, because the spread of education made self-expression possible, and because a larger number of these 10,000,000 people were raising themselves above the lowest poverty. The first sign of this renaissance was naturally a continuation of the self-revelations current during the abolition controversy in the slave narratives, of which Frederick Douglass's *Life and Times* (1892) was the most striking and Booker Washington's *Up from Slavery*, published in 1901, the last great example. Since 1910, other autobiographies have followed. In these later stories there is, of course, less of the older spontaneity, little of adventure and more self-consciousness. John R. Lynch published his revealing *Facts of Reconstruction* in 1913. Alexander Walters (a black bishop), R. R. Moton (the successor of Booker Washington) and many others published autobiographies.

A more careful consideration of the Negro's social problems has characterised the period 1910-26. This is perhaps best illustrated by the three or four volumes of essays published by Kelley Miller, the trenchant work of William Pickens, W.E.B. Du Bois's *Darkwater* (1920), and J. A. Rogers's *From Superman to Man* (1917), and especially by the files of the growing weekly Negro press. These general considerations have led to a number of scientific studies. Foremost among these are the series of Atlanta University studies covering 13 years and touching such matters as *Efforts for Social Betterment among Negro Americans* (1910); *The College-Bred Negro American* (1911); *The Common School and the Negro American* (1912); *The Negro American Artisan* (1913); *Morals and Manners among Negro Americans* (1915). There came also as a result of the Chicago riot the careful study of *The Negro in Chicago* (Illinois-Chicago Commission on Race Relations,

1922). The Tuskegee *Negro Year Book,* edited by M. N. Work annually since 1915, and the work of Dr. George E. Haynes have been along the same lines.

More striking work, however, begins with the rewriting of American history from the Negro point of view. The doyen of this effort since 1910 has been Carter G. Woodson, whose work has been prolific and painstaking. Beginning with 1916 he has published a considerable number of books, including the *Journal of Negro History,* 10 large volumes filled with documents, essays and research. Next comes Benjamin G. Brawley with his *Short History of the American Negro* (1913 and 1919), *Social History of the American Negro* (1921) and his study of *The Negro in Literature and Art in the United States* (1921). With these may be noted Steward's *The Haitian Revolution, 1791 to 1804* (1914), Emmett J. Scott's *The American Negro in the World War* (1919) and *The Gift of Black Folk: the Negroes in the Making of America* (1924), by W.E.B. Du Bois, published by the Knights of Columbus.

But not in propaganda, science nor history has the essence of the renaissance shown itself. Rather the true renaissance has been a matter of the spirit and has shown itself among the poets as well as among the novelists and dramatists. In poetry, there are a dozen or more writers whose output has been small but significant. George McClellan, with his somewhat didactic and conventional verse, forms the link between past and present. Then comes James Weldon Johnson, Claude McKay, Leslie Hill,

Joseph Cotter, Jr., Georgia Douglas Johnson, Countée Cullen and Langston Hughes, besides a half-dozen others. It is notable that already several critical anthologies (by James Weldon Johnson, Robert Kerlin, White and Jackson) have appeared. William Stanley Braithwaite has appeared as a widely read critic of poetry. The development in fiction is still newer and includes some earlier attempts like *The Quest of the Silver Fleece* by W.E.B. Du Bois (1911) and James Weldon Johnson's *Autobiography of an Ex-Coloured Man* (1912), and newer and more significant work by Rudolph Fisher, Jessie Fauset, Walter White and Jean Toomer. In the drama, Willis Richardson and one or two others have been writing effectively, while in the explanation and collection of Negro music and folk-lore we have J. Rosamond Johnson, T. W. Talley and J. W. Cotter.

Perhaps the extent of this renaissance of Negro literature can be summed up in two works. One is the 15 volumes of *The Crisis* magazine, which began publication in Nov. 1910, and has since been a compendium of occurrences, thoughts and expression among American Negroes. Most of the newer Negro writers found first publication in its pages. The second is the book called *The New Negro,* published in 1925 and edited by Alain Locke, in which some 30 contemporary Negro writers express the spirit of their day. All these things are beginnings rather than fulfilments, but they are significant beginnings. They mean much for the future.

EPILOGUE

As the need for workers in war-related industry increased during World War II, the Great Migration of African Americans to the cities of the North and West that had slowed somewhat during the Great Depression surged again—transforming the demographic, political, social, economic, and cultural landscape of the United States. The struggle for freedom and civil rights would continue to be waged in the South but also in the North. New generations of leaders would arise to take up the torch, African Americans would ascend to the highest levels of public and private office, and rich new works of literature, art, and music by African Americans would multiply exponentially in the last half of the 20th century and the beginning of the 21st. Ultimately, all of these successes would be products of the suffering, strength, courage, initiative, and genius of those whose efforts and accomplishments have been chronicled in this volume.

Timeline: 2nd Century CE to 1941

2ND CENTURY – 1789: OLD WORLD TO NEW

- 2nd–3rd century CE: Aksum becomes the greatest market of northeastern Africa.
- c. 600: The first of the great medieval western African trading empires is established as Wadagu, or Ghana. Its people act as intermediaries between the Arab and Berber salt traders to the north and the producers of gold and ivory to the south.
- c. 1100: The Great Zimbabwe (in what would later be southeastern Zimbabwe) begins some 400 years as the heart of a great trading empire.
- 1230: Sundiata, a West African monarch, establishes the western Sudanese empire of Mali, which flourishes for two centuries and lasts for three.
- 1307: Mansa Musa takes the throne of the great Mali empire.
- mid-14th century: A loose alliance, consisting of seven African states (Biram, Daura, Gobir, Kano, Katsina, Rano, and Zaria [Zazzau]), is formed. Known as the Hausa states, they flourish until the 19th century, when they are conquered by the Fulani.
- 1441: The first African slaves are transported to Portugal.
- 1464: Sonni 'Ali ascends the throne of the Songhai kingdom. By his death in 1492, the Songhai control a vast trading empire that lasts until the end of the 16th century.
- c. 1517: Black plantation slavery begins in the New World when Spaniards begin importing slaves from Africa to replace Native Americans who died from harsh working conditions and exposure to Old World diseases to which they had no immunity.
- 1562: Three hundred slaves are obtained by the British and taken to Hispaniola (later Haiti and the Dominican Republic).
- 1565: The Spanish take slaves to St. Augustine, the first permanent settlement in what would later be the state of Florida.
- 1619: A Dutch ship with 20 African slaves aboard arrives at the English colony of Jamestown, Virginia.

Inspection and Sale of a Negro, engraving from the book Antislavery (1961) by Dwight Lowell Dumond. Library of Congress, Washington, D.C.

- 1650: The Yoruba Oyo empire begins a century of ascendancy in what would later be southwestern Nigeria. The empire remains at its apogee for about a century.
- c. 1700: The Asante begin to supply slaves to British and Dutch traders on the southwestern coast of Africa (later southern Ghana) in return for firearms with which to support their territorial expansion.
- 1707: A South African census lists 1,779 Dutch settlers owning 1,107 slaves.
- 1735: Carolus Linnaeus begins his classification of all then-known animal forms, ultimately including humans with primates and providing a model for modern racial classification.
- 1739: The Stono Rebellion, one of the earliest slave insurrections, leads to the deaths of at least 20 whites and more than 40 blacks west of Charleston in the black-majority colony of South Carolina.
- 1746: Lucy Terry composes the poem "Bars Fight", the earliest extant poem by an African American. Transmitted orally for more than 100 years, it first appears in print in 1855.
- 1760: Jupiter Hammon writes an autobiography often considered to be the first slave narrative.
- 1770: Crispus Attucks, an escaped slave, is killed by British soldiers in the Boston Massacre. He is one of the first men to die in the cause of American independence.
- c. 1772: Jean-Baptist-Point Du Sable builds a fur-trading post on the Chicago River at Lake Michigan. Its success leads to the settlement that later becomes the city of Chicago.
- 1773: Phillis Wheatley, the first notable black woman poet in the United States, is acclaimed in Europe and America following publication in

England of her *Poems on Various Subjects, Religious and Moral*, the first book of African American literature.

- 1777: Vermont, not yet part of the United States, becomes the first colony to constitutionally abolish slavery.
- 1779: The first of a series of intermittent wars known as the Cape Frontier Wars is fought between the Cape colonists of South Africa and the Xhosa people. The wars last until 1879.
- 1789: Olaudah Equiano publishes his two-volume autobiography, *The Interesting Narrative of the Life of Olaudah Equiano or Gustavus Vassa, the African, Written by Himself*, pioneering the slave narrative.

1790–1863: THE ENSLAVEMENT OF AFRICANS

- 1790: Benjamin Banneker, mathematician and compiler of almanacs, is appointed by Pres. George Washington to the District of Columbia Commission, where he works on the survey of Washington, D.C.
- 1791: A slave revolt begins in Haiti and is joined by freedman Toussaint-Louverture.

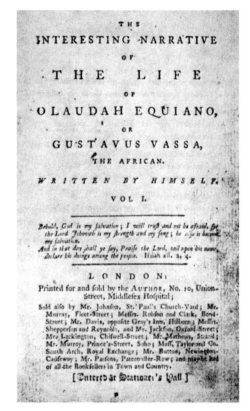

Title page from the first edition of The Interesting Narrative of the Life of Olaudah Equiano; or, Gustavus Vassa, the African, Written by Himself (1789).

- 1793: Congress passes the first Fugitive Slave Act, making it a crime to harbour an escaped slave or to interfere with his or her arrest.
- 1793: Eli Whitney invents the cotton gin, which is credited with fixing cotton cultivation, virtually to the exclusion of other crops, in the American South and so helping to institutionalize slavery.

- 1799: Richard Allen becomes the first ordained black minister of the Methodist Episcopal Church.
- 1800: Gabriel (Prosser) plans the first major slave rebellion in U.S. history, massing more than 1,000 armed slaves near Richmond, Virginia. Following the failed revolt, 35 slaves, including Gabriel, are hanged.
- 1816: The African Methodist Episcopal Church is formally organized and consecrates Richard Allen as its first bishop.
- 1817: The American Colonization Society is established to transport freeborn blacks and emancipated slaves to Africa, leading to the foundation of a colony that becomes the Republic of Liberia in 1847.
- 1820: The Missouri Compromise provides for Missouri to be admitted to the Union as a slave state, Maine as a free state, and western territories north of Missouri's southern border to be free soil.
- 1821: The African Methodist Episcopal Zion Church, developed from a congregation of blacks who left the John Street Methodist Church in New York City because of discrimination, is formally organized.
- 1822: Freedman Denmark Vesey plans the most extensive slave revolt in U.S. history. The Charleston rebellion is betrayed before the plan can be effected, leading to the hanging of Vesey and 34 others.
- 1829: Abolitionist David Walker publishes a pamphlet entitled *Appeal...to the Colored Citizens of the World* ..., calling for a slave revolt. Radical for the time, it is accepted by a small minority of abolitionists.

Frontispiece from the 1830 edition of David Walker's Appeal...to the Colored Citizens of the World..., first published in 1829.

- 1831: William Lloyd Garrison, a white man, begins publishing the antislavery newspaper *The Liberator*, which advocates emancipation for African Americans held in bondage.
- 1831: Nat Turner leads the only effective, sustained slave rebellion in U.S. history, attracting up to 75 fellow slaves and killing 60 whites. Some six weeks after the defeat of the insurrection, Turner is hanged.
- 1833: The American Anti-Slavery Society, the main activist arm of the abolitionist movement, is founded under the leadership of William Lloyd Garrison.
- 1834: Slavery is abolished in the British Empire.
- 1839: Slaves revolt on the Spanish slave ship *Amistad* in the Caribbean. After their arrest in Long Island Sound, former U.S. president John Quincy Adams successfully defends the rebels before the Supreme Court.
- 1840: The Liberty Party holds its first national convention in Albany, New York. In opposition to fellow abolitionist William Lloyd Garrison, members believe in political action to further antislavery goals.

Portrait of Joseph Cinqué, leader of the revolt aboard the slave ship Amistad; from a broadside dated 1839. Library of Congress, Washington, D.C.

- 1843: In a speech at the national convention of free people of colour, Henry Highland Garnet, abolitionist and clergyman, calls upon slaves to murder their masters.
- 1847: Joseph Jenkins Roberts, the son of free blacks in Virginia, is elected the first president of Liberia. In 1849 he secures British recognition of Liberia as a sovereign nation.
- 1847: Frederick Douglass begins publication of the *North Star*, an antislavery newspaper, which contributes to his break with abolitionist leader William Lloyd Garrison.
- 1848: The Free-Soil Party, a minor but influential political party—formed of Barnburners

and Whigs—opposed to the extension of slavery into the western territories, nominates former U.S. president Martin Van Buren to head its ticket.

- 1850: Speaking on behalf of the abolitionist movement, Sojourner Truth travels throughout the American Midwest, developing a reputation for personal magnetism and drawing large crowds.
- 1850: Harriet Tubman returns to Maryland to guide members of her family to freedom via the Underground Railroad. Later helping more than 300 slaves to escape, she comes to be known as the "Moses of her people."
- 1850: The U.S. Congress passes a series of compromise measures affecting California, Utah, New Mexico, Texas, and the District of Columbia in an effort to maintain an even balance between free and slave states. Part of the compromise, a new, stricter Fugitive Slave Act, contributes to the spread of the abolitionist movement.
- 1853: Episcopalian minister Alexander Crummell becomes a missionary and teacher in Liberia, advocating a program of religious conversion and economic and social development.
- 1853: William Wells Brown—a former slave, abolitionist, historian, and physician—publishes *Clotel*, the first novel by an African American.
- 1854: Author Frances E.W. Harper's most popular verse collection, *Poems on Miscellaneous Subjects*, is published, containing the antislavery poem *Bury Me in a Free Land*.
- 1855: John Mercer Langston, a former slave, is elected clerk of Brownhelm Township in Ohio. He is the first black to win an elective political office in the United States.
- 1856: Members of the Methodist Episcopal Church found Wilberforce University. After the university is closed during the Civil War, it is bought and reopened by the African Methodist Episcopal Church.
- 1856: In the ongoing contest between pro- and antislavery forces in Kansas, a mob sacks the town of Lawrence, a "hotbed of abolitionism," which leads to retaliation by white abolitionist John Brown at Pottawatomie Creek.
- 1857: In its Dred Scott decision, the U.S. Supreme Court

legalizes slavery in all the territories, exacerbating the sectional controversy and pushing the nation toward civil war.

- 1859: Harriet E. Wilson writes *Our Nig*, a largely autobiographical novel about racism in the North before the Civil War.

- 1859: The U.S. Supreme Court, in *Ableman* v. *Booth*, overrules an act by a Wisconsin state court that declared the Fugitive Slave Act of 1850 unconstitutional.

- c. 1859: Martin R. Delany, physician and advocate of black nationalism, leads a party to western Africa to investigate the Niger Delta as a site for settlement of African Americans.

- 1860: After the election of Abraham Lincoln, South Carolina secedes from the Union in December. It is followed in January 1861 by Mississippi, Florida, Alabama, Georgia, and Louisiana, and in February by Texas. As battle lines are drawn, Virginia, North Carolina, Arkansas, and Tennessee also choose to secede.

- 1861: The Civil War begins in Charleston, South Carolina, as the Confederates open fire on Fort Sumter.

- 1861: Harriet Jacobs's *Incidents in the Life of a Slave Girl*, the first autobiography by a formerly enslaved African American woman, candidly describes her experience of the sexual exploitation that made slavery especially oppressive for black women.

- c. 1861: Pinckney Pinchback runs the Confederate blockade on the Mississippi to reach New Orleans. There he recruits a company of black volunteers for the Union, the Corps d'Afrique.

- 1862: Future U.S. congressman Robert Smalls and 12 other slaves seize control of a Confederate armed frigate in Charleston harbour. They turn it over to a Union naval squadron blockading the city.

- 1862: The second Confiscation Act is passed, stating that slaves of civilian and military Confederate officials "shall be forever free," enforceable only in areas of the South occupied by the Union Army.

- 1863: Pres. Abraham Lincoln signs the Emancipation Proclamation on January 1.

- 1863: Worker discontent with the inequities of the Civil War draft leads to a four-day eruption of violence in New York City.

1864–C. 1916: RECONSTRUCTION AND THE START OF THE GREAT MIGRATION

- 1864: Southern outrage at the North's use of black soldiers flares up in Confederate forces capturing Fort Pillow, Tennessee, and massacring the black troops within; some are burned or buried alive.
- 1864: President Lincoln refuses to sign the Wade-Davis bill, which requires greater assurances of loyalty to the Union from white citizens and reconstructed governments.
- 1865: The Civil War ends in effect on April 9, after the surrender of the Confederate Gen. Robert E. Lee at Appomattox Courthouse.
- 1865: Congress establishes the U.S. Bureau of Refugees, Freedmen, and Abandoned Lands to aid four million black Americans in transition from slavery to freedom.
- c. 1866: The states of the former Confederacy pass "black code" laws to replace the social controls removed by the Emancipation Proclamation and the Thirteenth Amendment.
- 1866: The U.S. Army forms black cavalry and infantry regiments. Serving in the West from 1867 to 1896 and fighting Indians on the frontier, they are nicknamed "buffalo soldiers" by the Indians.
- 1866: With the complicity of local civilian authorities and police, rioting whites kill 35 black citizens of New Orleans, Louisiana, and wound more than 100, leading to increased support for vigorous Reconstruction policies.
- 1867: Howard University, a predominantly black university, is founded in Washington, D.C. It is named for General Oliver Otis Howard, head of the post–Civil War Freedmen's Bureau.

Howard University law school graduates, c. 1900. Library of Congress, Washington, D.C.

- 1868: The Fourteenth Amendment of the Constitution is ratified, guaranteeing equal protection under the law.

- 1868: The South Carolina General Assembly convenes with 85 black and 70 white representatives; a product of Reconstruction, it is the first state legislature with a black majority.
- 1868: Elizabeth Keckley, who rose from slavery in St. Louis, Missouri, to become the modiste and confidante of First Lady Mary Todd Lincoln, publishes her autobiography, *Behind the Scenes; or, Thirty Years a Slave and Four Years in the White House.*
- 1870: The Colored Methodist Episcopal Church is organized, four years after the first efforts among black members of the Methodist Episcopal Church, South, to develop an independent church.
- 1870: Hiram R. Revels of Mississippi takes the former seat of Jefferson Davis in the U.S. Senate, becoming the only African American in the U.S. Congress and the first elected to the Senate.
- 1870: Joseph Hayne Rainey is the first African American elected to the U.S. House of Representatives. This congressman from South Carolina will enjoy the longest tenure of any African American during Reconstruction.
- 1870: The Fifteenth Amendment to the U.S. Constitution is ratified, guaranteeing the right to vote regardless of "race, color, or previous condition of servitude."
- 1871: Brazil enacts the Law of the Free Womb, which grants freedom to all children born to slaves and effectively condemns slavery to eventual extinction. But immediate and complete abolition is demanded.
- 1872: John R. Lynch, speaker of the Mississippi House of Representatives, is elected to the U.S. Congress.
- 1877: Reconstruction ends as the last Federal troops are withdrawn from the South. Southern conservatives regain control of their state governments through fraud, violence, and intimidation.
- 1879: Author Joel Chandler Harris's story *Tar-Baby*, an animal tale told by the character Uncle Remus, popularizes the sticky tar doll figure of black American folktales. It draws on the African trickster tale.
- 1881: Tuskegee Normal and Industrial Institute in Alabama is founded on July 4

with Booker T. Washington as the school's first president.

- 1881: Tennessee becomes the first state to enact Jim Crow legislation, which requires blacks and whites to ride in separate railroad cars.
- 1883: Inventor Jan Ernst Matzeliger patents his shoe-lasting machine that shapes the upper portions of shoes. His invention wins swift acceptance and soon supplants hand methods of production.
- 1887: Florida A&M University is founded as the State Normal (teacher-training) School for Colored Students.
- 1887: Journalist T. Thomas Fortune begins editing the *New York Age*. His well-known editorials defend the civil rights of African Americans and condemn racial discrimination.
- 1888: On May 13, the princess regent of Brazil (in the absence of the emperor) decrees complete emancipation of some 700,000 slaves without compensation to the owners.
- 1892: The offices of the *Memphis Free Speech* are destroyed following editorials of part-owner Ida B. Wells denouncing the lynching of three of her friends.

- c. 1895: Cornetist Buddy Bolden, legendary founding father of jazz, leads a band in New Orleans, Louisiana.
- 1895: A merger of three major black Baptist conventions leads to the formation of the National Baptist Convention, U.S.A., Inc., in Atlanta, Georgia.
- 1895: At the Cotton States and International Exposition in Atlanta, educator Booker T. Washington delivers his "Atlanta Compromise" speech, stressing the importance of vocational education for blacks over social equality or political office.
- 1896: Believing African Americans to be the descendants of the "lost tribes of Israel," Prophet William S. Crowdy founds the Church of God and Saints of Christ.
- 1896: Mary Church Terrell becomes the first president of the National Association of Colored Women, working for educational and social reform and an end to racial discrimination.
- 1896: In the *Plessy* v. *Ferguson* decision the U.S. Supreme Court upholds the doctrine of "separate but equal."
- 1896: Paul Laurence Dunbar, acclaimed as "the poet laureate of the Negro race,"

publishes *Lyrics of Lowly Life*, containing some of the finest verses of his *Oak and Ivy* and *Majors and Minors*.

- 1899: Composer and pianist Scott Joplin publishes *The Maple Leaf Rag*, one of the most important and popular compositions during the era of ragtime, precursor to jazz.

- c. 1900: Originally a slaves' parody of white ballroom dances, the cakewalk becomes a wildly popular dance among fashionable whites as well as white minstrels working in blackface.

- 1901: Booker T. Washington dines with Pres. Theodore Roosevelt at the White House. The dinner meeting is bitterly criticized by many whites, who view it as a marked departure from racial etiquette.

- 1903: W.E.B. Du Bois publishes *The Souls of Black Folk*, which declares that "the problem of the Twentieth Century is the problem of the color-line," and discusses the dual identity of black Americans.

- 1903: In protest to the ideology of Booker T. Washington, W.E.B. Du Bois suggests the concept of the "Talented Tenth"—a college-trained leadership cadre responsible for elevating blacks economically and culturally.

- 1904: Joe Gans, perhaps the greatest fighter in the history of the lightweight division, loses to welterweight champion Joe Walcott in a 20-round draw.

- 1905: The Niagara Movement is founded as a group of black intellectuals from across the nation meet near Niagara Falls, Ontario, Canada, adopting resolutions demanding full equality in American life.

- 1905: Madame C.J. Walker (Sarah Breedlove Walker) develops and markets a method for straightening curly hair, on her way to becoming the first black female millionaire in the United States.

- 1906: Pres. Theodore Roosevelt orders that 167 black infantrymen be given dishonourable discharges because of their so-called conspiracy of silence regarding the shooting death of a white citizen in Brownsville, Texas, an event later known as the Brownsville Affair.

- 1906: After educator John Hope becomes its president, Atlanta Baptist College expands its curriculum and is renamed Morehouse College.

- 1907: Black Primitive Baptist congregations formed by emancipated slaves after the Civil War organize the National Primitive Baptist Convention, Inc.

- 1908: In Springfield, Illinois, the hometown of Abraham Lincoln, a major race riot occurs; the black community is assaulted by several thousand white citizens, and two elderly blacks are lynched.

- 1909: A group of whites shocked by the Springfield riot of 1908 merge with W.E.B. Du Bois's Niagara Movement, forming the National Association for the Advancement of Colored People (NAACP).

- 1910: *The Crisis*, a monthly magazine published by the NAACP, is founded. W.E.B. Du Bois edits the magazine for its first 24 years.

- c. 1910: Jazz begins to evolve in New Orleans, Louisiana.

- 1911: The National League on Urban Conditions Among Negroes (National Urban League) is formed in New York City with the mission to help migrating African Americans find jobs and housing and adjust to urban life.

- 1911: Anthropologist Franz Boas publishes *The Mind of Primitive Man*, a series of lectures on culture and race. His work is used often in the 1920s by those opposed to U.S. immigration restrictions based on presumed racial differences.

- 1912: The African National Congress is founded as the South African Native National Congress.

- 1913: Timothy Drew, known as Prophet Noble Drew Ali, founds the Moorish Science Temple of America in Newark, New Jersey. His central teaching is that blacks are of Muslim origin.

- 1914: The Universal Negro Improvement Association is founded by Marcus Garvey in his homeland of Jamaica to further racial pride and economic self-sufficiency and to establish a black nation in Africa.

- 1914: George Washington Carver of the Tuskegee Institute reveals his experiments concerning peanuts and sweet potatoes, popularizing alternative crops and aiding the renewal of depleted land in the South.

- 1915: Historian Carter G. Woodson founds the

Association for the Study of Negro Life and History in an attempt to assist the accurate and proper study of African American history.

- 1915: In Havana Jack Johnson, the first black heavyweight champion of the world, loses the title in 26 rounds to Jess Willard, the last in a succession of "Great White Hopes." Rumours claim he lost to avoid legal difficulties.
- 1915: A schism in the National Baptist Convention yields the National Baptist Convention of America, the largest black church in the United States.
- c. 1916: The period known as the Great Migration begins; between 1916 and 1970 some six million African American Southerners migrate to urban centres in the North and West.

1917–35: THE JAZZ AGE AND THE HARLEM RENAISSANCE

- 1917: Racial antagonism toward African Americans newly employed in war industries leads to a race riot in East St. Louis, Illinois, that kills 40 blacks and 8 whites.
- 1918: James VanDerZee and his wife open the Guarantee Photo Studio in Harlem. The portraits he shoots later become a treasured chronicle of the Harlem Renaissance.
- 1919: During the "Red Summer" following World War I, 13 days of racial violence on the South Side of Chicago leave 23 blacks and 15 whites dead, 537 people injured, and 1,000 black families homeless.
- 1919: A'Lelia Walker inherits the family business and estate upon the death of her mother, Madame C.J. Walker. In the 1920s she entertains the leading writers and artists of the Harlem Renaissance.
- 1920: Marcus Garvey, leader of the Universal Negro Improvement Association, addresses 25,000 blacks at Madison Square Garden and presides over a parade of 50,000 through the streets of Harlem.
- 1920: The Negro National League, first of baseball's Negro leagues, is established.
- 1921: Oscar Charleston, perhaps the best all-around baseball player in the history of the Negro leagues, leads his league in doubles, triples, and home runs, batting .434 for the year.

- 1921: *Shuffle Along*, a musical by Eubie Blake and Noble Sissle, opens on Broadway. It is the first musical written and performed by African Americans.
- 1922: Louis Armstrong leaves New Orleans, arriving in Chicago to play second trumpet in cornetist King Oliver's Creole Jazz Band. Armstrong's work in the 1920s would revolutionize jazz.
- 1922: Aviator Bessie Coleman, who later refuses to perform before segregated audiences in the South, stages the first public flight by an African American woman.
- 1923: Charles Clinton Spaulding becomes president of the North Carolina Mutual Life Insurance Company. He builds it into the nation's largest black-owned business by the time of his death in 1952.
- 1923: Pianist and orchestrator Fletcher Henderson becomes a bandleader. His prestigious band advances the careers of African American musicians such as Louis Armstrong, Coleman Hawkins, and Roy Eldridge.
- 1923: Poet and novelist Jean Toomer publishes his masterpiece, *Cane*, an experimental novel often considered one of

Bessie Coleman, U.S. commemorative stamp, 1995.

the greatest achievements of the Harlem Renaissance.

- 1923: Blues singer Bessie Smith, discovered by pianist-composer Clarence Williams, makes her first recording. She will eventually become known as "Empress of the Blues."
- 1924: Spelman Seminary, which began awarding college degrees in 1901, becomes Spelman College. The school began in 1881 with two Boston women teaching 11

black women in an Atlanta, Georgia, church basement.

- 1924: At a dinner sponsored by *Opportunity* magazine, black writers and white publishers mingle; the event is considered the formal beginning of the Harlem Renaissance, or New Negro movement.
- 1925: *The New Negro*, an anthology of fiction, poetry, drama, and essays associated with the Harlem Renaissance, is edited by Alain Locke.
- 1925: Singer and dancer Josephine Baker goes to Paris to dance at the Théâtre des Champs-Élysées in *La Revue nègre*, becoming one of the most popular entertainers in France.
- 1925: Countee Cullen, one of the finest poets of the Harlem Renaissance, publishes his first collection of poems, *Color*, to critical acclaim before graduating from New York University.
- 1925: In an era when Ku Klux Klan membership exceeds four million nationally, a parade of 50,000 unmasked members takes place in Washington, D.C.
- 1925: A. Philip Randolph, trade unionist and civil-rights leader, founds the Brotherhood of Sleeping Car Porters, which becomes the first successful black trade union.
- 1925: At a historic literary awards banquet during the Harlem Renaissance, Langston Hughes earns first place in poetry with *The Weary Blues*, which is read aloud by James Weldon Johnson.
- 1926: The literary journal *Fire!!*, edited by young writer Wallace Thurman, publishes its first and only issue. The short-lived publication remains highly influential among the participants of the Harlem Renaissance.
- *c.* 1926: Pianist, composer, and self-proclaimed inventor of jazz Jelly Roll Morton records several of his masterpieces, including *Black Bottom Stomp* and *Dead Man Blues*.
- 1927: James Weldon Johnson, poet and anthologist of black culture, publishes *God's Trombones*, a group of black dialect sermons in verse accompanied by the illustrations of Aaron Douglas.
- 1927: Poet and playwright Angelina Weld Grimké publishes *Caroling Dusk*, an anthology of her poetry edited by Countee Cullen.
- 1927: Painter Henry Ossawa Tanner, whose works include *The Two Disciples at the Tomb*, becomes the first African

American to be granted full membership in the National Academy of Design.

- 1927: Singer and actor Ethel Waters makes her first appearance on Broadway in the all-black revue *Africana*.
- 1927: The all-black professional basketball team known as the Harlem Globetrotters is established.
- 1928: Poet and novelist Claude McKay publishes *Home to Harlem*, the first fictional work by an African American to reach the best-seller lists.
- 1928: Evidence of the ancient Iron Age Nok culture is discovered on Nigeria's Benue Plateau.
- 1929: John Hope, noted advocate of advanced liberal arts instruction for blacks, is chosen as president of Atlanta University, the first graduate school for African Americans.
- 1931: Nine black youths accused of raping two white women on a freight train go on trial for their lives in Scottsboro, Alabama. The Scottsboro case becomes a cause célèbre among Northern liberal and radical groups.
- 1931: Walter White begins his tenure as executive secretary of the NAACP, his principal objective being the abolition of lynching. In the early

decades of the 20th century, there were often more than 60 lynchings nationally each year. By the time of White's death in 1955, lynchings would become a rarity.

- 1932: In Tuskegee, Alabama, the U.S. Public Health Service begins a study of the course of untreated syphilis in black men, not telling them of their syphilis or their participation in the 40-year study.
- 1932: Wallace Thurman, young literary rebel of the Harlem Renaissance, publishes his satiric novel *Infants of the Spring*.
- 1934: Wallace D. Fard, founder of the Nation of Islam movement, disappears, leading to the rise of Elijah Muhammad.

1936–41: ON THE EVE OF WAR

- 1936: Track-and-field athlete Jesse Owens wins four gold medals in the 1936 Olympic Games in Berlin. His victories derail Adolf Hitler's intended use of the games as a show of Aryan supremacy.
- c. 1936: Delta blues musician Robert Johnson makes his legendary and influential recordings in Texas, including *Me and the Devil Blues, Hellhound on My Trail,* and *Love in Vain.*

- 1937: Writer and folklorist Zora Neale Hurston publishes her second novel, *Their Eyes Were Watching God*, which receives considerable acclaim and criticism within the black community.
- 1938: In a knockout in the first round of their rematch, heavyweight champion Joe Louis wreaks vengeance on Max Schmeling of Germany, the only boxer to have knocked out Louis in his prime.
- *c.* 1938: Assisted by saxophonist Lester Young, her romantic companion during these years, jazz vocalist Billie Holiday makes several of her finest recordings.
- *c.* 1939: Count Basie leads his legendary Kansas City band, including saxophonist Lester Young, trumpeter Buck Clayton, guitarist Freddie Green, bassist Walter Page, and drummer Jo Jones.
- 1939: Singer Marian Anderson performs at the Lincoln Memorial before an audience of 75,000 after the Daughters of the American Revolution refuse to allow her to sing at Constitution Hall.
- 1939: The NAACP Legal Defense and Education Fund is organized. Charles Hamilton Houston spearheads the effort to consolidate some of the nation's best legal talents in the fight against legally sanctioned bias.
- 1940: Author Richard Wright publishes his masterpiece, *Native Son*. The stark, tragic realism of this novel immediately places Wright in the front ranks of contemporary American writers.
- 1940: Benjamin Oliver Davis, Sr., who in 1930 had become the first black colonel in the U.S. Army, becomes the first black general in 1940.
- *c.* 1940: Painter Jacob Lawrence begins work on his 60-panel Migration series, which depicts the journey of African Americans from the South to the urban North.
- *c.* 1940: Duke Ellington leads his greatest band, including bassist Jimmy Blanton, saxophonist Ben Webster, trumpeter Cootie Williams, and composer-arranger Billy Strayhorn.
- 1941: Following considerable protest, the War Department forms the all-black 99th Pursuit Squadron of the U.S. Army Air Corps, later known as the Tuskegee Airmen, commanded by Benjamin Oliver Davis, Jr.
- 1941: The United States declares war on Japan following the attack on Pearl Harbor, Hawaii.

GLOSSARY

ABO blood group system The classification of human blood based on the inherited properties of red blood cells (i.e., type A, type B, type O, or type AB).

abrogate To abolish or do away with by an official act.

accession The act of gaining a title; coming into power.

antebellum The period before the American Civil War.

anthropometry The study of human body proportions as a method of classification and comparison.

canon Any comprehensive list of books within a field or genre.

conflate To fuse two or more things into a single entity.

conjugal Pertaining to the relationship between a husband and wife.

Copperhead Democrat A Civil War–era pejorative term for Northern democrats who opposed the war and advocated restoration of the Union through settlement with the South. (A copperhead is a snake that strikes without warning.)

craniometry The science of measuring skulls.

de facto Existing as a matter of course, without lawful authority.

de jure Existing by right, according to the law.

desiccate To dry up.

entrepôt A warehouse, depot, or commercial centre.

epicanthic fold A fold of skin of the upper eyelid that covers the inner corner of the eye.

epithet A characterizing word or phrase associated with a person, place, or thing, often used in place of the actual name in a disparaging way.

ethnocentrism The belief in the inherent superiority of one's own ethnic group.

ethnography The branch of anthropology concerned with the scientific description of cultures.

etiology The study of cause and effect.

ex post facto After the fact.

fehmic court Judicial system of Germany in the Middle Ages.

gibbet law Medieval law started in the town of Halifax, England, that gave the Lord the power to try and execute any felon for thefts over 13½ pence.

heddle The principal part of the harness in a loom.

hokum Complete nonsense.

impunity Exemption from punishment.

indemnification The act of giving compensation for damages.

land-grant institution Colleges and universities established in the United States to receive the benefits of the Morrill Acts of 1862 and 1890, wherein the study of agriculture, among other fields, was funded by the federal government.

laudatory Expressing praise.

liminal In a state of transition.

MNS blood group system A human blood group system based upon presence of various antigens located on the surface of red blood cells.

mendacious Habitually dishonest or untrustworthy.

morphology The branch of biology concerned with the form and structure of organisms.

motif A recurring theme or feature.

mythos The underlying system of beliefs characteristic of a particular cultural group.

panegyric A lofty oration or writing in praise of a person or thing, often in the form of a eulogy.

phenotype The physical characteristics of an organism; in the case of those seeking to define differences among various human groups, this classification was applied to race.

pocket veto A veto of a bill brought about by the president's failure to sign it within 10 days of the adjournment of Congress.

provost A person appointed to superintend or preside.

rapine The seizure and carrying off of another's property; plunder.

Rhesus or Rh blood group system Clinically the second most important blood group system after ABO; it gives the blood type its "positive" or "negative" factor.

Spenserian stanza A stanza of eight iambic pentameter lines and a final Alexandrine, first used by the poet Edmund Spenser.

suzerain A dominant state exercising political control over a dependent state.

taxonomy The science of classifying organisms.

tenure The period or term of holding a position.

writ of error Issued by an appellate court to the court of record where a case has been tried, requiring that the record of the trial be sent to the appellate court for examination of alleged errors.

BIBLIOGRAPHY

Darlene Clark Hine, et al., *African Americans: A Concise History*, 3rd. ed. (2009); N.I. Painter, *Creating Black Americans: African-American History and Its Meanings, 1619 to the Present* (2006); Lerone Bennett, Jr., *Before the Mayflower: A History of Black America*, 8th ed. (2007); and John Hope Franklin and Alfred A. Moss, Jr., *From Slavery to Freedom*, 8th ed. (2000), are useful overviews of African American history. Roland Laird and T.N. Laird, *Still I Rise: A Graphic History of African Americans* (2009), is informative though the artwork is less satisfying than the text. Among the noteworthy works on special topics related to African American history and culture are A.L. Bower (ed.), *African American Foodways: Explorations of History and Culture* (2009); T.L. Brown, et al., *African American Fraternities and Sororities: The Legacy and the Vision* (2005); H.C. Covey, *African American Slave Medicine: Herbal and Non-Herbal Treatments* (2008); James Daley (ed.), *Great Speeches by African Americans* (2006); Howard Dobson and S.A. Diouf, comps. and eds., *In Motion: The African-American Migration Experience* (2004); Kathlyn Gay, *African-American Holidays, Festivals, and Celebrations* (2007); Joyce Hansen, *Women of Hope: African Americans Who Made a Difference* (2007); J.O. Horton and L.E. Horton, *Slavery and the Making of America* (2006); and Pamela Newkirk (ed.), *Letters from Black America* (2009).

Some of the richest analyses of African American culture can be found in studies of the literature of African Americans, including Dickson D. Bruce, Jr., *Black American Writing from the Nadir: The Evolution of a Literary Tradition, 1877–1915* (1989), and *The Origins of African American Literature, 1680–1865* (2001); Frances Smith Foster, *Written by Herself: Literary Production by African American Women, 1746–1892* (1993); and Jean Wagner, *Black Poets of the United States: From Paul Laurence Dunbar to Langston Hughes* (1973). William L. Andrews, *To Tell a Free Story: The First Century of Afro-American Autobiography, 1760–1865* (1986); and Frances Smith Foster, *Witnessing Slavery: The Development of Antebellum Slave Narratives*, 2nd ed. (1994), explore the American slave narrative, a deeply influential genre that captures vividly the lived experience of slaves during the 18th and 19th centuries in the United States. The Harlem Renaissance, one of the greatest flowerings of African American culture, is described in detail in Nathan Irvin Huggins, *Harlem Renaissance*, updated ed. (2007); David Levering Lewis, *When Harlem Was in Vogue* (1981, reissued 1997); Jervis Anderson, *This Was Harlem: A Cultural Portrait, 1900–1950* (1982, reissued 1993); and George Hutchinson, *The Harlem Renaissance in Black and White* (1995).

INDEX